Praise for *Testing for Kindergarten*

"This book is a gold mine of information—an invaluable resource for parents of young children who want to ignite their children's learning. With a unique talent for combining the latest scientific knowledge with her own real-world experience, Karen Quinn pulls back the curtain, revealing what educators look for when making admissions and placement decisions."

—**Dr. Marion Blank,** director of the A Light
on Literacy program at Columbia University

"It is 'the must have' book for every parent going through the kindergarten admissions process. The book is written with authority and experience from someone who knows what she is talking about. I will be recommending it to all parents of preschool children."

—**Lyss Stern,** Founder of Divalysscious Moms and
Editor In Chief of *Observer Playground*

"This is an extraordinary book, without question the best work for parents on the subject of getting a mind ready for schooling. This work needs to be read and applied by every parent of every preschool child. . . . The information is well grounded in science yet remarkably digestible and practical. Karen Quinn has made a terrific contribution, one that should enable countless minds to start school with the mental momentum they so need."

—**Mel Levine, M.D.,** author of *A Mind at a Time*

"Balmex, baby wipes, and this tell-all book . . . three diaper-bag essentials for every mom (and dad). Karen Quinn cracks the kindergarten testing code, and now you can too! Her smart strategies and practical knowhow will help you put your child on the path to school and life success. Wise, witty, and well researched, it's like getting sage advice from a seasoned, savvy, sisterly mom friend who has done her homework. In a word . . . *Testing for Kindergarten* ROCKS!"

—**Robin Gorman Newman,** founder of Motherhood Later . . . Than Sooner

"Bravo to Karen Quinn for an amazingly straightforward read into an elusive topic. New parents not knowing about the world of private schools are often so riddled with anxiety when they come into my office. Now, it is as if Karen can counsel them directly with this amazing read—and it's healthier than Xanax!"

—**Jasmine Lake,** director of admission, Miami Country Day School

"It's like cheating: it gives your child a leg up."

—**Victoria Goldman,** author of *The Manhattan Family Guide to Private Schools and Selective Public Schools* and *The Manhattan Directory of Private Nursery Schools*

"As teachers we are always happy when it is apparent that parents are doing the right thing . . . and following the suggestions in Karen Quinn's book is the surefire way to get your little one on the path to school success! I highly recommend this book."

—**Judy Mumma,** kindergarten teacher, Paulding Elementary School, Ohio

"Don't let the title fool you into assuming this is a book geared only for the wealthy elite who are fighting to get their kids into private schools—regardless of whether your child will attend public or private school, this book is for you. I'm the mom of a two-year-old and four-year-old who will with 100 percent certainty attend ordinary public school in the suburbs. This book explains for us regular parents just what a hard-core IQ test will cover, so we can gauge the preparation level of our tykes. Really and truly, this is a must-read for *every* mom of preschool-aged kids. Loved it!"

—**Colleen Padilla,** owner of Classymommy.com

"Until now, this information was available only to wealthy parents who hired consultants and tutors. With this book, Karen Quinn has leveled the playing field, making it possible for *any* parent to give their child an equal chance to get into the best possible school and to perform at the highest level. Whether you're thinking about public school, a gifted program, or private school, read this book!"

—**Candice Carpenter Olson,** cofounder of iVillage.com

"Thank you, Karen Quinn, for writing the only no-nonsense, beyond informative, useful, commonsense, and often laugh-out-loud book whose approach to kindergarten testing (and learning, in general) will manage to assuage the fears of masses of well-intended parents. As a pediatrician, I will recommend this to all parents!"

—**Dr. Jamie Wells,** pediatrician, New York City

"*Testing For Kindergarten* made me want to get back into the classroom. As a thirty-year public-school teaching veteran, I was shaking my head on almost every page because Karen Quinn got it so right. Not only is this a wonderful guide for parents, but it should be on the reading list for all prospective student teachers going into early childhood education. Well thought out, well organized, and well done."

—**Bonnie Edelman,** kindergarten teacher, Aurora Public Schools, Colorado

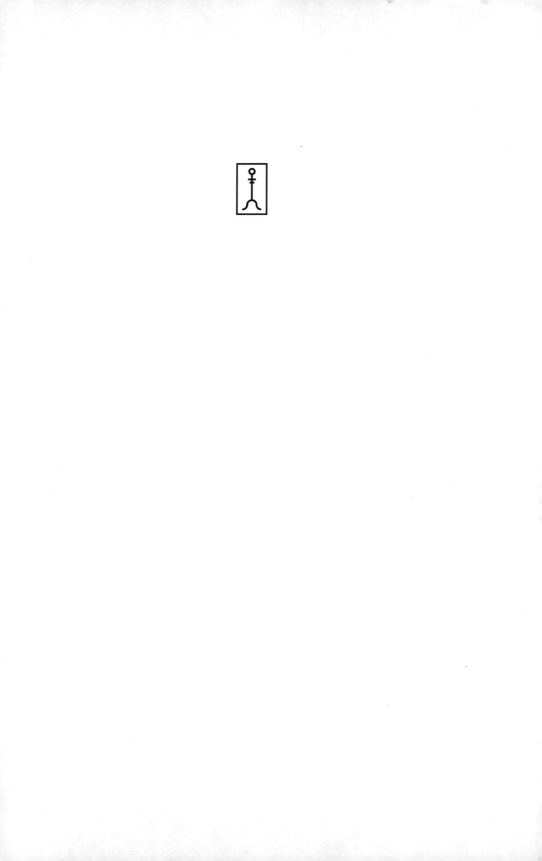

Testing for kindergarten

Simple Strategies to Help Your Child Ace the Tests for:

★ Public School Placement ★

★ Private School Admissions ★

★ Gifted Program Qualification ★

karen Quinn

A Fireside Book
Published by Simon & Schuster

New York   London   Toronto   Sydney

Fireside
A Division of Simon & Schuster, Inc.
1230 Avenue of the Americas
New York, NY 10020

First Fireside trade paperback edition July 2010

FIRESIDE and colophon are registered trademarks of Simon & Schuster, Inc.

For information about special discounts for bulk purchases, please contact
Simon & Schuster Special Sales at 1-866-506-1949 or business@simonandschuster.com.

The Simon & Schuster Speakers Bureau can bring authors to your live event.
For more information or to book an event contact the Simon & Schuster Speakers Bureau
at 1-866-248-3049 or visit our website at www.simonspeakers.com.

Designed by Ruth Lee-Mui

Manufactured in the United States of America

10   9   8   7   6   5   4   3

Library of Congress Cataloging-in-Publication Data
Quinn, Karen.
    Testing for kindergarten : simple strategies to help your child ace the tests for public school
placement, private school admissions, gifted program qualification / by Karen Quinn.
        p.   cm.
    "A Fireside book."
    Includes bibliographical references and index.
    1. Child development—United States—Testing.   2. Kindergarten—United States—
Evaluation.   3. Educational tests and measurements—United States.   I. Title.
    LB1131.Q85   2010
    372.126—dc22   2009053179

ISBN 978-1-4165-9107-8
ISBN 978-1-4165-9676-9 (ebook)

This book is dedicated with love to Dr. Shari Nedler,
a pioneer in the field of early childhood education
and (more important) my mother.

Contents

Author's Note

It's kind of sad, but kindergarten isn't all fun and games anymore. Today's kindergarteners are expected to perform at what used to be first-grade level. Whether it's for admission to private school, a gifted program, or placement in a public school ability group, almost every kindergartener is tested by the age of 5. So what's a parent to do? Should we prep our kids at home, sign them up for enrichment classes, and have them tutored, or would that be another example of over-the-top parenting? If we teach our preschoolers to draw triangles, circles, and squares so they'll be ready to write letters, are we dooming them to years of therapy? Some people would say yes. I'm not one of them.

If you're like other parents (and I'm pretty sure you are), you are deeply committed to your child's happiness and success. You want your little one to start his first school experience ready to hit the ground running with every ability he needs to soar, right? Certainly you hope he will qualify for the best educational opportunities you can make available to him. As much as you want this for your child, I'm guessing that you aren't willing to pressure him, or turn your home into a classroom (or yourself into Mom or Dadzilla) to achieve it. Good for you! That's unnecessary and will cause your friends and neighbors to make fun of you behind your back.

Giving your child the best possible academic start is infinitely doable. It doesn't take a lot of extra time and it can be pure (well, mostly) joy. All it takes is for you to get your arms around the 7 abilities every kid needs to succeed in school (Hint: These are the same 7 abilities every common intelligence test is designed to assess.) Then, each day, do focused activities together that instill these abilities in your child. We're talking about playing games, building with blocks, having stimulating conversations, reading picture books, doing art projects, and playing—lots and lots of playing. This book lays it out for you. The younger your child is when you start, the better, but it is never too late.

Will your little one's test scores improve if you follow the recommendations inside? I can almost guarantee it. But higher test scores aren't the point. The point is to help your child earn a coveted seat at the best school possible, a placement in the highest ability groupings where she can learn alongside equal or more able pupils, and early success in school that inspires a love of learning that will last a lifetime.

As you read on, refer often to my website at Testingforkindergarten.com. There, you'll find a direct link to every website address mentioned (saving you lots of tedious typing); a list of all the games, toys, and materials I recommend; references to all the studies and sources I relied on when writing this book; a place to sign up for daily IQ test prep questions for children ages 3 to 5 (they should take about a minute); and valuable bonus material that just didn't fit inside these chapters, along with additional information that hasn't come up yet, but will, and I know I'll want to share it with you in my blog.

In the coming pages, you'll notice that I randomly alternate between the female and male pronouns in my references to children. This was done for the sake of fairness, which, as you know, kids insist upon.

Finally, I genuinely want to hear from you. If you have questions, please ask me. If you want to recommend an ability-building activity that your child loves, let me know about it so I can share it with other parents (giving you credit, of course). If your mothers group would like to read this book and have me call in to your discussion, get in touch. Whatever you want to talk about, here's where you can reach me directly: karenquinn1@aol.com; on Facebook at www.karenquinn.net/facebook; on Twitter at karenquinnnyc.

Part I

The Secret World of kindergarten Testing

In this section, you will learn:

★ Why almost every child will be tested before age 5, whether he attends public or private school.

★ The 7 abilities every test covers (and every child must have) before starting kindergarten.

★ How these early tests can affect your child's entire education.

★ What IQ scores mean.

★ How simple changes to your parenting style can improve your child's IQ.

★ The different types of tests used by private and public schools.

★ Which tests are used to track children into ability groupings in public school.

★ How to prepare your child for testing.

★ What happens inside the testing room.

★ What is on the most common tests, section by section.

1. What Educators Know and Parents Don't

CONFESSIONS OF A MOM WHO HAD TO FIGURE THIS OUT FOR HERSELF

Did you know that by the age of 5 most children in America will have been given some kind of intelligence test? These tests cover all the abilities educators believe children *must* have to do well in the classroom. If you want your child to attend a top private school or a competitive gifted program, his scores will impact and in some cases determine whether he's in or out.

If you choose public kindergarten for your child, testing serves a different purpose. American public schools commonly engage in a practice known as "ability tracking," where students are grouped together by slow, average, and advanced skill levels and instructed differently depending on where they are assigned. Over time, children who make the advanced track get teachers who focus more on academic achievement and provide deeper, richer content. Those placed in slow groups are taught through drills, worksheets, and an easier curriculum, which limits their ability to handle harder work later. Their peers jump ahead of them and the gap between the two groups widen, limiting the educational opportunities of kids assigned to the slow track. Your child's ability group placement will depend on how he scores on the tests he'll be given when he starts kindergarten.

Considering how these high-stakes tests are used to make school placement decisions that affect our children's educational futures, you'd think we would be given a heads-up on what they cover. Instead, information about intelligence tests is as closely guarded as the Academy Award envelopes. Parents who want the best for their children don't understand what their kids need to know, much less how to make sure they've given them the right kinds of experiences to pick up these abilities. When I found out my daughter had to take one of these tests, she couldn't even draw a triangle. I had completely fallen down on the job.

The first time I heard that children her age could even be tested was at her end-of-school meeting at nursery school. Our preschool director had gathered the parents for a briefing on transitioning our children from preschool to kindergarten—"ex-missions," she called it. The word strikes terror in the hearts and minds of Manhattan parents.

In New York City—and many parts of the country—getting into a private kindergarten, a talented and gifted (TAG) program, and even many selective magnet or charter schools has become impossibly competitive. It seems absurd to test 4-year-olds for admissions. And yet, if that is the process where you live, your choice is to play the game or find the best public school program you can. In some markets, public school options are fantastic; in others, not so much.

Most parents who decide to jump through the hoops and apply their kids to more selective public or private schools go into it determined to retain their sanity. It's a noble intention that isn't always possible. These are our children we are talking about, our adorable, bright (in most cases genius) 4-year-olds who do not deserve to be judged by those wart-faced, fire-breathing admissions directors. I have seen icy-veined CEOs reduced to tears over this process.

Your kid can't spell her own name? Forget Yale.

But back to my first ex-missions meeting. Before I arrived, parents were offered tiny wooden seats next to pint-sized tables with coloring-box centerpieces. Me, I was late, so I sat cross-legged on the floor until my foot fell asleep. Standing, waiting for the numbness to subside, I gazed at the competition. There was Margarita Gonzalas-Baikov, Ben's mom. She had hired a Chinese nanny just so her son would learn to speak Mandarin before the age of 4. The kid already spoke Spanish and Russian. *Showoff*, I thought. After Kim Memolis' mother heard that shapes were on the test, she taught her daughter to make three-dimensional boxes and cones. *Was that really necessary?* According to his dad, Matthew Stein was already reading Dr. Seuss books. *Spare me! That little nose picker had memorized* Green Eggs and Ham *after hearing it sixty-eight times.* My future honor student, Schuyler, knew it after a mere fourteen readings. On the other hand, "Thkyler" (as she so adorably called herself), favored books she could easily stuff down the back of her underpants and couldn't spell her own name. I wondered, *Is it too late to change it?*

We lived in Manhattan, in a neighborhood with poor-performing schools, so we had three choices: apply her to private school, try for our local TAG program, or move to a different neighborhood zoned for a better kindergarten. The first two options would require she be tested. The third would not, at least not for admissions. Even so, when school started, her teachers would evaluate her for placement in the slow, average, or advanced ability groups.

Mark and I wanted to stay in our neighborhood, so our goal was to get Schuyler into either our local TAG program (which would be excellent and free) or a private school (which would be excellent and expensive). I asked our preschool director if there was anything we should be doing at home so she might score better on the all-important test. She gave me one of those "What kind of parent are you?" looks that you never want to get from your nursery school director the year you're depending on her to recommend your family to an in-demand kindergarten.

"Puh-leaze," she groaned. "It's one thing to prep a teenager for an SAT, but to tutor a child barely out of Pampers?" *You sicken me.* Her lips didn't say that, but her eyes did. "Relax," she said, "you just need to trust that between preschool and life, she has absorbed everything she needs to know to do well."

Obedient by nature, I followed my director's advice. She was the professional and I was the amateur. In the end, Schuyler tested well enough to get into private school, but not well enough to qualify for the TAG program. We were disappointed because private school was so expensive and a TAG program would have been free, but the outcome wasn't entirely unexpected (what with her habit of stuffing books down her pants and all).

Your Son Is No Baby Einstein

Over the next year, our younger son, Sam, suffered from recurring ear infections. I noticed that his language was developing more slowly than Schuyler's had. At 3, Sam often didn't look at me when I spoke to him, and he barely used words, pointing instead to what he wanted. When I brought this up with my pediatrician, he told me not to worry, that children develop at different rates, and Sam would naturally catch up with his sister.

Despite the doctor's assurances, I was secretly afraid that Sam might have autism or have some other devastating condition. The possibility that something was seriously wrong with my child was too much to bear. I ignored my doctor's advice and took Sam to a specialist.

The new doctor immediately ran a battery of physical and psychological tests. He told me there was good news and bad. The good news was that the delays stemmed from the fact that Sam couldn't hear, the result of fluid buildup from all the ear infections. That could be corrected with surgery. I jumped with joy and hugged the doctor.

"Not so fast. There's bad news," he said. "We gave Sam the WPPSI, the test he'll need to take to get into school next year. His scores were abysmal."

"So I guess that rules out TAG programs," I said.

"I guess it does. And with scores as low as his, there isn't a private school in town that will accept him," he declared. "You should look into the special ed program at your local school."

Now, I'm no snob. If I could have placed Sam in a fine (free!) public special ed program, I would have been first in line. However, we lived in one of the worst-performing zones in New York City. I wasn't about to put my precious son in their hands. "Isn't there *something* I can do?" I asked. "Can we fast-track his development and improve his scores for next year?" Surely there was some sort of "how-to" book for developmentally delayed darlings and the mothers who loved them.

The doctor spoke slowly and patiently to me as if I were the one with developmental delays. He explained that the WPPSI was an IQ test and that it was impossible to prep for these. Sam's intelligence was a trait like his beautiful blue eyes, his deep adorable dimples, and his funny cry. His IQ was set at birth and there was nothing I could do to change it. What I heard was, "Now, young lady, don't you go worrying your pretty little head about such things. I'm the professional; you're merely the parent. I proclaimed special ed and special ed it shall be."

A Mother's Got to Do What a Mother's Got to Do

Lucky for me, I had access to a second opinion. My mother happened to be a PhD and professor of early childhood education. She had written a book called *Working with Parents* that guided preschool teachers on helping mothers and fathers support their children's intellectual growth at home. Not only that, she had developed a preschool curriculum for children from low-income families who weren't "naturally" absorbing what they needed for school readiness. In opposition to theorists in her field, my mother's program advocated the active teaching of concepts and skills to preschoolers to make sure they met their intellectual milestones. A number of Head Start and other nonprofit early education programs across the country used her curriculum. The test scores for these kids improved significantly, and they were better prepared to enter kindergarten. Not only that, the preschoolers who were actively taught concepts did better on later standardized tests than those who weren't, proving that the effects of early intellectual support can be lasting.

If this book were fiction, the editor wouldn't let me have a mother like that. It would be too much of a coincidence for our protagonist to have the perfectly educated and experienced mother to get her out of her jam. But truth can be stranger than fiction, and in this case it was.

I called Dr. Mom. Was it true? Was there nothing I could do to help Sam, who (at age 3) trailed miserably behind his Pampered peers? "Nonsense," she told me. "The doctor doesn't know what he's talking about. Get Sam's hearing fixed. Then you can tackle his delays."

My mother explained that intelligence tests evaluate the extent to which a child has acquired the abilities he should have picked up by the age he's tested. Sam was behind because he couldn't hear what was going on around him. Other kids lag because they aren't in a good preschool or their parents don't talk to them enough. Kids of teachers test above expectations because teachers know how to impart the most important skills and knowledge to their kids. Mom said, "If you understand the abilities Sam should have by age four [when he would be retested for kindergarten], you can help him catch up."

My mother pulled back the curtain to reveal that there was no magic to the testing process. In fact, once I understood how it worked, it made perfect sense. With Mom's guidance and by studying the textbooks she used to train psychologists to assess young children, we mapped out a program I could do at home to strengthen Sam's abilities so he would test better and, more important, so he would be ready to enter a regular kindergarten program in a year.

With funding from the city, we were able to arrange for a special-ed teacher to assist Sam in the classroom a few hours each week. He was also given speech therapy and occupational therapy once a week. Then, every evening after I came home from work, the two of us nestled in my bed for a special activity time. To Sam, it was fun and games with Mom. But in reality, everything we did was selected to support his intellectual growth.

A year passed. Sam took the test again. Not long after, his nursery school director called. She was thrilled to report that Sam, her special-ed student, had made the top score in his class. He was admitted to the same private school his sister attended. Today, he is an excellent student. In fact, by first grade, his teachers were surprised to learn that he was ever behind.

Psychologists say that the home environment can impact IQ by 15 to 35 points. Sam's scores improved more than that. At age 3, his overall IQ was in the 37th percentile; at age 4, it was in the 94th percentile. His was an unusual case, but it showed me the enormous impact parents can have.

> **Ear infections** are among the most common illnesses in babies and young children. Middle-ear infections (acute otitis media) can lead to fluid buildup that results in hearing loss and can lead to delays in language and cognitive development. This is what happened to Sam. If your child suffers from recurring ear infections, work with your pediatrician to stave off recurrences. For Sam, the insertion of ear tubes did the trick, but there are other treatments. If your child has experienced this problem over a period of years, as Sam did, you may want to have him tested for developmental delays.

You Are Your Child's Most Important Teacher

Watching Sam blossom, I am convinced that parents working with their children to build abilities that intelligence tests measure is not only fair, but it is the responsible thing to do. We make it our business to understand nutrition so we can feed our kids in ways that will keep their bodies healthy. Shouldn't we understand intelligence so we can interact with them in ways that will nourish their brains? If we lovingly teach our children through play, at home, in the natural course of daily life, then why not?

After my experience with Sam, I cofounded Smart City Kids, a company devoted to helping families get their children into NYC's top gifted public schools and best private kindergartens. Through workshops and individual coaching, I taught scores of parents how to engage their own children as I had Sam. I figured if these activities could make such a difference with a mildly developmentally delayed child, think what they might do for kids who are where they should be. Time and again, parents followed the program, their children tested well, and they were admitted to NYC's most competitive public and private schools.

I am not suggesting that you turn your home into a classroom, use flash cards, or make every waking moment a learning opportunity. There's a balance to be struck. You read to your child every day anyway, but how can you do it so that you build his vocabulary and inspire him to become a voracious reader himself? How can you introduce math irresistibly into your dinner preparations? What games can you play in the car to build memory, vocabulary, and comprehension that will have your toddler begging for more? The activities I'm going to suggest are what every good parent should be doing to give kids the best chance to thrive in kindergarten and beyond. Better test scores are icing on the cake.

> Early childhood is the most critical and vulnerable time in any child's development. Our research and that of others demonstrates that in the first few years, the ingredients for intellectual and moral growth must be laid down. Children who don't get this are likely to be two or three steps behind no matter how hard we try to help them catch up.
>
> —Dr. T. Berry Brazelton

I am not a professional educator. I am a mother who was forced to figure this out to help her own child. Later, I became a professional, sharing what I knew with other parents so they could help their children, and they did. Now I'm passing it on to you.

This is the book I desperately wanted to read when I realized how much help Sam needed before he would be ready for school. If I only knew how to engage him in ways that would help him grow intellectually, I could get him back on track. It is my guess that you are already doing many of the types of activities I'm going to suggest. So much of this comes naturally to good parents. What you may not realize is *how* some of the different activities you're doing affect your child's intellectual growth.

You read her nursery rhymes, right? Do you know that nursery rhymes teach children phonological awareness, the ability to isolate individual sounds in words like "J-i-ll" and "h-i-ll?" This is an enormously important prereading skill.

Your child plays with different-shaped blocks, right? Did you realize that shapes are critical to learning letters, which are nothing more than lines, circles, squares, and triangles put together in different ways? When you read on, pat yourself on the back for the many right things you are doing now and then add some things you haven't tried.

Like many experts, educators and psychologists can be protective of "their turf." But don't ever let a school director or some fancy doctor tell you to leave your child's intellectual development "to the professionals." By being aware of what your child needs to learn and providing the right environment and stimulation, you are your child's most important teacher.

In the next chapter, you will discover specific things you can do and ways you can interact with your child at home that will naturally increase her IQ score and set her up for success in *any* kindergarten she attends, be it public, private, or gifted.

2. This Is Not About kinder-cramming

WHY PREPARING FOR KINDERGARTEN TESTING IS NOT "CHEATING"

So here you have it, the first manual on preparing 2- to 5-year-olds for kindergarten tests, written by a mother who turned herself into an expert out of desperation to help her own child catch up developmentally. It takes brass ovaries to tackle this subject because—let's face it—who doesn't love to bash those misguided moms and dads who push their kids, trying to mold them into prodigies they were never meant to be? Who doesn't shake their heads at those zealots that play Mozart to their fetuses and teach their babies how to read? My former neighbor did that, by the way. Last time we spoke, her 2-year-old was "reading" words from flash cards before the Latin tutor was due to arrive.

How Much Can You Affect Your Child's IQ?

I learned through experience that parents can affect their children's IQ scores, but what do the experts say about this? In the early 1900s, when Alfred Binet created the first test to measure intelligence in children, he was firm in stating that intelligence was fluid and could be increased. In the years that followed, scientists strayed from that belief and conventional wisdom became that a person's intellectual potential was genetic and fixed at birth.

In his meticulously researched 2009 book *Intelligence and How to Get It*, psychologist Richard E. Nisbett argues convincingly that intellect is principally determined by societal influences rather than genetics, and so is highly modifiable by parents and teachers. Nisbett deflates the notion that intelligence is hardwired at birth and offers ways parents can affect their child's cognition. For example, did you know that breast-feeding for 8 months is worth 6 points on a child's IQ test? Were you aware that if you exercise during pregnancy, you're more likely to have a bigger baby with a higher IQ because of his larger brain?

Nisbett's best evidence that intellect is influenced by environmental factors comes from studies showing that children born into higher socioeconomic status (SES) families have a 12- to 18-point IQ advantage over children born into lower SES families. This difference is meaningful when you consider that a person with an IQ of 100 might be expected to graduate from high school without distinction, whereas a person with an IQ of 115 is more likely to go to college and become a professional. However, when children born into lower SES families are adopted into higher SES families, they show IQ gains of 12 to 16 points. These gains can only be environmental in origin, the result of higher SES parents providing a richer cognitive home life than the child otherwise would have had.

Just as poor nutrition can stunt a person's physical growth, being raised in a weak cognitive environment can stunt a person's intellectual development. To explain the 12- to 18-point IQ score gap between lower SES and higher SES families, Nisbett relies on observational studies that compare how higher SES parents and lower SES parents interact with their children. These studies go a long way in establishing a causal relationship between parenting practices and higher intelligence in children, as outlined in the following table.

Higher SES Parent	Lower SES Parent
Talks to children more using advanced grammar; asks challenging questions; comments on child's world, her experiences, and emotions.	Talks to children less; more of what is said comes in the form of demands and reprimands that are unlikely to stimulate a child's intellectual curiosity.
Engages children in dinner table conversations, involving them in topics and issues adults are discussing.	Carries on adult discussion with the assumption that children would have no interest in the topic.
Speaks 2,000 words per hour.	Speaks 1,300 words per hour.
By age 3, typical child has heard 30 million words.	By age 3, typical child has heard 20 million words.
Makes six encouraging comments for every reprimand: encouragement supports the child's intellectual confidence and curiosity.	Makes two encouraging comments per reprimand.
Home has more books; reading begins as early as 6 months.	Few books in the home; reading begins later.

Higher SES Parent	Lower SES Parent
Relates material in books to objects and events in the child's life; asks child *what* and *why* questions about the story, encouraging the child to participate.	Doesn't relate material in books to the child's life; asks *what* but not *why* questions; views comments as interruptions and tells child to listen and pay attention.
Gives verbal instruction describing how to do something.	Physically demonstrates how to do something and is more likely to say, "Do it like this."
Will intervene in school to get accommodations for child's individual needs.	Unlikely to challenge authority, and teachers are viewed as authority.
Heavily involved in their child's world; chauffeuring them to activities, asking about teachers, coaches, friends.	Little involvement in child's free time. Unlikely to enroll them in lessons or take them to activities. Kids spend most of their time in self-directed play and watching TV.
Actively works to assess and foster child's talents, opinions, and skills.	Sees their role as making sure their kids are fed, housed, clothed, clean, schooled; lets child grow and develop on her own.
Engages in educational activities over the summer such as reading, conversing, going to the zoo or museums, resulting in an increase in IQ after summer.	Provides little educational and cultural stimulation over the summer, resulting in a decrease in IQ.
Raises children to have the kind of questioning analytical minds they will need as professionals, doctors, and CEOs. Teaches child social mores such as shaking hands, looking people in the eye, cooperating with others.	Raises their children to be workers where obedience and good behavior will satisfy employers who are not looking to be questioned or second-guessed.

Sources: *Intelligence and How to Get It*, by Richard E. Nisbett; *Unequal Childhoods: Class, Race, and Family Life*, by Annette Lareau; *Meaningful Differences in the Everyday Experience of Young American Children*, by Betty Hart and Todd R. Risley.

Nisbett concludes by suggesting simple things parents can do to raise their child's IQ score and intelligence: talk to him using high-level vocabulary, read out loud to him, make comments to encourage his curiosity, teach him to delay gratification, and value his efforts over his intelligence. Nisbett's bottom line—environmental influences can raise a child's IQ from a score that predicts barely graduating from high school to one that suggests a professional career—should convince you that interacting with your child in ways that will strengthen his intelligence is well worth the effort.

OTHER ENVIRONMENTAL FACTORS THAT INFLUENCE INTELLIGENCE

Spanking. According to a study by Murray Straus of the University of New Hampshire, 2- to-4-year-olds who were spanked scored 5 points lower on IQ tests than kids who weren't spanked. Children ages 5 to 9 who were spanked scored 2.8 points lower than those who weren't.

Sleep shift. Dr. Monique LeBourgeois of Brown University studies how sleep affects prekindergartners. She found that if young children are allowed to stay up one extra hour on weekend nights and are then given an intelligence test on Monday, there is a 7-point reduction in scores.

Lead Paint. A study conducted by Dr. Bruce Lanphear found that children with a lead concentration of less than 10 micrograms per deciliter of blood scored an average of 11.1 points lower on a Stanford-Binet IQ test. For every additional 10-microgram increase in blood concentration lead levels, there was a further 5.5 point decline.

Stimulate Your Child's Mind While Keeping It Fun

Recently I saw a follow-up report on the *Today Show* about a scary-smart girl named Elizabeth Barrett. They first featured her at 17 months because she had taught herself to read simple words. Now at 2.5 years old, she's reading the newspaper and the ticker that runs along the bottom of CNN. She knows all her state capitals. When her mother asked her what the capital of Maine was, she offered a classic gifted-child response, connecting two unrelated concepts by saying, "Augusta, just like [the month] August!"

Although Elizabeth hasn't taken an IQ test yet, I'll go out on a limb and declare her gifted. Did her parents push her? Did they subject her to in-utero tutoring and Baby Einstein videos at 3 months? Did they whip out the flash cards before she was out of diapers? No, Elizabeth came this way from God (or whatever higher power you believe in). She picked up reading naturally, asked questions, and continues to express deep curiosity about her world. Mom and Dad allowed her to take the lead, which is usually the case with these special children. If you explore any gifted child's history, they tend to be on a different developmental track from infancy on.

If you follow every piece of advice I'll be giving you in this book, odds are you will not mold your little one into another Elizabeth Barrett. James Delisle, a teacher and counselor for gifted children, put it this way: "The gifted child thinks, acts, and feels differently than other children. You can't 'train' children to be gifted . . . gifted children simply *are*."

Just because you can't turn your little one into a genius who gets to hobnob with Matt Lauer on the *Today Show* doesn't mean you shouldn't actively help her build her intelligence. The trick is to do it gently. Avoid pressuring her and setting unrealistic expectations that she can't meet. Mom- and Dadzillas who set the bar too high are often satirized in books and films; check out the movie *Parenthood* to see Rick Moranis drill his 3-year-old on chemical symbols, square roots, and world history. In my own novel *The Ivy Chronicles* I poke fun at mothers who sign up their kids for elocution lessons at Toastmasters for Tots or cooking at the French Kids Culinary Institute to give them an edge getting into New York City's top private schools.

Experts almost unanimously warn parents against focusing too much on learning in their daily interactions with kids at home. "Relax," they say. "Let your child enjoy his childhood. Leave academics to the educators. He'll pick up the skills he needs for school over time. Right now, he needs to flex his creative muscles, go out and catch fireflies, and smell the roses."

I am all for smelling the roses . . . *after* you teach your kid to categorize them by type, color, and smell, count the petals, and compare and contrast them to daisies. No, I'm just playing with you here. Speaking of play, kids need more of that. In fact, play may be as vital to a child's academic success as reading, writing, and arithmetic, but I'm jumping ahead of myself here.

The point is, you can support your child's intellectual development while leaving plenty of time for building forts and rolling in the grass. Several kindergarten teachers read early drafts of this book. Each told me that she wished the parents of her students were working with their children to build abilities as the book suggests. As one said, "There are twenty-five to thirty kids in my class, me, and two assistant teachers. We can't give each child the kind of individual attention that parents can. There's no substitute for one-on-one instruction. Parents have a responsibility to do this." Doing learning-focused activities for fifteen to twenty minutes on a regular basis can mean a lot. This is what I'm advocating. This, plus lots of playtime and love from parents and caregivers. If you learn how to stimulate your child's mind and build that into your daily life together so it becomes second nature, there will be plenty of time to smell the roses.

> A child educated only at school is an uneducated child.
>
> —George Santayana, philosopher

What Admissions Directors Say About Test Prep

In the last few years, a cottage industry has grown up around preparing children for kindergarten admissions exams. At worst, tutors teach children the answers to the test they'll be taking. At best, tutors are committed educators who teach kids the skills that tests measure. Some parents go so far as to have their little ones privately tested before the real thing just for practice, which is completely against the rules. Still, practice helps. Officials at Stanford-Binet say that preschoolers who have taken the test four months apart improved their IQ scores by an average of 8.2 points, enough to go from the 89th percentile (120) to the 96th (128).

Although intelligence tests aren't perfect, admissions directors rely on them as a common yardstick to compare applicants. They say that the test is just one indicator used to assess whether or not to admit a child. The importance of scores varies by schools. High scores won't necessarily get your child in, but low scores *may* keep her out—especially in areas where there are ten applications for every spot. Some kindergarten programs are more open to students with a wide range of scores and use the test only to eliminate children whose results are extremely poor or indicate a possible learning issue.

Since some nursery schools design their curriculum in ways that prepare their students for testing while others don't, children come to the exam with different levels of readiness. Add to that the variety of preschool experiences children have and the diverse educational, cultural, and socioeconomic backgrounds of applicant families, and you'll find a playing field for children taking admissions tests and ability group assessments that is unequal from the start. Given this, it is naïve to "trust" that your child will naturally absorb whatever she needs to know to test well.

Parents must cope with the fact that a test score earned on a single day of their young child's life could significantly affect her future. Until the inequalities in the system are magically evened out, moms and dads seeking the best educational opportunities for their kids feel compelled to do whatever they can to prepare their children to earn a seat at a good school or a place in a high-ability group.

The official word on test preparation is don't do it. Dr. Elizabeth (Babbi) Krents who heads admissions for the prestigious Dalton School in NYC, wrote an article for the *Parents League Review* on this very issue. Her arguments against preparation were: (1) your child may end up getting into a school requiring a higher level of performance than he can handle; (2) higher scores resulting from coaching give an inaccurate picture of the applicant, making it impossible for schools to assess whether they are a good match for the school; (3) even worse, "many psychologists . . . and other adults are actually teaching kids the exact answers to the test"; (4) a perceptive tester can tell when a child has been taught the answers and when this happens, the results are invalidated; and (5) children pick up on the stress of parents who go to great lengths for test preparation, and these kids may approach the test with great anxiety.

I agree with Dr. Krents that teaching children the answers to the test is wrong on many levels, starting with the fact that—*Hell-o!—it's cheating*! But that's not what I'm suggesting you do. *I am suggesting that you slightly adjust the way you interact with your child from the time he is very young and help him acquire the skills and abilities that educators agree he should have by the time he enters kindergarten.* If modifying your parenting practices enhances your child's intelligence to the point that he scores higher on an IQ test, the improvement is genuine, and the schools you apply him to will get an accurate picture of what he can handle.

As parents, we must deal with hyper-competitive admissions processes and educational systems that are imperfect and unfair. I did what it took to bolster my son's intellect so he would qualify for the best kindergarten program we could find for him. With the information in this book you can do the same for your child. This is *not* kinder-cramming. On the contrary; it is good parenting.

> In the next chapter, you'll learn about different types of intelligences, the various kinds of tests schools use to assess children, and how to prepare your child to do her best.

3. The Scoop on Intelligence Testing

WHAT TAKES PLACE BEHIND CLOSED DOORS

I promise to spare you a boring dissertation on intelligence testing. However, if you're interested in reading one of those, there are several references at Testingforkindergarten.com for texts written by professionals in the field. Be warned, however: your eyes may bleed. In these pages, I offer you the basics in plain English, which is really all we normal parents need to help our children.

IQ Tests Measure the Intelligence Needed to Succeed at School

The first IQ test, from which all modern tests derive, was developed in France in 1905. The developers based the test on the French school curriculum in order to determine which kids in the Paris public schools could handle the work and which needed special education. The French never intended for educators to rely on these tests to qualify 4-year-old applicants for competitive schools, and yet that is how they are being used today. *C'est la vie!*

Unlike the SAT, questions on IQ tests do not change from year to year. The Stanford-Binet 5 (Stanford-Binet), which can be administered to those age 2 to adulthood, has been revised only five times since 1905. The Wechsler Preschool and Primary Scale of Intelligence–III (WPPSI), which can be given to children ages 2 to 7, has been revised twice since it was developed in 1967.

From the beginning, IQ tests were designed to measure a specific kind of intelligence, the kind that children need to succeed in an *academic* setting. That kind of intelligence depends on language, knowledge, memory, mathematics, spatial, motor skills, cognitive abilities, and speed of thinking. They do not measure creativity, wisdom, honesty, persistence, or the ability to succeed in life.

Controversy over using these tests as criteria for entry into private schools and public gifted programs has been swirling since the 1950s. Experts agree that the tests favor children from advantaged homes. Kids from poor or immigrant backgrounds score lower than kids from middle-class families and native English speakers. Children whose parents read to them regularly, expose them to more language, and provide a richer cognitive environment score higher, too.

In New York City, there is a school called Hunter College Elementary. It is considered the *capo di tutti* of gifted programs in Manhattan, with insanely tough criteria for entry. Thousands of Manhattan children take the Stanford-Binet test to apply for the forty-eight places available annually. Only children scoring in the 98th percentile (meaning they scored as well as or better than 98 percent of children in the same age category) and above are asked back for an in-person visit where they are invited for—*ta-da!*—more testing! There, in groups of six or eight, deep inside classrooms with paper-covered windows so no one can see what's happening, the kids are evaluated on problem-solving and creative-thinking skills, verbal and mathematical abilities, leadership, and the ability to learn a new task and respond to complex directions. If your child is lucky enough to win a spot, it is like hitting the education lottery. She'll get a thirteen-year education as fine as those offered by the best private schools, but for free.

Naturally, when my daughter, Schuyler, was 4, we applied. There was no question in my mind that she was a genius. That runs in my husband's family, at least according to him. Imagine my shock when I opened the envelope and found out that Schuyler was (*gasp!*) average. *What?* Was the child I knew to be extraordinary (officially) ordinary? At the time, I didn't realize how scary a thought that was. Studies have shown that test scores can be self-fulfilling prophecies. When parents and teachers expect a child to do well or poorly based on his score, they treat the child in ways to make the prediction come true.

Shortly after my initial disappointment, I realized how silly it was to think differently about my daughter because of a test score. Today, Schuyler's genius has emerged in more venues than I can count. She performs aerial ballet. She sings. She dances. She acts. She writes. She has a wicked sense of humor and a personality that will take her anywhere she chooses to go in life. Did I mention that she played a baby on *As the World Turns* when she was 3 months old? Well, she did, and her performance was stellar. Everyone said so, not just me. I am telling you this not because I'm proud of my daughter (okay, I am), but because I don't want you to be disappointed if you discover that your wunderkind isn't a certified genius according to the Stanford-Binet.

High Scores Don't Mean Success; Low Scores Don't Mean Failure

IQ tests are not infallible. There is always a margin of error, meaning that your child's score could be higher or lower than reported. Scores are based on one performance on one day in the life of a preschooler. If your child has difficulty sitting still, is shy, tired, has a cold, or just isn't in the mood, that could be 20 points off her IQ score. If she's highly creative and decides to make her own block design when the tester asks her to copy the one he made, you can kiss Harvard good-bye. A friend of mine's son completely flubbed his kindergarten admissions test. Why? The child wanted to get out of the room as quickly as he could because the psychologist had "scary eyes and smelled like bellybutton."

It isn't until your child is 5 that her IQ score even begins to become predictive of her true level of intelligence. Only IQs measured at age 12 or older tend to be in line with adult scores. Several studies have shown that IQ scores can change anywhere from 10 to 30 points between the ages of 2.5 to 17.

Even if a child tests as having high academic intelligence, that doesn't mean she'll be motivated to work hard in school. An average-scoring child may grow up to be one of those tenacious kids who studies like crazy and brings home top grades. Many studies of motivation and self-discipline in children have concluded that these qualities are better predictors of academic success than IQ scores. When Thomas Edison was a schoolboy, his teacher told him he was too stupid to learn anything. Muhammad Ali graduated 376th from a high school class of 391 students. Winston Churchill failed sixth grade. Aren't you happy to know that your child doesn't have to be a card-carrying member of Mensa to make it in life?

Other Types of Intelligence

There are many types of intelligences, and academic is only one. Howard Gardner, a Harvard professor (who probably has a high IQ), developed the Multiple

Intelligence theory. According to Gardner, people possess eight different types of intelligence: linguistic (word smart), logical-mathematical (number and science smart), spatial (art and design smart), musical (music smart), intrapersonal (self-smart), interpersonal (people smart), body (athlete/dancer/actor smart), and naturalist (outdoor smart). The first two will serve you well in school. But if your genius is in the area of body, like Michael Jordan's, who cares if you can conjugate a verb? If your brilliance is as a naturalist, as I suspect Steve Irwin's was, do you really need to master trigonometry? Ray Charles dropped out of school at age 15, but his musical genius continues to be a gift to the world.

Robert Sternberg, a professor of psychology at Yale, believes that tests define intelligence too narrowly. He identifies three abilities needed to succeed not just in school, but in life:

> *Analytical intelligence* includes the linguistic and logical-mathematical skills necessary to excel in academic and problem-solving endeavors.
>
> *Creative intelligence* is the ability to deal successfully with new and unusual situations by drawing on existing knowledge and skills. While the analytically intelligent person might see a paper clip as an object for holding papers together, a creatively intelligent person would see it as a toenail cleaner, hem holder, Super Glue bottle unclogger, lock pick, hair clip, bookmark, or a hundred other things. Consider how important the ability to think in original ways is to making a mark in the world, and yet it isn't measured on intelligence tests!
>
> *Practical intelligence* enables people to understand what needs to be done in a situation and then know how to make it happen.

In other words: creative intelligence will help you come up with ideas, analytical intelligence will help you decide if the ideas are good, and practical intelligence will help you sell and implement them.

Daniel Goleman, in his 1995 book *Emotional Intelligence*, makes a strong case that qualities such as motivation, empathy, social skills, self-awareness, and self-regulation are as important (if not more so) to life success than a high IQ. Studies have supported this view, including research by Gregory Feist and Frank Barron presented in 1996. The researchers looked at eighty PhDs who underwent IQ testing, personality testing, and one-on-one interviews in the 1950s when they were students at Berkeley. Forty years later, they were tracked down, and their level of success in life was gauged based on their résumés and evaluations by their peers. It turned out that emotional qualities were four times more important than IQ in predicting success in life and prestige. Howard Gardner has said, "Many people with IQs of 160 work for people with IQs of 100 if the former have poor intrapersonal intelligence and the latter have a high one."

Why am I telling you this? Because I don't want you to get all hung up on your child's IQ score. Other more important variables determine whether or not she will succeed in life. Plus, IQ scores of young children turn out to be poor predictors of their ability to succeed in school. In their book *Nurture-Shock*, authors Po Bronson and Ashley Merryman cite research by Dr. Hoi Suen that finds intelligence test scores of preschool and kindergarten children have only a 40 percent correlation with later achievement test results.

The authors point out that the majority of school districts with TAG programs beginning in kindergarten rely on a single intelligence test for admission, never retesting kids to see if they still belong, never giving late bloomers a chance to test in. Bronson and Merryman find this practice appalling given the fact that children in these rarified programs are placed with smarter peers, given harder work, and cover extended curriculum. They describe a California study showing that kids in gifted classrooms make 36.7 percent more progress each year than those in regular classes. I agree with the authors. Testing young children whose brains are still forming and basing such a high-stakes placement on these results makes no sense.

Still, what are you going to do? Someday schools may change, but for now, it is what it is. You have to play the hand you're dealt (and all those other clichés). If your child is facing an intelligence test for private school, a TAG program, or ability placement inside her classroom, doing well could make a tremendous difference in the educational opportunities she's given. So what do you need to know to help her?

Types of Tests

INTELLIGENCE TEST

The term *IQ*, or *intelligence quotient*, refers to the composite intelligence test score that comes from combining all the subtest scores on the Stanford-Binet or another similar instrument such as the WPPSI.

The most popular intelligence tests are the WPPSI and the Stanford-Binet, which measure children's language, knowledge, memory, mathematics, spatial, fine-motor, and thinking abilities. A psychologist administers these one-on-one to children in a session that takes about an hour. Remember that bell curve from statistics class? If everyone's IQ scores are plotted, the scores are distributed in a bell curve, which means that about 68 percent of us fall somewhere in the middle, with 100 being the absolute center. Below, you'll see how IQ scores translate to percentiles:

An IQ Score of	Ranks Higher Than This Percentage of Population
65	1
70	2
75	5
80	9
85	16
90	25
95	37
100	50
105	63
110	75
115	85
120	91
125	95
130	98
135	99
140	99.5

Here are the generally accepted levels of intelligence based on IQ scores:

IQ Score	Level of Intelligence
180 and above	Profoundly gifted
160 to 179	Exceptionally gifted
146 to 159	Highly gifted
131 to 145	Moderately gifted
116 to 130	High average
85 to 115	Average
71 to 84	Moderate intellectual functioning
55 to 70	Moderately mentally retarded

READINESS TEST

These are also used to assess children's language, knowledge, memory, mathematics, spatial, fine-motor skills, and thinking abilities. They are administered one-on-one by trained professionals or in groups. For example, the Otis-Lennon School Ability Test (OLSAT) is given one-on-one to preschoolers, but in groups to older children. These are used to evaluate kids for TAG programs, private school admissions, or ability groupings in public schools. Other readiness tests include the Bracken School Readiness Assessment and the Gesell School Readiness Screening Test.

> ## BEWARE OF GROUP TESTS
> Tests administered in a group setting are less reliable than tests given one-on-one. If a major educational decision is made on behalf of your child based on results of a group test and you don't agree with it, get him retested.

DEVELOPMENTAL SCREENING

The third type of test your child may take is a developmental screening. These are administered in groups. It is impractical from a logistics and financial point of view for school districts to administer one-on-one intelligence tests to large populations of kids. Instead, they will use a developmental screening to select the kids who should go on for more in-depth testing for giftedness or learning disabilities. A few of these instruments used nationally are the Early Screening Inventory—Revised and McCarthy's Scales of Children's Abilities. Some districts create their own screening tools to evaluate children for ability groupings in public school.

INFORMAL ASSESSMENTS

A teacher using a checklist while observing each child in her classroom administers this type of test. They are most commonly used to assess children for ability groupings. The teacher might also use information gathered in informal assessments to design learning experiences appropriate to the children's level. Private schools and TAG programs use informal assessments (in addition to intelligence tests taken separately) during a child's "interview."

What Is It Like for Your Child to Be Tested?

TESTING AT SCHOOL

In some places, children are tested for private kindergarten admissions in their own nursery schools. When this is the case, you won't have to say a thing to prepare your child. The teacher will take care of it. This is ideal because your child is comfortable at school and will have had a chance to meet the tester ahead of time. The teacher is able to see when your child is having a good day and, ideally, that's when she will send her in for testing. However, if your child has a bad night or an emotional upset when testing may occur, be sure to tell the teacher. As a parent, you probably won't be told when your child will be assessed, so you won't inadvertently communicate any anxiety you feel about the process.

TESTING AT A PSYCHOLOGIST'S OFFICE

In many cities, you'll take your child to a psychologist's office to be tested. While their examination rooms tend to be inviting, their waiting rooms often resemble doctors' offices, so assure your child that she won't be getting a shot.

If you are able to choose your own psychologist for the test, ask your school or friends for a recommendation. Some districts provide a list of approved testers. Call and ask about their experience, advice they have to help you make your child feel at ease, or any other concerns. If your intuition tells you this isn't someone your child will relate to, listen to it and schedule with a different examiner. Here are a few suggestions to make your child's testing experience go more smoothly:

* **Health and restfulness.** Make sure your child is rested and feeling well on the day of the test. If she becomes ill within days of being assessed, contact the psychologist to let her know. If the results seem atypical for your child, the evaluation's validity should be questioned. If this happens, consider getting your child retested using a different instrument (retesting with the same test would be invalid, since the questions are the same). If these results are much better, you can offer them to the schools where you are applying.
* **Scheduling.** Avoid scheduling the appointment after she has had a long day at preschool and don't take her out of school to go for a test. If you drag her away from an activity she enjoys, she may be upset and uncooperative during the exam.
* **The waiting room.** Bring along some books and games in case you have to wait. In some cases, the psychologist may observe your child in the waiting room.

* **Separation.** If your child has trouble separating from you, have your spouse or caretaker bring her to the testing site. Whoever accompanies the child should assure her that she will wait for her the entire time.
* **What to tell your child.** Try not to use the word *test* when describing what will happen. You might tell her that you are going to "meet a special teacher who wants to find out just how smart 4-year-olds are. So do your best to answer her questions and show her how much 4-year-olds know." Kids usually take the responsibility seriously and give it their all. Explain that she'll be working with blocks and puzzles, pencils and paper, and that the teacher will ask her to draw some things and to answer some questions. Challenge her to try as hard as she can on every task. Let her know that many of the things she'll be asked to do will be fun. Don't tell her she will be playing games or she may not take the experience seriously.
* **Reward.** If your child is reluctant to go, you can promise to take him for something he considers special afterward (e.g., for ice cream, to the zoo), but don't make the treat *too* extraordinary or your child might rush through the test to get to the reward.

IN THE TESTING ROOM

Test designers have gone to great lengths to make sure that tests are administered the same way every time so results can be compared between children. Standard directions are given before each task, items (or tasks) are timed, and the tests are scored the same way. What test designers can't control for, however, is the consistency of the psychologists and examiners. Some are better at establishing rapport with children, which is why it is worth getting recommendations for testers. Here is what happens in the testing room:

* **Setting the stage.** When a child goes inside, she will be offered a pint-sized seat at a small table where she can easily work with materials. If your child has trouble separating, you can accompany her to the testing room and stay for a few minutes.
* **The examiner's introduction.** When your child feels at ease, the examiner will explain to her what she will be asked to do, tell her to try her hardest and have fun. She will assure her that she doesn't expect her to be able to do everything asked of her because some of the questions are really meant for older children.
* **Subtests.** The test your child will take is made up of several subtests in each category. For example, with the WPPSI, the verbal assessment is made up of subtests on information, vocabulary, and word reasoning. Sometimes the test has more

subtests than your child will get. It may be that the school requires only certain subtests or that your child isn't old enough to take all of them.

Ask the psychologist to explain your child's subtest results to you if you have questions. A child may have an overall score of 110, with a 99th percentile on information and vocabulary and a 40th percentile in spatial abilities. Knowing that, you can expect that she will do well in subjects with verbal-information components like reading and writing, but she may struggle in subjects with spatial aspects like math and science. If your child has inconsistent scores like this, keep your eye on her area of weakness and jump in with academic support if she begins to falter. The earlier you detect a learning issue, the easier it is to correct.

* **The process.** The examiner will give your child directions and often a practice item. She'll start with questions slightly below your child's abilities (the "floor") and will stop after he misses a few items in a row to be sure he has reached his highest ability on that subtest (the "ceiling"). She won't give away whether or not he is right or wrong in his responses. Instead, she might praise him with comments throughout like "Good job" or "I can see how hard you're trying."

* **Most children enjoy being tested.** Don't worry that you're scarring your little one for life by having him tested. Most kids enjoy it. I do know of one precocious child who dropped to the floor and feigned a heart attack mid-WPPSI, but that wasn't the tester's fault. The boy's parents were so stressed out about how he would perform that he picked up on their vibe and decided not to perform at all. It's too bad they weren't evaluating this kid for creative problem solving.

The Narrative Report

When a psychologist tests your child, she will include a report about the qualities she observed in him during the test (and possibly in the waiting room). This gives a glimpse into his social-emotional development as well as his work process.

If you feel there is something important that the tester should know about your child, tell her ahead of time. For example, tell the tester if your child is bilingual and it will be mentioned in the narrative report. If your child doesn't do as well as expected in the verbal subtests, his being bilingual may be relevant to understanding his score. Here are some of the things the tester might note:

* How well did she separate from her parent? Was she respectful, positive, clingy, overly independent, rude to the parent?

* Has she mastered common, simple social interchanges (e.g., politeness)? If not, were they never taught or might there be a clinical explanation? Did she make eye contact when conversing?
* How comfortable was your child with the tester? Friendly or shy? Talkative or quiet? Anxious or relaxed? Normally active or hyperactive? Overly demanding or too quick to attach?
* Did she respect bodily boundaries (e.g., not kicking, touching the tester)?
* How confident did she seem in her abilities? Self-assured or anxious? Enthusiastic or disinterested?
* What is her temperament? Cautious? Cooperative? Friendly? Motivated?
* Did she listen? Did tasks need to be explained over?
* Did she prefer easy or hard tasks? Did she need minimal encouragement or constant praise?
* As your child worked, was she absorbed or distracted? Was she persistent when the tasks got more difficult? Did she give up easily?
* How did your child respond to success? To failure?
* What was her problem-solving strategy? Was she impulsive or reflective? Did she learn from her mistakes?

Just as you feed your child from 5 food groups to nourish his body, you must also feed his brain from 7 ability groups to bolster his intellect. In the next chapter, you'll learn about each ability group and the impact it has on school and testing success. Later, you'll discover how to give your child a daily "serving" from each ability group through natural interactions such as reading a book, playing a game, or doing an activity together.

4. The 7 Abilities of Highly Successful kindergarteners

WHAT EVERY TEST MEASURES AND YOUR CHILD NEEDS TO KNOW: LANGUAGE, KNOWLEDGE/COMPREHENSION, MEMORY, MATHEMATICS, VISUAL-SPATIAL, COGNITIVE, AND FINE-MOTOR SKILLS

When my daughter was first evaluated, I remember wishing I could know the kinds of questions she would be asked and the information and skills she was expected to have, but I couldn't find books or articles that explained it in layman's terms. Had I pushed further, I would have discovered that psychologists consider the specifics of testing to be a closely guarded trade secret. They fear that this information, in the wrong hands (parents'!) could be used for evil purposes (teaching children) and, let's face it, that would spell the end of civilization as we know it. Okay, I'm kidding. Sort of.

In truth, psychologists are bound ethically to protect the security of the tests, which was why I couldn't find books or articles on the subject that didn't require a PhD to understand. Their concern is that the actual questions could get out and some unscrupulous parents would teach their children the answers, rendering their kid's test results meaningless. In this book, we are going to explore testlike questions (as an SAT prep book would), but not the real ones, so there is no danger of the answers getting out. When I was trying to help Sam, seeing the kinds of questions asked is what helped me get my arms around the underlying abilities he was expected to have. In this chapter, we will explore these abilities in depth.

What Tests Measure

There are two components to the kind of intelligence IQ tests measure. The first is *crystallized intelligence*, which depends on a child's knowledge of words, information, and the world around her—concrete things she has learned at home, at preschool, through life experience, exposure to language and her culture, to name a few influencing factors. In a testing situation, this might be evaluated in sections labeled "verbal skills" covering vocabulary, comprehension, knowledge, and mathematical word problems.

Tests also assess *fluid intelligence.* This does not require the use of real-world information. Instead it relies on a child's ability to reason through and solve visual, spatial, or abstract problems. On tests, fluid intelligence is evaluated by asking children to copy block patterns, complete two- and three-dimensional puzzles, or arrange visual images in meaningful order. These subtests often require a child to demonstrate fine-motor skills such as drawing shapes and folding paper. Test instruments assess fluid intelligence in sections they label "performance," "spatial," or "nonverbal" skills.

In testing (and life), almost every task requires both verbal and nonverbal skills. For example, in a block design subtest, a child is asked to use blocks to copy a design the tester showed him and then covered up. He will need receptive language to take in, understand, and follow the directions (verbal). He'll use short-term visual memory to remember what the design looked like (nonverbal). Then he'll rely on spatial reasoning to figure out how to create the pattern he saw from individual blocks (nonverbal). He'll use fine-motor skills to assemble the blocks (nonverbal).

> The ability to simplify means to eliminate the unnecessary so that the necessary may speak.
>
> —Hans Hofmann

For simplicity, I have combined an enormous list of technically defined abilities that various tests cover into 7 broader categories. For example, in the block design subtest just described, one textbook delineated 21 "mental ingredients" needed to do the task. One of these ingredients is "auditory perception of complex verbal stimuli" (receptive language), another is "cognition and evaluation of figural stimuli" (visual-spatial), and there are 19 more. When we examine this subtest later in the book, it will be in the visual-spatial section.

If your child has real trouble with blocks and puzzles at school, his teacher may suspect that he has some kind of spatial learning disability. However, blaming his weakness on a spatial learning problem would be premature until you understood which of the technically defined "mental ingredients" needed to do these kinds of tasks was giving him trouble. Maybe the problem isn't spatial at all. Maybe he has fine-motor difficulties. Only a trained psychologist would be able to tease out the specific abilities he is struggling with and suggest a learning plan to help him. But for our purposes, that level of detail isn't needed, so we will limit ourselves to 7 broader abilities. As you read about them, you'll notice that certain aspects of one ability may also be aspects of another. Sequencing, for example, is a component of both mathematics and cognitive thinking. Don't let the overlap throw you. Whether an ability is classified as mathematics, cognitive, or both, your child needs it to do well in school.

Finally, although intelligence tests cover much of the same ground, your child may score differently from one instrument to another. That's because different tests don't give equal weight to the same abilities. For example, the Kaufman Assessment Battery for Children (KABC) emphasizes problem solving and memory, the Otis-Lennon School Ability Test (OLSAT) stresses listening and following directions, and the WPPSI focuses on verbal and knowledge abilities. Depending on your child's strengths, she might do better on one test versus another.

The 7 Abilities Every Test Measures and Why They Matter

1. LANGUAGE

RECEPTIVE LANGUAGE This is your child's ability to tune in to and understand the language she hears (and later reads) all day. Kids develop receptive language before they can talk, at about 9 months. Ask a 1-year-old to point to the cow in a picture and he can, even though he may not be able to say the word.

Why is this important for school success? Language pervades English, math, history, and any class a student takes. Children need to be able to listen, pay attention, and understand verbal explanation and lectures (or the text they read in books) in order to comprehend the lesson being taught. They need receptive language to follow the teacher's instructions.

When your child is tested, examiners will observe how well he is able to listen to and follow directions, making each item a test of your child's receptive language skills. Plus several test items are specifically designed to appraise her ability to understand language. For example, when the examiner says, "Point to the thing that barks," receptive language is being assessed. For questions assessing receptive language skills, testers are instructed not to repeat the question, since it's the ability to listen to and understand spoken words that is being examined.

EXPRESSIVE LANGUAGE. This is your child's ability to use words orally (and later in writing) to express ideas and feelings in a clear, organized manner. Because you need to understand language before you can use it yourself, this develops after receptive language, at about age 1. If your child can't pronounce words correctly, this is called an "oral-motor" problem, which is a motor skill, not a language issue. A speech therapist can help with that.

Why is this important for school success? Whether they are talking or writing, students need to be able to answer questions, share ideas through words, and communicate with teachers and other students.

When your child is tested, the examiner will observe his ability to use language in the course of being evaluated. If a question requires your child to use spoken words to respond (versus drawing or pointing), his expressive language is being assessed. Plus, several subtests are designed to measure a child's expressive language capacity. When your child is asked, "What is a dog?" the examiner will evaluate the quality of the expressive language he uses in responding.

LANGUAGE ISSUES CAN LEAD TO EMOTIONAL DYSFUNCTION

Children with language difficulties have higher rates of social, emotional, and behavior problems. Inability to communicate causes kids to act out to get their needs met, fail to get along with peers, perform poorly in school, and feel inadequate. If you suspect your child has a language problem, have him evaluated. There is more at stake than good grades!

---

2. KNOWLEDGE/COMPREHENSION

This is your child's understanding of information, social standards of behavior, and common sense that kids his age generally understand.

Why is this important for school success? To get along in kindergarten, your child should know information like colors, shapes, seasons, holidays, farm animals, types of transportation, fruits, and vegetables—all the basics that children are exposed to through picture books, preschool, and life itself. He will be expected to demonstrate age-appropriate social standards and behavior. If he knocks over someone's art project, he should know to apologize and help pick it up. He will be expected to have acquired the same degree of common sense about getting along in the world as have his peers. For your child to acquire this fund of information takes time and your active involvement.

When your child is tested, the examiner might ask, "Why do we go to the dentist?" "Would you find a tiger in a zoo or on a farm?" "What should you do if you step on somebody's toe by accident?"

3. MEMORY

This can be verbal (information taken in by listening or reading) and visual (information taken in by seeing). According to learning expert Dr. Mel Levine, "More memory is needed for school success than is required in virtually any career."

LONG-TERM MEMORY. This is your child's ability to retrieve information that was learned in the past or after a delay.

Why is this important for school success? Long-term memory is critical to doing well in school. Kids are expected to remember multiplication tables, chemical symbols, state capitals, vocabulary, spelling words, rules of grammar, history, and procedures for solving different types of math problems. Students are constantly asked to attach new information to what they already know and to call up relevant facts or procedures learned in the past for assignments and tests.

When your child is tested, the examiner may ask, "Why do we brush our teeth?" Your child will remember his mother telling him how we clean our teeth to avoid cavities and will tell the tester. That's using long-term verbal memory. The tester may show your child a picture of a woman driving in an upside-down car and ask, "What is wrong with this picture?" If he says, "Cars don't drive upside-down," he is using his long-term visual memory.

SHORT-TERM MEMORY. This is your child's ability to retrieve information he was given in the last few seconds (e.g., "Can you repeat the numbers and letters I say? E, T, 7, 4, S." Answer: "E, T, 7, 4, S"). Working memory is your child's ability to retrieve information he was just given, hold on to it, and do something with it (e.g., "Listen to the numbers and letters I say and repeat them back to me with the letters first and the numbers second? E, T, 7, 4, S." Answer: "E, T, S, 7, 4").

Why is this important for school success? If the teacher asks a question, it will enter into a student's short-term memory and then move into working memory as she holds the question in her mind while simultaneously searching her long-term memory for the answer. Working memory is critical for academics because so many tasks involve taking in information and doing something with it. For example, a child will read a story or section in a textbook and be asked to answer questions about what she read; a math problem requires the child to remember the steps she's already completed while holding on to what she must do next; in sounding out a long word, a child must remember what the first part of the word is until she gets to the end.

When your child is tested, the examiner may show him a page of several geometric figures and ask him to point to the square that has the circle inside of it and the star over it. If your child can remember what the examiner said and point to the correct figures, he is demonstrating short-term verbal memory. The tester may ask, "What is a jet?" That requires long-term visual memory (if she's been on a jet or looked at pictures) or verbal memory (if she's read a book or heard someone talking about a jet). The examiner may string colored beads into a pattern and then unstring the beads and ask your child to re-create that pattern. That requires short-term working visual memory.

4. MATHEMATICS

MATH OPERATIONS. This is your child's ability to work with simple computational skills. *Math reasoning* is your child's ability to do the thinking needed for higher-order math work and includes concepts such as patterning, sequencing, ordering, classifying, and comparing. These same concepts are fundamental to three abilities: math reasoning and cognitive and language skills.

Why is this important for school success? Math reasoning helps children develop the critical-thinking and problem-solving skills they need to learn. From the moment your child starts school, math operations will be one of his important academic subjects.

When your child is tested, the examiner may show him a picture of eight apples and ask him to count them. The tester may ask a word problem such as, "If you had three cookies and ate one, how many would be left?" The tester may ask your child to arrange blocks from smallest to largest.

5. VISUAL-SPATIAL REASONING

This is the opposite of reasoning with words. It is your child's ability to reason and solve problems using pictures, images, diagrams, geometric shapes, maps, and tables. It involves interpreting and comprehending visual-spatial information (i.e., identifying shapes) and creating visual-spatial output such as drawing, doing puzzles, mazes, and other activities requiring fine-motor skills. Your child needs visual-spatial reasoning to organize his desk, notebook, or backpack.

Why is this important for school success? The ability to draw and identify triangles, squares, and circles is the basis for writing and recognizing letters and numbers. Differentiating between a circle and a triangle is the first step needed to recognize an O versus an A. The ability to notice differences in fine details of visual images is necessary to distinguish an F from and E. Children must be able to work within the margins of a page, start sentences on the left and go right, and space letters and words appropriately. When doing long division, your child must be able to line up the numbers as he solves the problem. Drawing shapes for geometry, recognizing countries for geography and chemical symbols for science, graphing for math and science, noticing if a word doesn't look like it's spelled right—all require visual-spatial thinking. The ability to organize your notes and materials is required for school success.

When your child is tested, she might be asked which of three dogs is different (two are identical, one has an extra spot). She might be asked to put together a puzzle or assemble four pattern blocks the way they are shown in a picture. She might be shown a drawing of a triangle and asked to copy it. The examiner may show your child a picture of two buildings and ask which is taller.

6. COGNITIVE SKILLS

These encompass brain functions that make it possible to "know." Thinking, processing information, analyzing, reasoning, learning, awareness, and judgment all require cognitive, or higher-order, thinking skills.

ABSTRACT/SYMBOLIC THINKING. This is your child's ability to make generalizations based on concrete experiences.

Why is this important for school success? This is truly the foundation for all intellectual endeavors. Students must learn that letters have sounds and these are used to create words, sentences, and stories that have their own meanings beyond the letters themselves. The number 5 looks nothing like five cookies, but your child learns that the number is an abstract representation of any five items. If the teacher asks your child what he did last summer and he recounts his adventures, he is thinking abstractly by visualizing himself in another time and place and telling her about it. The best way for a young child to learn abstract thinking is through play (e.g., using a block to represent a car) rather than instruction. As your child gets older, he must master abstract language, which are words that represent something you cannot see or hear, words like *danger, democracy, joyful,* and *irony.* Abstract terminology pervades math, science, literature, and social studies classes.

When your child is tested, the examiner may point to a picture of a dog and ask what it is. He is demonstrating abstract thinking when he assigns the word *dog* to what is clearly not a real dog. An examiner may ask him what the word *freedom* means.

SEQUENTIAL THINKING. This is your child's ability to think about information presented in a particular order, to recognize patterns, and anticipate and predict what comes next.

Why is this important for school success? When learning to read, your child will discover that letters in words and words in a sentence are read from left to right and must be placed in a particular order to make words and logical sentences. For example, *art* and *rat* are made up of the same letters in a different sequence. Children observe sequences in the environment (e.g., a butterfly evolves from an egg to larva to pupa to butterfly). Logical order and sequencing skills are needed to write essays and stories. In math, numbers are in sequential order. History is taught in chronological order, lists are put in alphabetical order. Teachers give multistep directions or present concepts that build upon each other. Schedules are a form of sequencing. So much in school is set in a sequence: the steps to solve a long division problem, a school project, or a science experiment. Children must manage their time in order to take tests, do class assignments, homework, and long-term projects.

When your child is tested, he might be shown three cards—one with a barefoot child, one with a child who has her shoes and socks on, one with a child who has only her socks on—and asked to put the cards in the correct sequential order. An examiner might show the child a row of shapes—square, circle, square, circle, square—and ask him to predict what comes next.

CONCEPTUAL THINKING. A concept is a set of features that together form a category of ideas or objects. A car is a tangible concept whose features include four wheels, a steel frame, windows, seats, a motor, a steering wheel, windows, and a class of transportation. Certain features distinguish this from a boat or bicycle, although they share some features and serve the same function. There are also intangible concepts such as a poem whose features include a composition, verse, recited, beautiful language, artistic expression, conveying ideas in a vivid way. Certain features distinguish this from a song, although they share features as well.

Being able to conceptualize relies on your child's ability to identify and group together concrete objects and ideas with like attributes (i.e., color, size, texture), to classify them into groups (vegetables, animals, letters), to recognize and compare similarities and differences in objects and ideas (chocolate versus vanilla, plays versus movies, Barney versus Arthur), and ultimately to evaluate and judge different concepts or use critical thinking (e.g., Musicals are better than plays because they have a story like a play, but they also have singing and dancing, so you get more for your money).

Why is this important for school success? Conceptual thinking allows your child to compare things for a report: farm animals versus wild animals, democracy versus communism, for example. It makes it easier to reason. If trees and flowers are both plants, then they both need water and light to live. If communist countries don't allow voting, and Russia is a communist country, then they must not allow their citizens to vote. In English class, your child will learn how to create metaphors and analogies in writing, which require conceptual thinking.

When your child is tested, similarity and difference, matrix and analogy questions are often used to assess conceptual thinking. The tester may say, "Apples and oranges are both what?" Or she might ask an analogy question such as, "Dog is to bark as lion is to what?" She may show a child a row of four items (a doll, a ball, a jack-in-the-box, and a plant) and ask him which one doesn't belong.

PROBLEM SOLVING. This is your child's ability to respond when faced with a challenge involving unfamiliar information or processes. How does he assess the problem, formulate ideas to solve it, evaluate the best solution, try a solution, and accept or reject what he learns if what he tries doesn't work until he discovers a satisfactory answer?

Why is this important for school success? In school, your child will constantly be faced with problems to solve, experiments to conduct, and hypotheses to prove. Once he learns the rules of grammar or mathematics, he will need to apply them to new problems or in fresh pieces of writing. To solve a science problem, he will need to think creatively and generate several options to consider before beginning.

When your child is tested, the examiner may give him a puzzle to put together or a picture of a block configuration to re-create. The tester will observe and note how he approaches the problem. Does he use trial and error? Does he learn from his mistakes? Does he plan ahead and work slowly and methodically? Or is he impulsive, rushing into the task? When the task becomes difficult, does he persist even if frustrated? Your child's approach to problem solving will be noted in the narrative report that accompanies the test results.

7. MOTOR SKILLS
FINE-MOTOR SKILLS. This is your child's ability to control his hands and fingers. These are needed for activities such as playing an instrument, cutting, tying a bow, folding, buttoning and unbuttoning, tying shoelaces, playing with small toys or cards. Graphomotor skills involve the use of hand and finger muscle movements necessary to write with a pencil.

Why is this important for school success? At school, your child will be expected to write papers, take tests, complete projects, type on a computer, and work with manipulatives (beads, blocks, rods) for math. A study by Joanne Landy and Keith Burridge in 1999 concluded that 60 to 70 percent of children's schoolwork requires fine-motor skills.

When your child is tested, he may be asked to draw something, re-create a block pattern, or put a puzzle together. (Note: Gross-motor skills involve movement of large muscles needed to run, skip, and jump. These are not evaluated in intelligence tests, although kindergarten teachers will informally assess these abilities when your child starts school.)

TESTERS ALSO LOOK AT . . .

PROCESSING SPEED. Processing speed captures how quickly your child can perform the activities on the test. It isn't a separate skill that your child can work on. As he becomes more adept with the 7 abilities, his processing speed will naturally increase. Faster processing speed means that your child is able to absorb information and master material at a quicker pace, thus moving him through his intellectual milestones more rapidly.

Why is this important for school success? Being able to work quickly requires your child to focus his attention, scan, discriminate, and manipulate visual information in his mind. It depends upon the ability to quickly and easily process verbal information. It involves planning, motivation, motor skills, and the ability to work under pressure. Children whose brains work faster are viewed as "smarter" kids. They are more likely to be placed in advanced-ability groups and TAG programs and to take higher-level and honors classes in later grades.

When your child is tested, certain visual-spatial tasks are timed. It is done discreetly so the child doesn't feel pressured.

ATTENTION CONTROL. This is your child's ability to regulate or control his level of mental activity, the amount of information and stimuli he takes in, and the way he works and acts. Children with attention control problems are often overactive and have short attention spans. They may experience difficulty slowing their minds and bodies and controlling their impulses.

Why is this important for school success? At school, your child needs to behave appropriately, sit at his desk for extended periods, pay attention and process what the teacher says, retain in his mind what he reads and sees, think through the best way to solve a problem before leaping in, identify what is important in written material, shield himself from distractions that take his mind away from schoolwork, concentrate when studying and taking a test, think through the possibilities when assigned an original story to write rather than jumping in with his first idea, work mindfully so as to avoid careless mistakes, keep his papers organized, and much more.

When your child is tested, the evaluator will note if he repeatedly misses questions and then gets the next (harder) one right, as an attention problem might explain his missing the easier ones. She will observe if your child asks for tasks to be explained repeatedly and watch the way he solves problems, noting if he plans ahead or impulsively dives into tasks. She will watch his level of activity during the test. Attention issues will affect a child's score negatively and will be noted in the narrative report.

Dr. Mel Levine says, "It is rare to encounter a student who has trouble with attention unaccompanied by other kinds of dysfunction. Weak attention control is almost always one member of a little cluster of dysfunctions. Therefore, whenever a parent spots problems with attention control, he should always ask, 'What else does she have?'"

If a psychologist suspects an attention problem, she will be able to suggest ways to help your child. While attention symptoms can start by age 3, Attention Deficit Disorder (ADD or ADHD, which includes hyperactivity) cannot be diagnosed until age 7 because so many of the symptoms are within the range of normal for active young children. Still, studies have shown that more than any psychiatric disorder, ADD has the strongest negative impact on a child's academic success. If you suspect that your child has attention issues, seek advice from his teacher or a psychologist. There are many effective ways to help kids with attention issues, but you will need guidance.

In the next chapter, we will review the types of questions asked on the most common tests given for kindergarten.

5. What Is on the Test?

BREAKING DOWN THE MOST COMMON TESTS, SECTION BY SECTION

How Do Different Tests Work?

In the next pages, I'm going to describe for you three of the most commonly used tests: the Wechsler Preschool and Primary Scale of Intelligence III, the Stanford-Binet Intelligence Scales 5, and the Otis-Lennon School Ability Test. We'll talk about what they cover and how they do it. (Appendix I contains information on three additional tests: the Woodcock-Johnson Test of Cognitive Abilities, the Bracken Basic Concept Scale, and the Kaufman Assessment Battery for Children.) The summaries of each test are not the "official" descriptions from the test publisher. After researching each test, I've presented the information in non-technical language. The sample questions included are not actual questions but do illustrate the *kinds of information* and *style of questions* typical of each test when given to children between the ages of 4 and 5.

While each test gets at a child's abilities using different types of questions and different names for subtests, they cover much of the same ground. All evaluate language and fine-motor development. All assess thinking abilities. All examine the knowledge and information your child has acquired up until now. After you read what these tests cover and see how much they overlap, you can feel comfortable that no matter what instrument is used to appraise your child, educators are measuring the same abilities.

A sample of a *public school informal assessment* that a teacher might use to evaluate the children in her classroom for placement in ability groupings can be found in chapter 22. These tend to be more limited in scope than commercial tests, focusing on individual areas such as reading, writing, math, fine-motor, or thinking skills.

The Wechsler Preschool and Primary Scale of Intelligence III (WPPSI)

The WPPSI has two major sections: verbal and performance.

Verbal Section

INFORMATION SUBTEST

Your child is shown a series of pictures and asked to point to the thing that "says moo" or that "you wear on your feet." *Assesses language, knowledge/comprehension, memory, visual-spatial reasoning.*

Point to the thing that meows.

INFORMATION AND VOCABULARY SUBTEST

Your child answers questions like "What is an apple?" or "What is a shoe?" or "What does *vacation* mean?" These questions generally go from easier to harder. On *all* verbal subtests that require your child to answer a question or explain something, she is given extra points for more specific answers. So, for example, if she says that an apple is "fruit," she might earn one point. If she says that an apple is "red, fruit, crunchy," she would score two points. *Assesses language, knowledge/ comprehension, memory.*

COMPREHENSION SUBTEST

Your child is asked a question relating to herself, her world, social or practical standards most children her age would know. For example: "Why do you need to take a bath?" "Why do we wear coats in the winter?" "Why do dogs wear collars?" "What should you do if you break something that belongs to your neighbor?" *Assesses language, knowledge/comprehension, memory.*

SIMILARITIES SUBTEST

The tester might ask how two things are alike. "How is a coat like a shirt?" or "How is a pencil like a crayon?" *Assesses knowledge/comprehension, memory, cognitive skills.*

WORD REASONING SUBTEST

Your child is asked to identify a common object or concept after being given clues: "This is something you eat." "This is something you eat that has a yellow skin that you peel." "This is something you eat and has a yellow skin that you peel and is a fruit." If the child answers correctly after the first clue, the tester moves on. If not, she'll give a second clue, and so on. *Assesses language, knowledge/comprehension, cognitive skills.*

RECEPTIVE VOCABULARY SUBTEST

Your child is shown four pictures and asked to point to the one that best depicts the word that the tester says aloud. *Assesses language, knowledge/comprehension, memory, visual-spatial reasoning.*

Point to the fish.

PICTURE NAMING SUBTEST

Your child is shown a picture such as a flower, pair of scissors, or toothbrush and asked to say the name of the item. *Assesses language, knowledge/comprehension, memory, visual-spatial reasoning.*

What is this?

Performance/Nonverbal Section

BLOCK DESIGN SUBTEST

Your child copies geometric designs made from 2-, 3-, or 4-pattern cubes while viewing a model or picture of what she is supposed to copy. There is a 90-second time limit for copying the design. Most 4-year-olds can copy only designs using solid block as opposed to triangular patterns. *Assesses visual-spatial reasoning, cognitive skills, fine-motor skills.*

MATRIX REASONING SUBTEST

Matrix questions are used to assess logic and reasoning skills. They are the visual version of verbal analogies (e.g., "Big is to small as tall is to . . . ?"). With a matrix question, your child must infer the relationship between the two items on top and then apply that relationship to the items on the bottom. For example, in a box that has been divided into four squares, there is a picture of a hand and a ring on top (you wear a ring on your hand), a foot on the bottom left, and an empty box next to it. Your child is shown a picture of a shoe, a glove, a pair of pants, and a jacket and asked to select which belongs in the empty box (you wear a *shoe* on your foot). ***Assesses memory, visual-spatial reasoning, cognitive skills.***

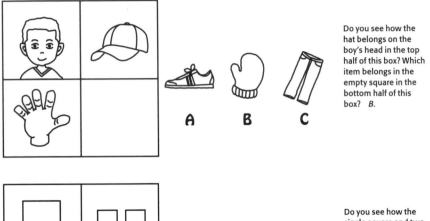

Do you see how the hat belongs on the boy's head in the top half of this box? Which item belongs in the empty square in the bottom half of this box? *B.*

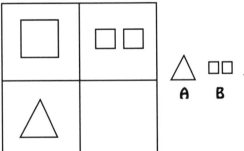

Do you see how the single square and two squares in the top half of the box go together? Which of the pictures to the side of the box goes with the single triangle the same way? *C.*

PICTURE CONCEPTS SUBTEST

Your child is shown two or three rows of pictures and asked to choose one picture from each row to form a group of items with common characteristics. For example, within the three rows, they may select all toys, all things that are red, or (below) all flowers. *Assesses memory, visual-spatial reasoning, cognitive skills.*

SYMBOL SEARCH SUBTEST

Your child is shown a symbol. Then she is told to scan a row of three symbols and asked if the symbol she was shown is in the row. *Assesses memory, visual-spatial reasoning.*

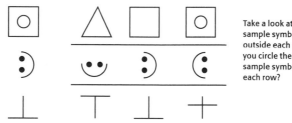

Take a look at the sample symbol outside each row. Can you circle the same sample symbol inside each row?

CODING SUBTEST

Your child is given a key and told to draw a specific symbol inside a shape. For example, when she sees a triangle, she should draw an "–" in it. When she sees a circle, she should draw an "I" in it. When she sees a square, she should draw an "o" in it. She is instructed to work in the order the shapes are presented (e.g., not to do all the circles first, then the triangles). She has 120 seconds to complete this. *Assesses visual-spatial reasoning, memory, fine-motor skills.*

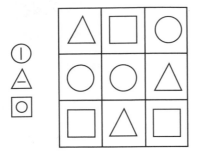

Key
Anytime you see a ○ draw a | inside it.
Anytime you see a △ draw a — inside it.
Anytime you see a ☐ draw a ○ inside it.

PICTURE COMPLETION SUBTEST

Your child is shown a picture of something she would know that has an essential part missing: a tiger with three legs, a face without a nose, a wagon without a wheel. She is asked what is missing. *Assesses knowledge/comprehension, memory, visual-spatial reasoning.*

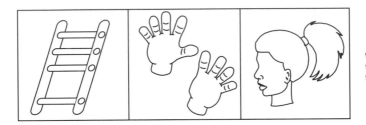

What is missing from the ladder, hands, and face?

OBJECT ASSEMBLY SUBTEST

Your child is shown pieces of a frameless puzzle (e.g., a horse that has been divided into four pieces). She is given 90 seconds to fit the pieces of the puzzle together to form the complete image. *Assesses memory, visual-spatial reasoning, cognitive skills, fine-motor skills.*

Take a look at this hat.

Can you put these puzzle pieces together to make it look like the hat I showed you?

The Stanford-Binet Intelligence Scales—5th Edition (Stanford-Binet)

The Stanford-Binet divides its test into verbal and nonverbal sections.

Verbal

KNOWLEDGE SUBTEST

This is like the Comprehension subtest on the WPPSI (see page 42).

VOCABULARY SUBTEST

This is like the Information and Vocabulary subtest on the WPPSI (see page 43), along with these additional types of questions:

1. Your child is asked to identify facial features and body parts on herself (e.g.:, "Point to your nose") and on a picture of a person. Girls identify features from a picture of a girl, while boys identify features from a picture of a boy. *Assesses language, knowledge/comprehension, memory, visual-spatial reasoning.*

Can you point to the girl's eyes?
Can you point to the girl's feet?
Can you point to the girl's two hands?

2. Your child is asked to identify common objects shown to them in pictures or with small toys. *Assesses language, knowledge/comprehension, memory, visual-spatial reasoning.*

What is this?   *Pencil.*
What is this?   *Balloons.*
What is this?   *Ring.*

VERBAL ABSURDITIES SUBTEST

The tester makes a statement that doesn't make sense and your child is asked what is silly about what she said (e.g., "I'm going to wash my puppy in chocolate pudding"). *Assesses language, memory, knowledge/comprehension.*

VERBAL REASONING

What goes together? The tester shows your child a pile of chips with pictures on them. The tester pulls out three things that go together such as a red rose, a red fire truck, and red lips. Your child is then asked to create as many groups of three chips as he can that share at least one common characteristic and to explain how they go together. *Assesses memory, visual-spatial reasoning, cognitive skills.*

What three things belong together?   *A—cupcake, C—gingerbread man, D—cookie.*

What's happening? Your child is shown a picture of a scenario and asked to describe what is going on. The tester is looking for an answer describing cause and effect or what is happening between characters, not just a naming of objects or people in the picture. (E.g., with a picture of a child crying at the table with a glass of spilled milk at his place, the tester would look for a response such as, "The boy is upset because he spilled his milk.") *Assesses language, knowledge/comprehension, cognitive skills.*

What is happening in this picture?
The girl fell down and hurt her knee. She's sad.

VERBAL QUANTITATIVE REASONING

Your child is asked to name numbers and solve simple verbal addition and subtraction word problems, such as "If you had three marbles and I gave you two more, how many would you have?" *Assesses mathematics.*

RELATIVITY SUBTEST

Your child is asked to show basic understanding of relativity concepts (e.g., *shorter, taller, more, less*). *Assesses visual-spatial reasoning.*

Which bowl has more apples?
The first bowl.

MEMORY FOR SENTENCES SUBTEST

Your child is asked to repeat a sentence exactly as it is said to him. The sentences start out short and get longer. Or in a "last word" subtest, your child is asked a yes/no question such as: "Are some shoes made of leather?" If the child answers the question correctly, it is assumed that he understands the last word of the question (*leather*). *Assesses language, memory.*

MEMORY FOR WORDS AND NUMBERS SUBTEST

Your child is asked to repeat a series of words or numbers exactly as it is said to him. (E.g., "tiger, ice cream, basketball, rose," or "3, 6, 2, 8.") *Assesses language, memory.*

Performance/Nonverbal

OBJECT SORTING SUBTEST

Your child is asked to sort and classify various pictured objects. (E.g., he may be given pictures of animals, plants, and items of clothing and asked to divide these into categories.) *Assesses knowledge comprehension, memory, visual-spatial reasoning, cognitive skills.*

PICTURE ABSURDITIES SUBTEST

Your child is presented with a picture of something absurd (e.g., a person driving a shoe) and asked what is odd about this picture. *Assesses language, knowledge/comprehension, memory, visual-spatial reasoning.*

What is odd about this picture?
The boy has cheese on his head!

PROCEDURAL KNOWLEDGE

Your child is asked to demonstrate something: "Show me how you brush your teeth." Or a child is shown a picture of something (a key) and asked to show what you do with it. The child uses gestures to demonstrate knowledge of the activity. *Assesses knowledge/comprehension, visual-spatial reasoning.*

Show me what you do with this.
Demonstrate digging.

COUNTING, ADDITION AND SUBTRACTION, RELATIVITY

Your child is asked to demonstrate quantitative reasoning skills using blocks and small objects (for counting, estimating, addition), rods (comparing length). *Assesses mathematics.*

How many oranges are in this bowl? *7.*

VISUAL-SPATIAL REASONING

Your child is asked to identify spatial relationships such as *ahead, behind, above, below.* The tester gives the child a verbal command such as, "Can you place that ball on [or behind, in front of] the block?" *Assesses visual-spatial reasoning.*

PUZZLES SUBTEST

Your child is asked to put puzzle pieces into a form board (your typical puzzle where the piece fits into an indentation). *Assesses knowledge/comprehension, memory, visual-spatial reasoning, cognitive skills, fine-motor skills.*

Your child is also given pieces that when combined make recognizable pictures such as an animal, child, car, boat, shape, person, or face. This is just like the Object Assembly subtest on the WPPSI (page 46).

PATTERNS SUBTEST

Your child is asked to re-create a design that the tester shows her using form pieces in various shapes. Or your child is shown a general design that he must re-create using separate pattern puzzle pieces (e.g., two half circles will combine to make a circle). *Assesses knowledge/comprehension, visual-spatial reasoning, cognitive skills, fine-motor skills.*

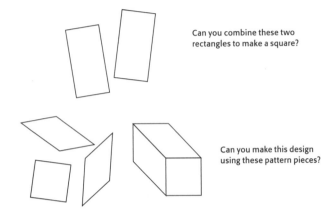

Can you combine these two rectangles to make a square?

Can you make this design using these pattern pieces?

WORKING MEMORY SUBTEST

Your child is shown blocks placed in a sequence and must re-create that pattern from memory. *Assesses memory, visual-spatial reasoning, fine-motor skills.*

Toys or blocks are placed under opaque plastic cups and the cups are repositioned (like a shell game). Your child is asked where a particular toy or block is now located. *Assesses memory, visual-spatial reasoning, cognitive skills.*

Block tapping. Your child taps blocks set out in two rows in the same tapping sequence as the tester. *Assesses memory, visual-spatial reasoning, fine-motor skills.*

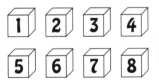

The tester taps block numbers 2, 6, 3, and 8, and the child must tap the same blocks in that sequence.

Bead Patterns. Your child is shown a picture of beads set up in a pattern and asked to replicate it from memory. *Assesses memory, visual-spatial reasoning, mathematics, cognitive skills, fine-motor skills.*

Can you make the same bead pattern using these beads?

MATRICES SUBTEST

This is the same as the Matrix subtest on the WPPSI (see page 44).

BLOCK DESIGN

This is similar to the Block Design subtest on the WPPSI (see page 43).

The Otis-Lennon School Ability Test (OLSAT)

The OLSAT is divided into verbal and nonverbal sections.

Practice Test

The OLSAT is one of two tests that the New York City Public School system uses to assess children for their gifted and talented program. An OLSAT practice test can be found at: http://schools.nyc .gov/Documents/Offices/GT/LevADOE.pdf.

Verbal

LISTENING AND FOLLOWING DIRECTIONS

Your child is asked to listen to, remember, and follow the tester's instructions. *Assesses language, memory.*

Here is a puppy, a cat, and a mouse. The puppy wants to play. The cat wants to wash his fur. The mouse wants to eat.

What does the cat want to do? *Wash his fur.*
What does the mouse want to do? *Eat.*
What does the puppy want to do? *Play.*

67   **6**6   **77**   76

Look at these numbers. Can you point to the two numbers that are the same but are different sizes? **6**6
Can you point to the two numbers that are different but are the same size? 76

Another task assesses understanding of relational concepts such as *above*, *next to*, and *between* along with your child's listening skills. (E.g., in a chart with five boxes across and five boxes down, each filled with a shape, a number, or a letter, the tester might ask, "Which number is above the triangle but below the heart?") Since receptive language is being assessed here, the tester will not repeat the question if your child can't remember. *Assesses language, memory, visual-spatial reasoning.*

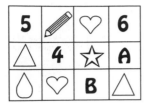

Can you show me the heart that is next to the number?
Can you show me the triangle that is on top of the drop?
Can you show me the letter that is below the star?
Let's pretend that you are the 4. What shape are you above? *Heart.*
What two shapes are you in between? *Triangle and star.*

Look at these shapes. Can you circle the picture that shows a big square and a small circle with hearts on both sides? *D.*

AURAL (HEARING) REASONING

Your child is asked to make sense of a situation that has been described orally. (E.g., he may be shown a picture of a cat, a horse, a fish, and a bunny.) The tester says, "Mary and Joey each have pets, but not the same kind. Mary's pet wears a saddle. Joey's pet does not live in the water and does not purr. What is Joey's pet?" Answer: bunny. *Assesses language, memory, knowledge/ comprehension, visual-spatial reasoning, cognitive skills.*

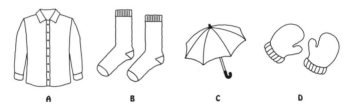

It was a rainy day. Janie already had something to keep her body and feet dry. She went back inside to get something that would keep her head dry. Circle what Janie got to keep her head dry. *C.*

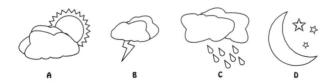

Billy went out on a partly sunny day. Suddenly it got darker. Billy looked up and saw a flash of light and then heard thunder. What did Billy see when he looked up? *B.*

ARITHMETIC REASONING

Your child is asked to solve verbal math problems that stress numerical reasoning as opposed to computational skills. (E.g., a picture of three cookies next to pictures of one cookie, two cookies, three cookies, and four cookies.) The child is told, "Sam ate three cookies. If Mary ate one cookie less than Sam, point to the picture that shows exactly how many cookies Mary ate." *Assesses language, mathematics, visual-spatial reasoning.*

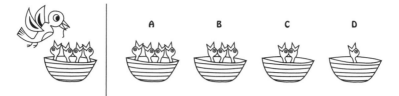

There are four hungry baby birds. The mama bird had two worms to feed them. After feeding two of her babies, she was out of food. Circle the picture that shows the number of birds that did not get fed.   *C.*

Nonverbal

PICTORIAL REASONING

Picture Classification. Your child is asked which picture in a series of five "does not belong" with the four others. He is looking for the similarity between the four items that the fifth doesn't share. *Assesses knowledge/comprehension, mathematics, visual-spatial reasoning, cognitive skills.*

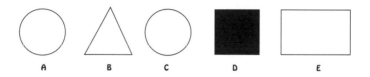

Which one of these is most different from the others?   *The square because it is black and the other shapes are white.*

FIGURAL ANALOGIES, PATTERN MATRIX, AND PICTURE ANALOGIES

These are very similar to the Matrix questions on the WPPSI (see page 44).

PICTURE SERIES

Your child must predict what comes next in a series of pictures. (E.g., he is shown a series of four little boys that go from baby to toddler to child to teenager.) Then he is shown four other pictures of a girl, a man, a grandmother, and a toddler, and asked which of these comes next in the first sequence. Answer: the man. With this type of question, the series typically fits a pattern (red, white, red, white), shows movement (e.g., a clock at 12 o'clock, 3 o'clock, 6 o'clock), increases or decreases in size or number, or tells a story. *Assesses knowledge/comprehension, mathematics, visual-spatial reasoning, cognitive skills.*

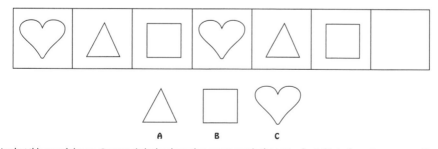

Look at this row of shapes. Can you circle the shape that comes next in the pattern?   *C. (Note: for patterns, suggest to your child that she say each shape aloud as that will help her know what comes next. "Heart, triangle, square, heart, triangle, square . . .")*

Which picture comes next?   *A, because the baby bird that was just born is now standing outside the egg.*

FIGURAL CLASSIFICATION

Your child is asked which geometric shape or picture in a series of five does not belong with the others. *Assesses mathematics, visual-spatial reasoning, cognitive skills.*

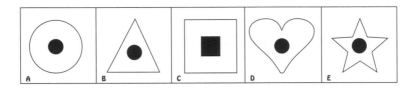

Which shape does not belong?   *C. It's the only shape with a square inside of it.*

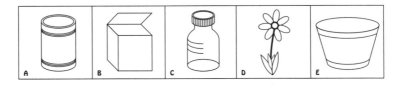

Which one of these doesn't belong?   *D. Everything can hold something else except the flower.*

FIGURAL SERIES

Your child must supply the next step in a geometric series in which the shapes change according to a rule that he must infer. *Assesses mathematics, visual-spatial reasoning, cognitive skills.*

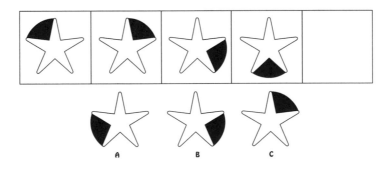

Which of the three pictures below the line of boxes belongs in the empty box?   *A, because the dark oval is moving clockwise around the star. (Your child won't say this but will notice that the oval is moving in one direction.)*

Free Daily Practice Test Questions

If you'd like to receive a daily IQ test prep question you can do with your child (it should take about a minute), go to Testingforkindergarten.com and subscribe.

In the next chapter, we will explore how to know if your child is ready to learn a particular skill by paying attention to the milestones he has hit.

Part II

Prepare Your Child to Succeed—At Tests and in Life

In this part you will learn:

★ What abilities your child should have at ages 3, 4, and 5.

★ DVDs, CDs, computers, workbooks, and other tools to help you work with your child at home.

★ The 4 magic keys to building all abilities at once: read, music, talk, listen!

★ The top language activities to support talking, listening, and literacy.

★ Knowledge and comprehension: Everything your child must know by age 5—what are you waiting for?

★ How to build your child's mathematics and visual-spatial skills.

★ Memory-building games your child will love.

★ How to raise a thinking child.

★ Occupational therapists' secrets for strengthening your child's fine-motor skills.

★ A step-by-step plan to build these activities into your life.

★ The 20 most important activities if your child is about to be tested.

★ Forget testing! What does your child need to succeed at life?

6. Milestones That Matter for School Success

HOW TO RECOGNIZE WHAT YOUR CHILD IS READY TO LEARN

At 9 months, did your baby start to crawl? At 12 months, did he take his first step and say at least one word? Perhaps your baby talked at 9 months and didn't take a step until 14 months. That's okay. Developmental milestones fall within a range of several months. Kids develop according to their own unique timetable, but abilities do tend to emerge in a certain order and by a certain age.

Children Acquire Individual Skills over Time

Take writing, for example. A child will pick up a crayon with his fist and move it over a page to make random markings or scribbles. As he develops better motor control, shapes and patterns start to emerge. He'll draw pictures that become more recognizable with practice. Drawing people, he'll start with only the head, adding eyes, nose, mouth, and hair. When he begins to draw arms and legs, they will sprout directly out of the head (psychologists call these "tadpole people"). Eventually, he'll represent a body with a stick figure that will evolve into a person with a body, arms, legs, hands, and fingers. As he matures, he will learn to hold a crayon with his fingers instead of his fist. After he has a familiarity with the alphabet and words, he will make letterlike forms, trying to write his name. Later, with practice, his letters become more accurate.

It is important to know when to expect milestones. If your child is a bit late picking up a skill, it's probably not a cause for worry, since there is a wide range of times in which children develop. A child's motor skills may outpace his verbal abilities. Then, his verbal abilities may surge ahead like a sprinter leaving the starting gate. As you saw by watching your child go from infant to baby to toddler, development does not happen at a steady pace.

Milestones Represent Abilities Your Child Can Develop

When looking at milestones for a given age, think of them as abilities that a typical child of that age has the capacity to develop. With writing, you can certainly teach your child to hold a crayon with her fingers at 3 because the capacity to master that skill is there. If you try to teach your 2-year-old the same thing, you are both likely to be frustrated.

In the next pages, you'll see lists of intellectual and social-emotional milestones for children ages 3, 4, and 5. These lists are lengthy but not exhaustive. Go through them and check where you think your child is right now. By knowing where she is today and what abilities she has the capacity to develop, you'll know which activities to introduce and which to postpone.

Many of the ideas I'll suggest can be done at any age, like reading to your child. Other activities, such as asking her to play certain memory games or to put together a multipiece puzzle, will have to wait. If you think your child is ready for any of the games or ideas suggested, go for it. If it's a hit, that's great. If not, you might improvise and make it simpler or try again in a few months.

> There are many who hold, as I do, that the most important period of life is not the age of university studies, but the first one, the period from birth to the age of 6. For this is the time when man's intelligence itself, his greatest implement, is being formed.
>
> —Maria Montessori

By End of Age 3, a Child Should

LANGUAGE

speak at least 300 words, understand 2,000 words

speak so that nearly everything he says can be understood

speak in sentences of three to five words: "Mommy kiss Daddy"

tell personal experiences with a focus on the main event, leaving out details

learn nursery rhymes and songs that feature lots of repetition

follow a series of two-step oral directions

name and describe simple objects and pictures

describe simple experiences and events

describe simple functions of objects

KNOWLEDGE/COMPREHENSION

count to 10 and recite ABCs by rote

recognize his name as a sight word

recognize some letters and numbers

name basic colors

know his name and address

MEMORY

remember what happened yesterday

retell simple stories he's heard over and over

memorize the text of books she hears often

reproduce a sequence of three items from memory

laugh at silly ideas like milking a horse (and remember what's real)

MATHEMATICS

count three objects, assigning one number to one object

classify, label, and sort objects by one quality at a time (color, shape)

sequence objects by size

recognize patterns in daily routines

recognize similarities and differences in objects

start to understand time sequences (get up, go to school, come home, eat dinner) and environmental patterns (night comes after day)

VISUAL-SPATIAL

assemble a simple puzzle

move from scribbling to writing letterlike designs

begin to draw objects such as a house or person (a head with sticks for legs and arms)

recognize basic shapes (circle, square, triangle)

duplicate a simple three-dimensional design with objects (beads, cubes)

understand size concepts such as *more, less, bigger, smaller*

understand relational concepts such as *top, bottom, in front of, behind*

understand opposite meanings (*in-out, hot-cold*)

understand time concepts of *now, soon,* and *later*

COGNITIVE

ask and answer simple *who, what, where* questions; may have difficulty with concepts of *when, why,* and *how* since they require more abstract thinking

make simple inferences

play make-believe with dolls, animals, people

FINE MOTOR

hold crayons or markers with fingers instead of fist

manipulate clay

paint using a brush or fingers

copy simple shapes, like a circle or cross

cut simple patterns with scissors (fringe, straight line)

stack blocks up to nine high

place small objects in small openings

string large beads

begin to write letters of his name; may reverse letter orientation

---

By End of Age 4, a Child Should

LANGUAGE

speak 1,000 to 1,500 words, understand 4,000 words

know the vocabulary associated with information children his age commonly understand

speak more complex sentences: "Mommy kissed Daddy and said good-bye"

talk about important things like family, preschool, friends, field trips, interesting experiences engage in give-and-take conversations

identify 4 to 5 pairs of words that rhyme

name 4 to 5 words that start with the same sound

follow a series of three-step oral directions

learn and sing songs, finger plays, and rhymes

sit for longer periods to listen to more complex stories

describe and compare experiences and events

describe functions of objects in detail

MEMORY

repeat a sequence of at least three words or numbers from memory

retell the events of a three- to four-step sequence in a story

reproduce a sequence of at least four items from memory

KNOWLEDGE/COMPREHENSION

correctly name some colors

recognize numbers from 0 to 9

recognize that there are upper-case and lower-case letters

know about seasons and holidays

know some but not all the information listed on pages 115–16

MATHEMATICS

count three objects, assigning one number to one object

count to 10 but not always in correct order

solve simple verbal addition and subtraction problems

match, sort objects in various shapes, sizes, and colors on the basis of more than one characteristic

classify pictures by category

recognize similarities and differences in a variety of pictures

sequence objects and pictures by size

string beads and create simple patterns

identify and reproduce repeating patterns in blocks, shapes, numbers, and sounds

VISUAL-SPATIAL

assemble an eight-piece puzzle in a frame

understand that writing goes from left to right, top to bottom

draw simple shapes including circles, squares, and triangles

draw a person with four to six body parts (head, body, arms, legs)

duplicate two- and three-dimensional designs with objects, cubes, or pattern tiles

identify missing parts in shapes and pictures

understand and use time words (*yesterday, tomorrow*), money words (*penny, nickel*)

understand and use relativity and space concepts (*more, less, bigger, smaller*)

understand and use relational words (*in front of, behind, near, far, first, last*)

COGNITIVE

ask and answer *who, what, where, why, how*, and *when* questions

understand mental state words (*I wonder, don't know*), emotional words (*sad, happy, surprised*)

develop vocabulary for thinking, problem solving, and observing

grasp that pictures and symbols can represent real objects

start to develop logical thinking

begin to recognize cause and effect

use simple reasoning

engage in fantasy play

understand that letters translate into
sounds

predict what will happen next in a story
by using clues

solve problems through trial and error

enjoy riddles, jokes, and silly language

FINE MOTOR

Grip a writing tool with fingers instead of
fist (many can, but not all)

print many letters, mostly upper-case,
but will start to form some lower-case

write his first name in upper-case letters

write some numbers

cut more complex patterns with scissors

pour sand and liquid into containers

use table utensils skillfully

build complex block structures that
extend vertically

discriminate items through touching
various textures, shapes, sizes

perform simple paper-folding tasks

draw simple shapes like circle, square,
triangle

By End of Age 5, a Child Should

LANGUAGE

speak 1,500 words or more, understand
5,000 to 8,000 words

speak without pronunciation errors for
the average child (may have trouble
with a few sounds like *th* or L)

develop a vocabulary to describe
personal experiences and feelings, tell
stories, engage in dramatic play, and
make complex observations

learn multisyllabic words associated
with special areas of interest, such as
dinosaur names or car models

construct long, detailed sentences
("We went to the aquarium today and
Tiffany ate three cotton candies and
threw up")

speak fluently, correctly using plurals,
pronouns, and tenses

take turns in speaking and listening to
what another person is saying

know words to many songs

generate pairs of rhyming words

show growing fluency in expressing
ideas and experiences in detail

tell long, involved stories with detail

follow a series of four-step oral
directions

KNOWLEDGE/COMPREHENSION

correctly name 6–8 colors

recognize and read numbers from 0 to 19

recognize letters of alphabet, upper- and
lower-case

know sounds that letters and pairs of
letters make

know about things used every day in the
home (money, food, furniture)

understand the basic information listed
on pages 115–16

MEMORY

repeat a sequence of at least five words
or numbers from memory

retell a long story in the correct
sequence

reproduce a sequence of at least five
objects from memory

recount things that happened in the past

MATHEMATICS

count through the teens to 20 (many
children will be able to use repeating
patterns of numbers to count to 100)

use one-to-one correspondence (line up parallel sets of objects) to count sets of 5, 10, then 20 items

understand estimation terms (*near, about*)

mentally determine sums adding up to 4 (1 + 3 = 4) and solve verbal math problems (*four cookies and two cookies is six cookies*)

sequence objects, pictures, and symbols from left to right

reproduce a complex rhythm pattern

identify and describe sequences of objects or events

discriminate objects and pictures by properties (color, size, shape, length)

describe objects by properties (red things, soft things)

VISUAL-SPATIAL

assemble a 12-piece puzzle

build a three-dimensional block structure

sight read some common words like *stop*

create more complex drawings including people

identify and describe similarities and differences in pictures

identify missing parts of objects, shapes, letters, numbers, and pictures

learn right from left

recognize shapes of various sizes and orientation (triangle right side up and upside down)

COGNITIVE

compose simple fictional stories

ask and answer complex questions

use information learned in various experiences to solve problems

draw on past experience to describe, compare, and talk about the present and anticipate the future

FINE MOTOR

cut and paste shapes as directed by adult

grip a pencil like an adult

print recognizable upper- and lower-case letters, plus numbers and shapes

write his name, words, and short sentences; use some punctuation; understand that spaces go between words

make horizontal lines, vertical lines, and diagonal lines

color within lines

use computer keyboard

tie his shoes

fold paper diagonally

draw a person with six parts

Social and Emotional Milestones Important for School Success

These milestones will not be evaluated per se, although the narrative report accompanying any test administered by a psychologist will mention social-emotional behaviors observed during the exam. If your child doesn't make eye contact with the tester or if he has little frustration tolerance when tasks are difficult, the examiner will note that. Many private schools will ask for comprehensive reports about applicants from the nursery programs they attend. In these reports, all aspects of your child's development will be covered: intellectual, physical, fine- and gross-motor skills, and social-emotional development.

Between the Ages of 3 and 4, a Child Should

play cooperatively with other children versus playing alongside other children (parallel play)

use objects symbolically in play (e.g., using dolls to have a pretend tea party)

participate in simple group activities

start to share and take turns

begin to follow rules

listen to and follow simple directions

separate from parent and caregiver

communicate his needs to adults

respond appropriately to adult authority

label his feelings and understand that feelings have causes

express feelings, needs, and opinions in difficult situations

help other children who are in need or upset

begin to understand moral reasoning: *good versus bad, fair versus unfair*

begin to accept compromise to resolve conflict

begin to tolerate frustration

help with simple tasks like cleanup or serving snacks

say "please" and "thank you" appropriately

Between the Ages of 4 and 5, a Child Should Also

learn coping strategies to manage emotions (drawing, fantasy play, using words)

express his feelings and needs

successfully enter a group of children who are already playing

begin and sustain pretend play scenarios

attend to tasks for increasingly longer periods of time

assume independent responsibility for completing tasks

show willingness to attempt successively more difficult tasks

engage in discussions and activities involving adults and children in the classroom

make eye contact when speaking

sustain a conversation

listen without interrupting

follow directions

work for delayed reward

use compromise and discussion to resolve conflict, suggest solutions to problems

begin to develop real friendships

use polite and courteous behavior

By 5, When Your Child Starts Kindergarten, He Should Also

listen and respond appropriately to teacher-directed tasks
follow classroom and safety rules
go to the bathroom himself
dress himself
wait his turn
share
spend extended time away from parents
use words instead of being physical when angry

follow routines
put toys away when asked
run, jump, skip
walk backward
walk up and downstairs using alternating feet
know his address, phone number, mother's and father's first names, birthday

In the next chapter, we'll look at the various ways you can work with your child on skill building: both hands-on learning and education tools.

7. Sneak Learning into the Moments You Already Spend with Your Child

NO EXTRA TIME NEEDED!

I worked full-time when Schuyler was a toddler. Every evening after a long day at the office, we'd have dinner, a bath, and then play for a few hours before it was bedtime. I'd sit on the floor while she would run around playing with whatever intrigued her at the moment. If she got involved with her Little Tykes kitchen, I'd pretend to eat what she cooked. Sometimes we'd play Go Fish or Candy Land. Often I'd read her a favorite book or we'd recite nursery rhymes.

Although it was a treat to spend time together every night, I remember not knowing and yet really *wanting* to know what I should be doing with Schuyler. When I read to her, should I have been pointing out letters or was I supposed to wait until she learned them in school? Who knew! When we strung colored beads, should I have shown her how to make patterns or was that even important? I wasn't sure. At age 4, she still grasped crayons in her fist. Should I have corrected her? I had no idea. Nursery rhymes made no sense to me. A woman living in a shoe? I mean, really! I wondered if nonfiction books would be better.

I don't want you to stumble the way I did. In the coming pages, I'm going to show you special things you can do while you're reading to your toddler and talk more about how nursery rhymes help your child. I'll give you ideas for mixing beading and learning, suggest games you can play, activities you can do, and new ways of interacting that will support your child's intellectual development and naturally prepare her for testing and kindergarten success.

KINDERGARTEN MAY BE THE MOST IMPORTANT YEAR IN YOUR CHILD'S SCHOOLING

- It is here that the foundation for her entire academic career will be established: reading, writing, math, and socialization.
- If she starts out ready, she'll develop the love of learning and experience success. Her confidence will soar. If she begins without critical skills, she'll be playing catch-up from day one. Her confidence will suffer.

When helping your child get ready for testing and school success, there are three important Dos

1. **Do make plenty of time for play.** Play is as important to promoting your child's thinking, problem solving, and creative skills as any enrichment experience you might give him. The American Academy of Pediatrics recently issued a statement that parents should limit their children's structured activities and, instead, give them more time to play. Children's brains need time to process and ponder everything they see, hear, and experience. As they lie in the grass and watch clouds, swing at the park, and make their own general store or bake mud pies, they come up with ideas, connect the many pieces of their lives, and solve problems. Later, we'll discuss how the best way for children to master language and math skills is through play—but you must make time for it!

   Play supports development across every domain, among them symbolic and abstract thinking (e.g., using a rectangular block as a cell phone), initiative (e.g., choosing what to do next), imagination and literacy (e.g., dressing up and acting out stories), decision making (e.g., deciding how to construct a block structure, who plays what part in a game of house), math (e.g., sorting beads by color, matching in a game of Go Fish), small motor skills (e.g., drawing, pounding clay), social skills (e.g., taking turns, sharing)—the list goes on and on. Play teaches problem solving, creativity, and independence; it strengthens attention spans and self-control. Active play is essential to fighting the obesity epidemic that plagues one out of three children in the U.S. But don't think about all that. Instead, just set aside time and space, make a variety of toys and materials available, and let your child's imagination take him where he wants to go.

2. **Do follow your child.** This is a Maria Montessori tenet. You have a sense of where she is, what she can do now, and what she is ready to take on. Start there. Work with her in ways that keep her engaged and interested. If you see

she's not into what you're doing, make it more enjoyable or move on to something else.

3. **Do have fun while working together.** One of my favorite books of recent years is Jessica Seinfeld's *Deceptively Delicious*, a cookbook that teaches you how to hide veggies in foods children love. The recipes allow you to make your kids secretly healthy dishes that taste great. That's what I want you to do with the activities I'm going to suggest. Your child never has to know that the games you're playing together are educational. They're just plain fun.

Make More of the Time You Already Spend with Your Child

If you are working outside the home as I did, you may be concerned that you don't have time to do this. Not to worry! Many things I'm going to recommend will become ways of being with your child that won't take a minute extra. Lots of suggestions can be done in the car, on the street, while waiting in line—again, no extra time. The other games and activities in the book can be enjoyed when you would have otherwise been playing with your child. In chapter 19, I'll show you how to introduce these ideas into your life in tiny, bite-sized pieces. If you want to set aside extra "special" time to try some of my suggestions, that's great, but you don't have to.

I'll be sharing two kinds of activities with you. The first type can be weaved into your life with no fuss or additional time on your part. Those are called **"Daily Life Lessons."** Setting the table offers an opportunity to count how many people are coming, to sort silverware into categories, and fold napkins into rectangles. A walk in the city is the perfect time to look for shapes of buildings, signs, windows, and wheels. Daily Life Lessons are ways of being together that should permeate your interactions and become so routine that you don't have to think about it.

The second type of activity can be incorporated into your regular playtime, drive time, standing-in-line time, bedtime, and out-and-about time. These are called **"Games and Activities."** I always played with my kids when I came home from work. Instead of watching Schuyler randomly string beads, I might have challenged her to a game of letter Bingo. If she started to whine while waiting at the post office, I could have gotten her to play I Spy. By the way, if your child loves any particular ability-building games and activities that I don't mention, please tell me about them. You can reach me at karenquinn1@aol.com. I'll post them on my website for other parents to try (giving you credit, of course).

Every game and activity has been chosen to help strengthen the **7 Abilities** intelligence tests measure and kindergarten teachers look for when evaluating children. Here how to make the most of the suggestions:

* ★ **Start early.** Some of these activities can begin when your child is a baby, some when she's 2, 3, or 4. When your child is younger, your assistance will be required. When she's older, she'll be able to do some activities independently.

* ★ **Assess readiness.** I've made age suggestions for each activity, but your child may be ready for something earlier or later, depending on the milestones she's reached.

* ★ **Watch for choking hazards.** Always supervise if an activity requires small objects such as beads, coins, crayons, and so on.

* ★ **Don't try to do everything.** I'm giving you lots of choices so you can choose the games and activities that will interest *your* child. Remember, fifteen to twenty minutes a day is all you need.

* ★ **Substitute other activities that build the same skills.** If a suggestion doesn't appeal to you, look for other games and activities designed to build the same skills. Many learning retail websites organize their materials and games into categories like math, language, and thinking. Check out Lakeshorelearning.com, Etacuisenaire.com, Wonderbrains.com, Melissaanddoug.com, Backtobasictoys .com, and Teachchildren.com.

* ★ **No boot camp.** If your child is taking his test next week and you haven't begun this work, don't engage in a seven-day kindergarten prep-boot camp. I say this from (an embarrassing to admit) experience. A mother once came to me a few weeks before the test in hope that I could help her daughter cram. I was gently bombarding the child with questions such as, "Why do we have doors?" "If you had two bananas and I gave you one more, how many would you have?" The little girl held up her tiny palm and said, "Stop! Can't you see I'm only four?"

* ★ **Make it enjoyable for both of you.** Keep everything light and playful. When a child is exposed to something new and has fun at the same time, the learning will stick. It's important to find a way to make it fun for *you* as well. If you're bored silly by an activity, you won't be motivated to keep it up.

* ★ **Teach your child to tolerate boredom.** Speaking of boredom, some children will not sit still for a book. Others shy away from puzzles. It can be a red flag if your child resists certain types of activities. This may be an area of weakness for him.

Let's face it, in school we often have to do things that don't interest us or that we aren't good at. You can help your child strengthen weak skills and build his boredom tolerance "muscles" by engaging him in activities he prefers not to do. Work on those for three minutes a day (gradually increasing to ten) three times a week and his skills will improve. Kids who work at things that don't come easily to them become better learners. Caveat: Make activities he avoids as enticing as you can by tying them into his special interest or characters he loves (see next suggestion).

★ **Tie the activities to whatever your child loves.** When I worked with Sam, he was crazy about Batman. I bought a Batman coloring book and cut, pasted, photocopied, reduced, and enlarged the pictures to use in the activities we did together. For example, I created a page featuring Batman, Robin, the Joker, the Penguin, and Mr. Freeze (all different sizes). Then I asked Sam, "Which one is taller? Shorter? Fatter? Smaller?" I cut out five pictures of Batman and used them to illustrate math concepts. "If you have three Batmen and add one more, how many would you have?" In those days, mazes were on the WPPSI (they aren't now). I would draw my own mazes and paste a Batman at the start and tell Sam that he had to help Batman save Batgirl or Robin, who was imprisoned in the middle. I would cut out a large picture of Batman, paste it to a piece of cardboard, then cut it into four pieces to create a borderless puzzle. Sam could not get enough of any activity tied to Batman.

Years later, I read about a British study on using popular culture, media, and new technologies to teach young children. They reported that when they put Batman logos on white paper and made it available in the classroom, boys couldn't write enough, whereas when they placed white paper without logos in the same areas, the boys ignored it. The use of the superhero motivated the boys to engage in literacy and language activities that would not have otherwise interested them. The study concluded that integrating children's favorite media characters into skill-building activities makes learning more pleasurable, relevant, and interesting to children. It certainly worked for Sam.

★ **Build from where your child is.** This is known in the education biz as *scaffolding*. Present experiences that challenge your child in a positive way and help take him to the next level, higher than he would be able to go on his own. For example, if your child asks how to spell his name, write it out for him. Let's say it starts with a *T*. Later, when you are reading a book, ask if he can find more *T*s in the text.

★ **Learn in context.** Any child can memorize the alphabet or how to count from 1 to 10. That is not true learning. True learning is understanding that *A* is a symbol in words that makes the *ah* or *ay* sound, that 3 means *one Cheerio and one Cheerio and one Cheerio* that together make *three Cheerios.* Any child can name the four seasons, but there is nothing like trudging through the snow in January to teach a child what winter *is.* Learning is most powerful and permanent when it occurs experientially and in context.

★ **Your child's learning style will impact his ability to take in information.** Each person has a preferred learning style by which information is more easily processed. We know that 40 percent of people are *visual learners.* In a classroom, they need to sit close and see a teacher's body language and facial expressions. They respond to seeing the information presented in pictures or charts or on film. You will often see these learners taking copious notes during a lecture because that is the only way they will be able to integrate the information. Another 20 percent to 30 percent are *auditory learners.* They must hear information presented to process it. They benefit from having text read to them or listening to lectures. Everyone else is a *tactile learner.* For them, touching, feeling, and experiencing is the optimal way to take in information. They are often unable to sit still for long periods and are easily distracted. Most young children entering kindergarten learn best this way.

In later grades, a preference for visual or auditory learning may develop. At this point, you probably don't know which learning mode will emerge most strongly within your child. Until you do, be cognizant of presenting information and teaching skills all three ways: through visuals, sound, and hands-on experience. Using the different tools described in the next section allows you to do this.

★ **Involve your child's caretaker or your spouse.** Share this information with everyone who regularly interacts with your child. If they're not the types to read a book like this, fine. They don't have to understand which abilities an activity will build. Just ask them to play Candy Land, dominoes, or Go Fish or do puzzles, build with blocks, or make shape cookies with your child. I used to ask my husband to let Sam sort laundry with him. Mark had no idea he was helping his son with cognitive and motor skills.

CHILDREN NEED REPETITION

Before a child can process and retain information or a new skill, he needs lots of repetition. Do you notice how your child loves to read the same book over and over again? Each time he takes something new from it. Watch *Sesame Street* and you'll see how they come back to the same lessons over and over again, but in different ways. One day, the Count may sing about his love of the number 5, the next week, 5 may be selected as the number of the day, and the next day Lefty the Salesman may try to sell Ernie five pairs of pants. When working with your child, it will take many times and different approaches before he truly understands a concept.

Learning Tools: DVDs, Computers, Workbooks, and Other Media

Developing brains learn most easily by actively participating in real-life activities. Experts will tell you that math is best absorbed using manipulatives such as blocks, and literacy skills are more easily grasped through reading. Nothing beats getting down on the floor to play with your child or taking her to a zoo or museum. That doesn't mean that you can't vary your presentation from time to time to keep things interesting. Since kids need repetition, using DVDs, computers, workbooks, and other tools in small doses is a good way to present the same information in different ways:

MUSIC

For children who are auditory learners, your basic concepts can be taught by music. There is *Sesame Street Platinum All-Time Favorites, Schoolhouse Rock, Letters and Numbers* from the Twin Sisters label (they have a whole series covering weather, insects and spiders, dinosaurs, and more), *Here Come the ABCs* and *Here Come the 123s* by They Might be Giants, and the Little People CDs from Fisher-Price. For a large selection of CDs that teach basic preschool concepts, visit Songsforteaching.com.

EDUCATIONAL TV AND DVDS

For children who are visual learners, educational DVDs allow them to see concepts brought to life, which assists such kids in processing and internalizing the information. There is a slew of educational DVDs available, many featuring your child's favorite characters. Disney's Winnie the Pooh and Nick Jr.'s Blues Clues offer DVDs on shapes, colors, numbers, and letters. Leapfrog makes some excellent learning DVDs such as *Leapfrog Letter Factory* and *Math Circus. Meet the Numbers* from Preschool Prep Company is also popular with kids.

There is research to back up the educational benefits of shows like *Sesame*

Street, *Blues Clues*, and *Barney* for children ages 2 and older. Studies have shown that children who regularly watch *Sesame Street* do better on tests for cognitive skills and socioemotional awareness than kids who don't. Children as young as 27 months who watch Barney test better on vocabulary, manners, and health awareness than nonviewers. Studies prove that the best shows for young children have stories that are linear and easy to follow, a slow and steady pace, fewer cuts between scenes, and research to back up their claims of learning. As long as your child is 2 or older, he can benefit from well-designed and researched programs like Nick Jr. and Noggin's *Blues Clues*, *Barney*, *Dora the Explorer*, *Sesame Street*, *Dragon Tales*, and *Mister Rogers'* among others.

If you do let your child watch TV, it is important that you monitor the shows that she watches. In a 2008 study, media experts Dr. Jamie Ostrov and Dr. Douglas Gentile found that the more educational TV children watched, the more relationally aggressive they were (e.g., bossy, lying, saying "shut up," excluding other kids, acting manipulative). They studied programs on PBS, Disney Channel, and Nickelodeon, noting that many seemingly tame shows spend most of the episode building up a relational conflict between characters that is quickly resolved at the end. They speculate that young children focus on the bad behavior but do not attend to or remember the conflict resolution. They recommend that parents talk to their children about relationship problems they see depicted on TV, help them grasp the ultimate resolution, and teach them that these behaviors are harmful and shouldn't be copied.

CHILDREN'S EDUCATIONAL SOFTWARE

If your child is 2.5 and older, there is excellent software available that teaches all the preschool basics in entertaining, interactive ways. Working on the computer helps your child build fine-motor skills and actively engage with media (versus watching TV or listening to music, which are more passive). You can purchase a child-sized mouse and colorful keyboard that is easier and more fun for kids to use. There are learning programs that your child may enjoy, programs from series such as Reader Rabbit, Math Blaster, Leapfrog, and JumpStart. If your child is working at the computer, you will want to supervise at first. Eventually, children get so adept that they are able to work independently for short periods. Warren Buckleitner runs a website that reviews and sells children's software at Childrenstech.com. Two excellent sites for purchasing educational software for children ages 3 to 5 are Kidsclick.com and Cdaccess.com. They have learning software featuring every character your child could want.

FREE INTERACTIVE CHILDREN'S SITES

Here are my favorite free, interactive sites full of colorful games and activities that will help your child learn all the information children are expected to know before kindergarten:

* PBSkids.org (leads you to separate sites featuring all your child's favorite PBS programs, including *Curious George*, *Sesame Street*, *Caillou*, *Mister Rogers' Neighborhood*, *Clifford*, *World World*, *Martha Speaks*, *It's a Big, Big World*, *Sid the Science Kid*, *Hooper*, and others).
* Bobthebuilder.com
* Primarygames.com
* Nickjr.com
* Barbie.com
* ABCya.com
* Uptoten.com
* Scholastic.com
* Funschool.kaboose.com/preschool
* Internet4classrooms.com

ONE HOUR A DAY FOR MEDIA

The American Academy of Pediatrics (AAP) recommends that children younger than 2 should watch no TV at all, no matter what the educational claims of its producer. Why? For one thing, a University of Washington study found that among children ages 8 to 16 months, each hour per day spent watching Baby Einstein and similar "baby education" videos translated to a 17 percent *decrease* in vocabulary acquisition! Other studies show that TV exposure at ages 1 through 3 is associated with attention problems at age 7. For children 3 and older, the AAP recommends no more than two hours a day of high-quality screen time (TV, computer, or video games).

WORKBOOKS

Pick up age-appropriate workbooks packed with activities and games that teach ABCs, numbers, letters, shapes, colors, beginning sounds, sorting, matching, sequencing, and thinking skills. If your child isn't working with a pencil yet, show him the question and have him point to the answer. For children with older siblings who "get" to do homework, workbooks can be offered as an opportunity for a preschooler to do her own special homework. DK Publishing makes workbooks featuring characters kids love. Their *Math Made Easy* workbook is one of the best I've seen. Workbooks that cover the basics include the *Big Preschool Workbook* (Big Get Ready Books Series), by Barbara Gregorich and Joan Hoffman, and *Summer Bridge Activities: Preschool to Kindergarten*, by Julia Ann Hobbs and Carla Fisher. The superbly produced *Brain Quest Workbook: Pre-K* features a wide assortment of learning exercises children really enjoy.

An enormous variety of workbooks are available. Start with one that you think your child might enjoy and if he does, pick up more. To save money, you can print free workbook pages off the Internet at Edhelper.com, ABCteach .com, and Education.com.

> The ages between birth and age 5 are the foundation upon which successful lives are built.
>
> —Laura Bush

BOARD GAMES

Children enjoy competition, and board games offer them the chance to win and learn to lose (with grace, we hope). When children play board games they are strengthening their mathematical, vocabulary, and memory skills—and that's just for a start. By rolling dice and moving their player that number of spots on the board, children gain greater numerical understanding. Moving five more spaces helps them master counting and addition. Games like Clue help build deductive reasoning skills and Cranium Cariboo teaches letters, numbers, shapes, and colors. Games show children how to follow rules, take turns, devise strategy, and exercise fine-motor control when moving game pieces around the board. My personal favorites are:

Candy Land. Children as young as three can play this one. Kids draw colored cards and move their game piece along the candy path. The first to reach the candy castle wins.

Connect Four is like vertical tic-tac-toe. The goal is to get four checkers of the same color in a row. Players take turns dropping a checker down one of several adjacent slots at the top of an upright grid. This is an excellent game for developing thinking and fine-motor skills.

Memory. Using 72 picture cards, children take turns making 36 pairs of elephants, puppies, fruit, and other colorful images. When children are 2, you can let them make matches with the cards faceup. At 3, you might want to play with half the deck since 72 cards may be more than they can keep in their memory. When your child is ready, he can play with the whole deck.

Hiss. Here, kids build a snake from a stack of partial snake cards (heads, tails, middles). This helps with pattern recognition, color matching, and thinking skills. It's also a lot of fun.

Chess. These days, even preschoolers are learning to play chess. Study after study has proven that playing chess strengthens critical thinking, spatial skills, numerical abilities, memory, decision making, patience, logical thinking, ability to recognize complex patterns, and more. Children who play the game score higher on standardized reading and math tests, which is why it is required curricula in thirty countries. If you think your child may enjoy chess, give it a try (if not now, later).

In the next four chapters, we'll look at things you can do that will impact *all* 7 Abilities your child needs for testing and school success (reading aloud, playing music, talking, listening). If you do only these four things, your child will make substantial gains in intelligence. Read on and you'll get ideas for strengthening each of the 7 Abilities: language, knowledge comprehension, memory, mathematics, visual-spatial reasoning, cognitive, and fine-motor skills. Chapter 19 offers a plan for introducing these activities into your child's life a little bit at a time. If your child is taking an intelligence test within the next year, go right to the Express Prep Schedule, page 174.

8. Reading to Build All 7 Abilities

READ ALOUD IN A NEW WAY TO SUPERCHARGE YOUR CHILD'S INTELLECT

A parent once asked Albert Einstein, "How can we improve our child's IQ?" He said, "Read Aesop's fables to them from infancy." He didn't say to drill them with flash cards, teach them math, or practice spelling. "Read them stories," he said. Stories inspire the imagination, introduce children to new worlds, and arouse their curiosity. The rewards of reading to your child cannot be overemphasized. Start when he is just a baby and continue as long as he's willing to sit and listen. I read Harry Potter books to Sam when he was in fifth grade. Entire books have been written about the value of reading to your child, but let's review just a few of the benefits:

★ **Builds the 7 Abilities.** By reading to your child, you'll bolster his receptive and expressive language, sharpen his vocabulary, boost his listening skills and attention span, strengthen his memory, support his understanding of sequencing, and build his fine-motor skills as he turns the pages.

★ **Teaches the skill of coherence.** Coherence refers to knowing how sentences link even when they do not share any words. This is one of the most vital language and communication skills your child needs to learn. In stories, sentences *relate* to each other. For example, these two sentences are coherent because the second builds upon the first: "The little bird was worried. He could not see his mother." These two sentences are not coherent because the idea expressed in the first does not lead to idea expressed in the second sentence: "The little bird was red. He could not see his mother." Your child needs coherence skills to help him learn to think abstractly and make inferences.

★ **Teaches preliteracy skills.** When you read to your child, he learns that books are read from front to back, that words and sentences are read from left to right, that letters are symbols that make sounds, and that pictures represent real objects. He hears how sentences are structured and is able to express himself more confidently, clearly, and correctly both orally and (eventually) through his own writing. He becomes familiar with the letters that make up words. This will help him when he begins learning how to read and write these letters himself.

* **Enhances knowledge.** When you read aloud to your child, he is introduced to all kinds of new facts, topics, ideas, people, places, ideas, and things. His fund of knowledge about the world is expanded.

* **Creates an emotional connection.** Reading aloud to your child is a wonderful opportunity to cuddle, create warm memories that will last a lifetime, and just have fun together.

Daily Life Lessons

DIALOGIC READING

Earlier this year, I saw myself in the mirror and realized that I resembled a ball. At that moment, I decided to lose thirty pounds. My strategy for dropping the weight was twofold. I would eat 1,200 calories and walk five miles on the treadmill each day. For the first two weeks, I followed my plan to the letter. But when I weighed myself, I had dropped one measly pound. I'd heard that as you got older, it was harder to lose weight, but this was just sad.

When the trainer at the gym saw me weeping (only a slight exaggeration) by the scale, he offered to teach me a special technique for making my routine work doubly hard. He told me about a 3-month study where one group of participants walked five miles a day and the second group put in three miles, but walked and ran in alternating one-minute intervals. The second group lost twice as much body fat as the first. So the next week, I tried this method for three miles instead of five. By the end of the week, I'd lost four additional pounds. I immediately adopted this technique and the weight came off at a fast and steady clip.

Reading aloud to your child is very much the same. You can read books the traditional way, and your child will absolutely benefit from the experience. However, there are techniques you can adopt to make your reading do double duty. One such method is called dialogic reading, developed by Dr. Grover J. Whitehurst.

In dialogic reading the adult both reads to the child and has a conversation with him about the book. It works like this. As you read a picture book, you will gently guide your child through questions and expansions on what he says, while paying attention to what interests him most and his ability to answer questions (but without pressuring him or turning reading into a test). Once every page or two, you'll initiate the PEER (Prompt, Evaluate, Expand, Repeat) sequence that follows:

1. PROMPT YOUR CHILD TO SAY SOMETHING ABOUT THE BOOK.
FOR 2 TO 3-YEAR-OLDS

★ Give him a sentence and ask him to fill in the blank: "Look at that dinosaur. His legs are short, but his neck is _____?"

★ Ask a *who, what,* or *where* question: "Who is that?" "Where do you think the dinosaur will go now?" "What was the queen's name?"

★ Ask him to point to all the *m*s on a page or to find specific things in an illustration: "Can you point to the thing that says 'moo'?" "Can you show me the rain clouds?" "Can you point to the thing that rhymes with *loon*?" "Can you point to something that starts with the *m* sound?"

FOR 4 TO 5-YEAR OLDS

★ Ask a *when* or *why* question: "Why do you think the dinosaur cried when the little boy said good-bye?"

★ Ask him to recall something about the story at the end or the beginning if you're reading something he's read before: "What happens when the dinosaur comes alive at the museum?"

★ Ask him an open-ended question about what is happening in the story: "What else do you see in the picture?" "What do you think this other dinosaur is doing in that tree?" If your child doesn't respond, you can help him. "I think that dinosaur is going to fly out of the tree."

★ Ask him to connect something in the story to his own life: "Remember when we went to the museum? What did we see?"

★ Ask him to describe what is happening in the illustrations: "Can you tell me what is going on in the picture?"

★ In the middle of the story, ask him to predict what he thinks will happen next.

★ Ask math or spatial questions about pictures in a book: "How many people are in the picture?" "How many noses can you count in the picture?" "Which is the biggest/smallest animal in the picture?"

★ After you have read a passage, ask him to put into his own words what just happened.

It's best to focus your prompts on something in the book that your child has already expressed an interest in. For example, if he gets excited about a picture of a dancing polar bear, your prompt should be about that.

2. EVALUATE YOUR CHILD'S RESPONSE. If he gets the answer right, praise and encourage him: "That's right, that is a dinosaur." If he isn't right, you can correct him without saying he made a mistake: "That does look a lot like a lizard, but it really is a dinosaur."

3. EXPAND ON WHAT YOUR CHILD SAYS BY REPHRASING OR ADDING A BIT OF INFORMATION. "Yes, that is a dinosaur. He's called a brontosaurus."

4. REPEAT THE ORIGINAL PROMPT IN A WAY THAT INCORPORATES THE EXPANSION: "Can you say brontosaurus?"

DIALOGIC READING WORKS!

Grover Whitehurst studied the effectiveness of his technique by dividing children (who were comparable in language skills) into two groups: a control group, whose mothers simply read to their children daily, and a treatment group, whose mothers were trained in dialogic reading and used it when they read to their kids each day. After four weeks, the children in the treatment group *scored 6.5 to 8 months ahead* of the children in the control group on two measures of expressive language in an IQ test. They scored marginally ahead of the control group on measures of receptive language.

Here are some examples of dialogic reading.

Parent: What is that doggy doing? [prompt]
Child: Barking.
Parent: That's right. [Evaluates response] The doggie is barking at the moon. [expansion] What is he barking at? [repeat]
Child: Doggie barking at the moon.

Parent: What is happening to the bear? [prompt]
Child: Bear has a temperature.

Parent: Yes, he does [evaluation]. The bear has a temperature and a bad cold [expansion]. What's wrong with that bear? [repeat].

Child: He has a cold.

Parent: Remember when you had a cold? How did you feel?

A similar model to dialogic reading goes like this:

1. Make a comment. Wait for your child to respond.
2. Ask a question. Wait for your child to respond.
3. Expand on what your child says. Wait for your child to respond.

Let's say your child showed an interest in the picture of the fire engine on a page you read aloud.

Child: Fire engine!

Parent: That is a fire engine. It's red. [comment]

Child: Red fire engine.

Parent: What color is the fireman's jacket? [question]

Child: Yellow.

Parent: That's right. It's bright yellow just like your school bus [expansion].

VIDEOS TO WATCH

To see a marvelous example of a parent actively reading to her child, go to the PBS series on reading at Readingrockets.org/shows/launching/roots ("Reading as Dialog" video). If you go to Youtube and search for "dialogic reading," you'll see examples of parents using this technique with their own children. These videos may change the way you read to your child forever.

RECOMMENDED WORDLESS PICTURE BOOKS

Wordless picture books, where a sequence of illustrations tells the story, are wonderful for young children. Without words, the child can follow complex sequencing ideas and decipher what the story is about. Older children can build vocabulary and comprehension by "reading" the books aloud. By telling the stories, children learn that stories have a beginning, middle, and end. Here are some your child will love:

A Boy, a Dog, and a Frog, Mercer Mayer (part of a series)

Good Dog Carl, Alexandra Day (part of a series)

Changes, Changes, Pat Hutchins

Clown, Quentin Blake

Do You Want to Be My Friend, Eric Carle

Good Night Gorilla, Peggy Rathmann

Have You Seen My Duckling? Nancy Tafuri

Pancakes for Breakfast, Tomie dePaola

Picnic, Emily Arnold McCully

The Red Book, Barbara Lehman

RECOMMENDED PICTURE BOOKS

In 1999 the National Education Association selected 100 books as great reading for children. Below are some of their top-rated books for young children, along with a few books that didn't make their list but were my kids' all-time favorites.

Alexander and the Terrible, Horrible, No Good, Very Bad Day, Judith Viorst

Amelia Bedelia, Peggy Parish

Arthur, series, Marc Tolon Brown

Are You My Mother? Philip D. Eastman

Barnyard Dance, Sandra Boynton

Brown Bear, Brown Bear, What Do You See? Bill Martin Jr.

Caps for Sale, Esphyr Slobodkina

Chicka Chicka Boom Boom, John Archambault, Bill Martin, Jr., Lois Ehlert

Corduroy, Don Freeman

Curious George, Hans Augusto Rey

Danny and the Dinosaur series, Syd Hoff

Everyone Poops, Taro Gomi and Amanda Mayer Stinchecum

Fox in Sox, Dr. Seuss

Goodnight Moon, Margaret Wise Brown

Green Eggs and Ham, Dr. Seuss

Guess How Much I Love You, Sam McBratney

How the Grinch Stole Christmas, Dr. Seuss

If You Give a Mouse a Cookie, Laura Joffe Numeroff

Ira Sleeps Over, Bernard Waber

Jumanji, Chris Van Allsburg

Junie B. Jones series, Barbara Park and Denise Brunkus

Love You Forever, Robert N. Munsch

Madeline, Ludwig Bemelmans

Oh, the Places You'll Go, Dr. Seuss

One Fish Two Fish Red Fish Blue Fish, Dr. Seuss

Strega Nona, Tomie dePaola

Stellaluna, Janell Cannon

Sylvester and the Magic Pebble, William Steig

The Berenstain Bears, series, Stan Berenstain and Jan Berenstain

The Cat in the Hat, Dr. Seuss

The Complete Tales of Winnie the Pooh, A. A. Milne

The Going to Bed Book,
    Sandra Boynton

The Little Engine That Could,
    Watty Piper

Millions of Cats, Wanda Gag

Moo, Baa, La La La! Sandra Boynton

The Paper Bag Princess,
    Robert N. Munsch

Pat the Bunny, Dorothy Kunhardt

The Rainbow Fish, Marcus Pfister

The Runaway Bunny, Margaret Wise

The Snowy Day, Ezra Jack Keats

The Story of Babar, Jean De Brunhoff

The Story of Ferdinand, Munro Leaf and
    Robert Lawson

The Tale of Peter Rabbit, Beatrix Potter

The Velveteen Rabbit, Margery Williams

The Very Hungry Caterpillar, Eric Carle

There's an Alligator Under My Bed,
    Mercer Mayer

Where the Wild Things Are,
    Maurice Sendak

Don't forget the classics—Aesop's fables, Grimm's fairy tales, and the stories of Hans Christian Andersen. You can find these online, but it is more enjoyable to read them from picture books. Choose books on topics for which your child has a deep affinity, like cars, dinosaurs, princesses, or superheroes. Nonfiction books that deal with going to the doctor, the dentist, or school for the first time are fascinating to kids. You don't have to spend a fortune. Your library lends them out for free. If you want to own them, check with your local elementary schools or churches. They often hold tag sales of clothes, toys, and books and you can pick up many of the titles mentioned above for fifty cents or a dollar each.

> There are many little ways to enlarge your child's world. Love of books is the best of all.
>
> —Jackie Kennedy

More Tips on Getting the Most Out of Reading to Your Child

- ★ Even while practicing dialogic reading, you should still snuggle up with your child in a quiet, comfy place and make the experience as cozy as possible.
- ★ Read the same book as often as your child likes. They get to know a book and can often recite it from memory. That is a form of prereading. Books with lots

of repetition (like *Brown Bear, Brown Bear*, by Eric Carle) are easy for kids to learn.

★ Gradually increase the amount of time you spend reading stories to your child. This will help him develop his listening and attention skills.

★ Let your child select the book he wants to read.

★ Give him time to look at the pictures as you read.

★ Before you read a book for the first time, look through all the pictures. Point things out on various pages and ask, "What is this?" "What's he doing?" "Where are they?" "What do you think this story is going to be about?" Before the end of the book, ask, "Can you guess how the story will end?" Later, after you read it to him, you can see if his predictions were right.

★ At the climax of a story, ask your child what she thinks will happen next.

★ Pause at the end of repetitive phrases and let your child fill in the blanks: "Run, run as fast as you can, you can't catch me, I'm the _____?"

★ Let your child turn the pages as you read.

★ Act out the story as you're reading it. Change your voice for different characters. Show the emotions of the characters as you read. Ham it up!

★ Explain words to your child that are new to her. Building vocabulary is an important part of the reading experience.

★ When reading to your child, follow the text with your finger to help her learn that the symbols she sees correspond to the words that you are saying. This also helps her learn that text is read from left to right, top to bottom.

★ If your child has a hard time sitting still and listening to books, try reading at bedtime when he is tired.

★ Don't practice dialogic reading all the time. Sometimes, just read a book straight through and keep the experience light and fun.

Another Daily Life Lesson

READ NONFICTION BOOKS WHEN YOUR CHILD IS AGE 5 AND OLDER

When children reach fourth grade, their success in school is largely based on their ability to read and comprehend books with expository text. These are books with a higher-level vocabulary and "invisible connections" between sentences requiring coherence skills (the ability to infer the missing information or hidden logic connecting sentences). Nonfiction books allow children to practice recognizing implicit meanings within text. According to Dr. Marion

Blank, a leading expert in reading from Columbia University, "If parents begin at about five years old to introduce interesting expository text into their bedtime reading [stories about the *Titanic* or the Trojan War, a true story like Joy Adamson's *Born Free* where a lion is raised at home and then taught to live in the wild, books about space, biographies of leaders, et cetera] they will be doing something of enormous value for their children's school success." Choose nonfiction books related to your child's life. If you are traveling soon, read a book about where you're going. If you're planning a visit to the planetarium, a book about space is perfect.

SHOULD YOU TRY TO TEACH YOUR PRESCHOOLER HOW TO READ?

Remember Elizabeth Barrett, the gifted toddler who began reading at age 1? At 2.5 years old, she was reading the newspaper and the CNN headline feed. Elizabeth taught herself, with no help from Mom and Dad. But these days, well-meaning parents are pushing their kids to leap ahead of their Pampered peers to gain every possible intellectual advantage. Many have signed up their 3-month-olds for one of those "Teach Your Baby to Read," programs, drilling them with flash cards every day. Is this necessary?

Child development experts say no. Responding to flash cards at such an early age isn't really reading. Unlike Elizabeth, kids trained to read this way have merely memorized what is on each card. These children do not understand that each squiggle has a corresponding sound, that words are made of discrete sounds and segments that combine to create a word like /m/a/n/. If the last letter of this word were changed to /p/, the baby who could "read" /m/a/n/ wouldn't be able to decipher /m/a/p/ until she'd memorized the new word. Studies show that any early advantage these kids have disappears a few years later.

According to Maryanne Wolf, head of Tufts University's Center for Reading and Language Research, most children aren't ready to read until about age 5. The visual, auditory, linguistic, and conceptual brain functions required for reading aren't fully integrated until then. She says, "The best predictor of how a child will do in school is not reading ability but size and richness of a child's vocabulary. Reading books out loud and making connections between what is on the page and in the child's own world is the most effective way parents can help children build their vocabulary."

Hyperlexia is an autism spectrum disorder where children may recite the alphabet as early as 18 months, read words by age 2, and sentences by age 3. These kids are often overly fascinated with books, words, and numbers. They have problems understanding language and learning to speak. Parents often delay seeking help for hyperlexia because they are thrown off track by their child's advanced reading performance.

At the opposite extreme are parents who don't think about working on reading skills until their child starts kindergarten. It turns out that the time to focus on reading is earlier, from birth to age 5. The emphasis should not be on teaching reading per se, but on imparting *preliteracy skills*, which consist of:

* a good vocabulary
* the ability to retell a story that was read to him aloud
* the ability to make up stories based on pictures in a picture book
* the ability to tell his own story with a beginning, middle, and end
* an understanding that words are made of discrete sounds and the ability to work with those sounds (phonological awareness)
* an understanding of what text is (print awareness)
* knowing names of letters and their sounds
* knowing the difference between letters and numerals, upper- and lower-case letters.

Phonological awareness must be in place before a child will be able to crack the code of reading. Phonological awareness relates to sounds of *spoken* words. It is the ability to notice, hear, and work with the discrete sounds that make up our spoken language. It is a prerequisite to understanding phonics, which relate to the sound and spelling associated with *printed* words.

There are 44 phonemes, or individual sounds, in the English language. Some sounds are made from two letters, such as *sh* and *ng*. A child who can recognize that the word *mat* has three sounds (/*m*/*a*/*t*/), or who can change the /*m*/ sound at the beginning of *mat* to the /*r*/ sound and know the word is *rat* is demonstrating phonological awareness. Prereaders who learn to identify the beginning sound of a word, segments in words such as syllables, and clusters of words that make up rhymes have phonological awareness.

Activities that will help your child develop phonological awareness include:

* listening to nursery rhymes and alliterations ("Peter Piper picked a peck of pickled peppers")
* looking at pictures of three items (sun, star, moon) and knowing which one starts with a different letter
* hearing three words and knowing which one doesn't rhyme (moon, soon, dog)
* clapping syllables in a word
* counting discrete sounds in a word
* blending words and syllables: "What word is this? /m/ . . . /at/?"
* segmenting word sounds: "What word is this? /s/ . . . /a/ . . . /t/?"
* making rhymes by changing the first letter of a word: "What happens to the word *top* when you replace the *t* with an *m*?"

A child with print awareness understands that books are read from left to right, top to bottom, that the squiggles on the page represent letters that make sounds that combine to make words that come together to make sentences that carry meaning when read. She knows that there are spaces between words and that print is used in storybooks, signs, menus, grocery lists, posters, calendars, labels, and articles. Help your child experience the power of print by letting him dictate emails or letters to people he loves and then reading aloud the responses he gets back.

Experts recommend that you spend time building these preliteracy skills rather than attempting to teach a child who isn't ready to read. With a strong preliteracy foundation, your child will learn to read when the time is right. The last thing you want is for him to start kindergarten lagging in these abilities. The research is clear that children who start school behind their classmates in language and early literacy skills are unlikely to catch up and are at high risk for reading failure.

SIGNS THAT YOUR CHILD MAY BE AT RISK FOR A READING OR WRITING DELAY

* lacks phonological awareness
* can't learn letters, letter sounds, and number symbols in preschool
* is unable to recognize rhyming patterns in nursery rhymes or can't pick the odd word out in *ham/bug/sam* or *bed/red/bat*

- doesn't like to listen to stories
- shows little interest in letters or words
- gets words mixed up (says "bump bed" instead of "bunk bed" or "beanut put-ter" instead of "peanut butter")
- has trouble recognizing words that start with the same sound
- has difficulty remembering people's names
- says "Get me that thing," has difficulty remembering names of things
- points to what he wants instead of using words
- can't "cross the midline" (i.e., right-handed child can't reach over and pick up something on his left side)
- has difficulty with time terms like *yesterday, today, tomorrow*
- has trouble holding a crayon or pencil
- cannot write his name from memory by age 5

If you see these signs, carefully monitor your child's progress as he learns to read. If he's struggling, get him help as soon as possible.

Games and Activities

BUILD YOUR CHILD'S STORYTELLING SKILLS
- ★ Get wordless picture books and have your child "read" these stories to you.
- ★ After you read a book to your child, have her tell you the story in her own words.
- ★ Give your child a catalog or magazine and ask her to make up stories about the pictures.
- ★ Prompt your child to tell her own stories by asking her to tell you the funniest thing that happened today at school or asking, "Do you remember the day such and such happened. Tell Grandma that story."
- ★ Let your child finish a story you start. For example, "Once upon a time there was a little girl who was born with bright blue hair. It never bothered her until her first day of school when—what happened?" Be enthusiastic and responsive to her telling. **Age 3+.**

GET A SET OF THREE- AND FOUR-SCENE SEQUENCING PICTURE CARDS. These cards feature a ministory with a beginning, middle, and end. Your child puts them in logical order. Look for them at TeachChildren.com and Funiqtoys.com.

You can find free sequencing activities online. Check out Funschool.kaboose.com/preschool (my favorite for online). **Age 3+.**

PICK UP A COPY OF *WHAT YOUR PRESCHOOLER NEEDS TO KNOW*, edited by E. D. Hirsch Jr. and Linda Bevilacqua. Filled with songs, poetry, stories, history, science, and art lessons that are age-appropriate for the prekindergarten child, *What Your Preschooler Needs to Know* specifically demonstrates active reading techniques. **Age 2+.**

READ RHYMING BOOKS Rhyming words like *cat* and *bat* can draw your child's attention to component sounds within words. A great way to help your child see that different words can share component sounds is to read him nursery rhymes (*Bo Peep* and *sheep, Jill* and *hill*) and Dr. Seuss books (*hop* and *pop, cat* and *hat*). Research conducted at Oxford University showed that the greater a child's experience with nursery rhymes, the greater his phonological awareness. **Age infant+.**

SING CHILDREN'S SONGS AND NURSERY RHYMES. For lyrics and music to more than 2,000 children's songs and nursery rhymes, go to Bussongs.com. Also check out Enchantedlearning.com/rhymes/coloring/. They offer hundreds of songs and nursery rhymes you and your child can read together. Pictures replace nouns, so your preschooler can "read" with you. **Age infant+.**

PLAY RHYMING GAMES
1. "Rhyme or Reason." Say three words to your child. If all three rhyme, tell your child to clap and nod his head. If one word doesn't rhyme, tell him to give you the thumbs-down sign and shake his head no. Then he has to tell you which word didn't rhyme. For example, "blue-glue-boot" ("no!—boot"); "fish-dish-wish" ("yes!"), "nail-shoe-pail" ("no! shoe").
2. "Is It a . . ." You start.
    You: Is it a shirt? [Your child makes a rhyme from that.]
    Child: No, it's dirt.
    You: Is it a pear?
    Child: No, it's hair.
    You: Is it a spoon?
    Child: No, it's a balloon.

3. "Rhyming Riddles." Think of a word that has an easy rhyme and give a clue about it: "I'm thinking of something that rhymes with *boy* and is something you love to play with?" *Toy!*

4. "I Spy Rhymes." Take turns looking around the room and spotting rhymes: "I spy with my little eye . . . something that rhymes with head." Bed! **Age 3+.**

BEEP BEEP! Recite a nursery rhyme or poem that your child knows but reverse the words, substitute new words, or switch words around. When your child hears the mistake, he should yell "Beep beep" and tell you what was wrong. For example:

> *Ring around the rosie*
> *A pocket full of posey*
> *Ashes, ashes, we all fall up!*

> *Cat-a-pake, cat-a-pake, baker's man!*

> *Twinkle, twinkle, little guitar*

> *The eensy weensy spider climbed up the water spout*
> *Out came the sun to dry the spider out.* **Age 3+.**

ROBOT VOICE Start with words that you say to your child sound by sound and see if they can guess the word. Emphasize every word sound. For example: "e . . . l . . . e . . . ph . . . a . . . n . . . t, c . . . a . . . t, f . . . i . . . sh." When they get good at guessing words, try a short sentence: "L . . . e . . . t . . . s g . . . o p . . . l . . . a . . . y." **Age 3+.**

WHAT STARTS WITH . . .

You: I'm thinking of something that starts with B, banana.
Child: Banana, boat.
You: Banana, boat, bottle.
Child: Banana, boat, bottle, box [and so on].

If you mix up the order or can't think of a B word, you lose! **Age 3+.**

"I SPY" LETTERS

You: [Take turns looking around the room and spotting letter sounds.]
I spy with my little eye something that starts with the *c* sound.

Child: Clock?

You: Yes!

BIPPITY BIPPITY BOP. Start a chant with your child: "Bippity bippity bop, how many parts has this word got?" Then, call out a word and clap it with your child. Let your child say how many parts the word has.

You: Bippity Bippity bop, how many parts has this word got: El-e-phant!
[clap to each part].

Child: Three!!! **Age 3+.**

READ *DR. SEUSS'S ABCS* The good doctor uses alliteration to teach the alphabet: "Aunt Annie's alligator . . ." In *Alligators All Around*, Maurice Sendak does the same thing. It was one of my children's favorites.

ENVIRONMENTAL WORDS. Before your child can read, he recognizes certain words in his environment: the *Stop* on a stop sign, the McDonald's logo, the word *Cheerios* on a box of cereal. Make a book that your child can "read" to you using environmental words you've written down or cut out of magazines. **Age 3+.**

BOB BOOKS. If your child is **4 or older** and just beginning to read, a good series to start with are the Bob Books. These books are extremely short and simple with cartoon drawings. For example, the words that make up the first story in the Bob Book Beginning Reader Series have just four letters (*M, A, T, S*) so kids can easily learn how to sound out the words used in the story: Mat, sat, Sam. The Bob Books teach reading concepts in tiny, measured bites over five book sets with eight to twelve paperback booklets per set.

MY TWO ALL-TIME FAVORITE READING PROGRAMS

★ **For prereaders, check out Story Smarts,** by Marion Blank, PhD, and Laura Berlin, PhD, Storysmarts.com. Story Smarts is a wonderful prereading program designed to build your child's reading readiness skills. Ideally suited for children **age 4+** (although a **precocious 3-year-old** might be ready for it), the program also supports receptive language, expressive language, memory, and sequential thinking. It helps children build their comprehension and storytelling abilities. The series has thirty colorfully illustrated stories that start out very simply (a three-picture sequence) and become more complex (a five-picture sequence). When you purchase them (in bundles of six for less than $2 per story), you can immediately download them to your computer. To sample one of these stories for free, and try the accompanying activities with your child, go to Testingforkindergarten.com.

★ **Reading Kingdom.** If your child is **4+** and seems ready to read, the best program I've seen is online at Readingkingdom.com. It is based on years of research into how children learn to read and is extremely kid-friendly. Your child begins with a skill assessment. Based on the outcome, the program automatically starts at the right place for him. Unlike most programs that focus on phonics, this one covers six key skills needed for reading: sequencing (letter order), keyboarding, phonology (sounds), semantics (meaning), syntax (grammar), and text (books). Reading Kingdom is great for new readers and for kids struggling with reading up to age 10. Children enjoy doing the program and ask to do it after they get started. You can try it through their free trial and then sign up for a modest fee if it is working for your child. If he hasn't exhibited all the prereading abilities we talked about earlier in the chapter, save this program for later.

In the next chapter, we'll talk about how learning a musical instrument will affect almost every ability a child needs to succeed in kindergarten and beyond.

9. Instruments to Strengthen All 7 Abilities

PLAYING AN INSTRUMENT: THE SECRET, ALMOST AUTOMATIC WAY TO A SMARTER CHILD

When I was 5, my mother signed me up for piano lessons with Mrs. Baskin. Once a week, I'd go to her house and suffer. Despite my best efforts, I couldn't learn to read or play music. Eventually, Mrs. Baskin told my mom to stop wasting her money. (I was thrilled!) Knowing what I know now, I realize that I lacked something called basic music competence (BMC), the ability to sing in tune and move with accurate rhythm. A child can't learn to play an instrument without it. Sadly, I still don't have it. Oh well. A child without BMC may not recognize if she's playing the right melody or understand if she's keeping a steady tempo. This is a skill children can pick up as early as age 3 if their parents give them experiences learning to sing in tune and move with accurate rhythm. To help your child gain BMC, here are a few things you can do:

Daily Life Lessons

- ★ Play all kinds of music at home from Mozart to the Beatles, creating a soundtrack for your child's life. **Age infant+.**
- ★ Sing songs together and clap with the rhythm. **Age infant+.**
- ★ Sing songs with hand movements like "The Itsy Bitsy Spider," "The Wheels on the Bus," "Where Is Thumbkin." **Age infant+.**
- ★ Listen to songs and get your child clapping, dancing, marching, rocking, tapping, and moving to the beat. **Age infant+.**
- ★ **Singing conversation.** Instead of talking, sing a conversation with your child.

MUSIC: NECESSARY OR JUST NICE?

There is an enormous amount of research showing that learning to play an instrument will strengthen your child's intellectual skills, from math to spatial to language abilities. Notwithstanding my experience as a failed music student, I recommend that if your child enjoys music and is willing to give it a try, consider signing him up to learn an instrument. Kids can take violin lessons using the Suzuki method beginning at age 3 or 4, but you should gauge your own child's readiness. I'm not a believer in enrolling little kids in too many enrichment classes, but if you're going to choose one thing, this is a good one. Just take a look at some of these studies.

* In a 1994 University of California (Irvine) study, preschoolers having eight months of keyboard lessons showed a 46 percent improvement in spatial reasoning skills on an IQ test.
* A 1993 Swiss study of 1,200 students showed that young kids involved in music lessons were better at languages and learned to read more easily.
* Students who play instruments scored 53 points higher on verbal and 61 points higher on math on the SAT.
* A Wisconsin school district now requires music lessons for K-5 students after kindergarteners who took piano lessons scored 43 percent higher on solving puzzles and 53 percent higher on block patterns than those who did not have lessons.
* Students who learn music consistently outperform students who do not on math and reading achievement tests. Skills such as reading, memory, listening, predicting, concentration, eye-hand coordination, and fine-motor abilities are developed through playing music.

Musicians are particularly successful in fields beyond music. Physician and biologist Lewis Thomas reported that music majors are accepted to medical school more than any other field of study. Two-thirds of music majors who apply to medical school were accepted. The next largest group is biochemistry majors; 44 percent of those applicants were admitted.

Beyond music's intrinsic artistic beauty and impact on intellectual development, it gives children a chance to express themselves, putting them in touch with who they are and what they feel. Self-expression does wonders for a child's confidence. Kids who play in orchestras or bands learn teamwork. They also develop excellent work habits as they commit to continued learning, stretch beyond current abilities, practice what they haven't mastered, rehearse, and perform.

You may have heard of a theory called "the Mozart Effect," which contends that listening to Mozart improved children's scores on tasks designed to measure spatial IQ. It turns out that the effect lasts only ten to fifteen minutes, so passively listening to music is not sufficient for enhancing spatial intelligence. Playing an instrument, however, is a different story.

Finally, it is reported that Einstein was a mediocre student until he learned to play violin. Later, he said that some of his greatest inspiration came while playing the instrument. It liberated his brain and allowed his imagination to soar.

For more information on studies that show the intellectual advantages of music lessons in children, visit Mustcreate.org.

Games and Activities

HOMEMADE BAND. Give your child rattles, bells, drums, shakers, xylophones, cymbals, pots, sticks, and wooden spoons so she can experience making sounds. Play lively CDs such as Ricky Martin's "Livin' la Vida Loca" or Gloria Estefan's "Conga" and let your child add to the orchestration. **Age 1+.**

CLASS. Take an age-appropriate music class together. **Age infant+.**

SCARF DANCING. Get brightly colored scarves for you and your child. Play classical music and dance while twirling the scarves in the air. Really get into the feeling of the music and the beauty of the designs made by the flowing scarves. **Age 2.5+.**

HOMEMADE MARACAS. Take colorful plastic Easter eggs that open up and fill them with pennies, beans, pebbles, paper clips, and other small items. Listen to music and shake them to the beat. **Age 2+.**

In the next chapter, we will talk about the one thing you can do to have the most profound impact on your child's verbal skills: talk to him about everything and anything that is happening in his world.

10. Conversing to Support 6 Abilities

**THE "RIGHT" AND "WRONG" WAYS TO HAVE A CONVERSATION
(THIS CHAPTER ALONE COULD BE WORTH 38 IQ POINTS!)**

The year Schuyler was born, a woman in my apartment building had a son named Aaron. This woman was extremely weird, in my opinion. We'll call her Sandy because that was her name and I don't live in the building anymore anyway.

Sandy used to have a loud, one-sided running dialog with Aaron about everything and anything they encountered. They would be walking down the hall to go up to their apartment and Sandy would say, "We're walking down the hall, Aaron. Now we're getting in the elevator." The boy would squeak "Elevator." "What floor do we live on?" Sandy would ask. "Seven," he'd say. "That's right. Can you press the seven button?" Aaron would press it. "Now we're going up. The doors are opening now." "Open," a high voice would peep. They'd step out of the elevator and I'd hear, "The doors are closing now. Let's walk left to our apartment. Which way is left? What letter is our apartment . . ."

I think we can all agree that Sandy was obnoxious. Me, I was too polite to inflict my parenting dialogs on neighbors like that. Sure, I talked to Schuyler while we were at home or out and about, but I rarely engaged her in front of strangers. When I did, I always used my spa voice. This was partly because I felt silly carrying on with a toddler who could hardly keep up her end of the conversation.

From the time Aaron was born, I'd see them at the grocery store. Sandy would be pushing Aaron in the shopping cart, jabbering away about everything they encountered. "Aaron, what is this orange fruit I'm holding? It's called an orange. Feel how rough and bumpy the skin is. And these yellow bananas, are they fruits or vegetables? They're fruits. We get our fruits and vegetables first and our frozen foods last because we don't want the frozen foods to melt. What kind of cereal shall we buy today? Let's not get Cocoa Puffs; they're full of sugar. Let's get Cheerios. They're made from whole grain and whole grain is healthy." She did this even before the kid could talk! Not only that, when all Aaron could do was babble, she'd respond with a question or comment to every "ga ga" and "goo goo" that passed his lips. When she was pushing him in his stroller outside, she would point out letters in signs, colors of cars, relative sizes of people, breeds of dogs, makes of cars, types of flowers—there was no end to Sandy's commentary. The woman was ridiculous. I did not invite her to be in my new mothers' group.

Imagine my surprise when, a few years later, Aaron got into Hunter College Elementary and Schuyler didn't. As you may recall, that is the most prestigious gifted and talented program in Manhattan; getting in is like hitting the educational lottery.

Experts Agree That Talking to Your Child Is Critical

Sandy convinced me that talking to your child is one of the most important things you can do for his intellectual development. I'm not the only one who believes this. Drs. Betty Hart and Todd Risley analyzed more than 46,000 hours of speech between parents and children ages 7 months to 3 years old. Their research showed the average number of words a typical 4-year-old born into various family income levels has heard. In a professional family, it's 45 million words; in a working-class family, it's 26 million words; in a family living in poverty, it's only 13 million words.

According to their research, children raised in a "low language" environment had an average IQ of 79, children raised in a "medium language" environment had an average IQ of 107, and children raised in an "enriched language" environment had an average IQ of 117—*a 38-point difference between low- and high-language homes!* The authors found that at age 9, academic success was correlated to the number of words they had heard when young. They concluded that the variation in children's IQs, language abilities, and academic success were directly related to the number of words the parents spoke to their kids (that's live words; TV doesn't count). They also found that parent talkativeness was more predictive of IQ than socioeconomic status or race.

Daily Life Lessons

Here is my advice: Do what Sandy did and what Drs. Hart and Risley recommend. Talk to your child as much as you can about anything and everything. Surround him with language. If you work full-time, make sure that your caretaker is a talker; don't entrust your child to a shrinking violet! Tell her to turn off her cell phone, BlackBerry, or iPod when she is with your little one.

You can't start this kind of talking too early. From the time your child is an infant until he is about 3, he has what Maria Montessori called an *absorbent mind*. He learns by absorbing what he sees, hears, touches, smells, and feels. It is an unconscious kind of learning. No one actively teaches him how to speak or understand his language. He picks it up without effort.

After age 3, he still learns by absorbing, but now he becomes actively involved in gaining knowledge and skills. He asks questions, explores, and discovers more and more through exercising his own curiosity. During this time, the more you talk to him, the more language, information, and understanding of his world he will absorb. When you talk to him, use high-level vocabulary—and no sing-songy baby talk after age 2!

Even if your child can't talk back, bring up an interesting book you are reading or something funny you saw. Describe your day at work, what you did, and whom you saw. At the doctor's office, talk about what it was like when you went to the doctor as a child. Narrate your life when you are out together. Think out loud when making your grocery list or deciding what to do or where to go.

If your very young child is babbling, pointing, or gazing at something, pay attention to what is coming from her and respond accordingly. When she looks at a small object, pick it up, wiggle it, and tell her what it is: "This is a book." As she points to something on the shelf, ask her, "Do you want cereal, raisins, or crackers?" Watch for her response, even if it is a smile or eyes that light up, and answer her: "Ah, you want cereal." If she makes consonant or vowel sounds, respond to her with a question like, "Oh really, is that what you think?" Acknowledge her by saying, "Mmm, I see." Or, imitate her vocalization, giving her a kiss or an affectionate touch to show her that you are listening and interested in what she is saying. When a child is just beginning to communicate, this kind of back-and-forth or turn taking is a critical step in teaching her that words, sounds, gestures, and expressions have meaning. Make sure she sees your eyes, lips, and face as you respond to her since children learn language both visually and orally.

If she is just beginning to talk and says something simple like "more," use that as an opportunity to respond in complete sentences: "Oh, do you want more Cheerios? I'll pour them in your bowl now." Children learn vocabulary and syntax within the context of meaningful experiences. It may not seem like your child is listening (especially if she can only say a few words), but she is absorbing more than you can imagine.

HOW TO TALK TO YOUR CHILD

After your child really starts to talk, you should engage him in conversations. A particularly powerful way of strengthening his verbal skills is through Ping-Pong dialog. Sandy did it quite naturally. Here's all it is. The mother *listens* to what her child is saying, then *expands* on it in her response. As the conversation goes back and forth, it gets richer and richer. Here is an example:

Aaron [*patting Sandy's belly*]: Baby sister.

Sandy: You're going to stay with Aunt Helen when I go to the hospital to have your baby sister.

Aaron: No sister. Have a puppy.

Sandy: You're silly. Dogs have puppies, not mommies. Mommies have children. Puppies and children are both babies.

Aaron: I want puppy.

Sandy: Someday you'll get one. What kind of puppy do you want? A boxer? Poodle? Collie? Golden retriever?

Aaron: Boxer that barks.

Sandy: Yes, puppies bark. And babies cry and coo. Your new sister will cry and coo.

Through this kind of back-and-forth interaction between mother and child, the child innately begins to understand the power of language to communicate. Here is another Sandy-and-Aaron conversation that I overheard in the elevator. Notice how Sandy lets Aaron drive the conversation, listens, and then expands on what was just said:

Aaron: Where's Daddy?

Sandy: Daddy went to pick up Aunt Helen. He and Aunt Helen will be home for dinner tonight.

Aaron: Dinner.

Sandy: Yes, there will be four of us for dinner: you, me, Daddy, and Aunt Helen. What do you think we should have to eat?

Aaron: Chicken.

Sandy: Good idea. Daddy loves meat. Chicken is meat. Should we have fried chicken or barbecued chicken or baked chicken?

Aaron: Fried chicken.

Sandy: Fried chicken it is. How about baked beans, too?

Aaron: Yum. Baked beans.

Sandy: Would you like to help me make the baked beans?

Aaron: Yay!

Sandy: What ingredients will we need to make baked beans?

At this point, the elevator got to their floor. Not only was Sandy a real pro at conversing with Aaron in a way that would build his language skills, but she made baked beans from scratch. I hated her.

In the course of running Smart City Kids, I observed many young mothers talking to their toddlers. Often the conversations went more like the one below, and I point it out to you as an example of a *less effective* dialog. Why? Because the mother isn't listening to her child.

Mom: Sally, look at that car.

Sally: Car.

Mom: See the lady over there and her big dog?

Sally: Me pet doggie.

Mom: What do you think we should have for dinner tonight?

Sally: Doggie.

Mom: Let's order Chinese.

Remember, *listen* and *expand* on what *your child* says as you converse. Sandy had that right. However, while Ping-Ponging with your child this way, try not to annoy your neighbors as she did. Still, if you follow this model, you will not believe how many of your child's skills will be strengthened. The conversations between Sandy and Aaron affected his:

- ★ **Expressive language:** He learned to say new vocabulary words (*boxer*).
- ★ **Receptive language:** He understood more advanced vocabulary words because he heard them used in the context of a meaningful conversation (*ingredients*).
- ★ **Knowledge:** He learned that chicken can be baked, fried, or barbecued. He learned dogs come in different breeds.
- ★ **Similarities:** He learned that dogs bark and babies cry and coo.
- ★ **Classifications:** He learned that puppies and children are types of babies; chicken is a kind of meat; boxers, poodles, collies, and golden retrievers are types of dogs.
- ★ **Math:** He learned that he, Mommy, Daddy, and Aunt Helen added up to four people.

Depending on the conversation, talking to your child can affect every ability children need before kindergarten except their fine-motor skills! Sandy didn't actively think about teaching Aaron all of these lessons. She just listened and spoke to him in a way that kept expanding on each thing that was said.

As Aaron got older and his language skills developed, I watched Sandy change the conversation model a bit. She would *listen*, *expand* what Aaron said, and then ask Aaron to *elaborate* or *make connections* between the topic and experiences in his life.

Aaron: Time for school.
Sandy: Yes, and we have to walk fast this morning or we'll be late.
Aaron: Not supposed to be late.
Sandy: That's right. How many more blocks to get to school?
Aaron: Three.
Sandy: Right, and you need to be in your seat by nine. It's five minutes until nine. Can we walk three blocks in fine minutes?
Aaron: Uh huh.
Sandy: Do you remember what we were late for yesterday?
Aaron: Rachel's party.

With her first response, Sandy inspired Aaron to expand on the topic of being late to school. With her second and third questions, she injected a little math lesson. Then she asked Aaron to relate the topic of being late to school to a previous experience. By helping Aaron make connections between being late to school and being late to a party, Sandy was helping her son strengthen his thinking skills.

If you build this way of conversing with your child into your life, he will absorb, remember, and appropriately apply much of the language and information exchange as he develops his verbal skills.

> ## THE FOREIGN LANGUAGE MYTH
> If you think you have only a small window of time to teach your child to speak a foreign language, relax. It just isn't true that very young children pick up languages more easily than older children. Several studies have shown that older students learn a second language more quickly, although younger students develop native-like accents more easily. (Source: the Center for Applied Linguistics.)

ALWAYS SAY WHY

As long as you are going to talk to your child more, remember this: whenever you're doing something together, explain *why* you are doing it. First, the more he understands why, the more cooperative he'll be. Second, by kindergarten, children are expected to have acquired the same degree of common sense and understanding of their world as other kids their age. For him to have amassed this fund of information takes time and verbal explanations on your part. Almost all intelligence tests have a comprehension section where a child is asked questions about his world that he should know from experience. Here are some examples (they go from easy to harder):

> Why do we wear coats in the winter?
> Why do houses have roofs?
> What is a house made of?
> Where does milk come from?
> What is a cake made of?
> What should you do if you break your friend's toy?

So, if you are talking to your child about going to the dentist, you'll want to say something like, "We are going to the dentist so he can clean your teeth and check to see if you have cavities." This way, if a tester asks your child why he goes to the dentist, he won't say, "Because Mommy says I have to."

OTHER TIPS FOR TALKING WITH YOUR CHILD

* **Name things that your child notices.** Name common objects at home, in nature, or outside that your child looks at or points to. For example, name body parts, colors, numbers, and letters that he sees.
* **Keep sentences short.** Five to seven words are perfect for younger children.
* **Low-key his mistakes.** When your child makes a grammatical error or uses baby language like "dindin" instead of "dinner" or mispronounces a word, don't be critical. Just repeat correctly what he was trying to say.
* **Never ask, "How was school today?"** That is too broad a question for most preschoolers to answer.
* **Children respond better to comments.** Questioning a child can feel like an interrogation to him. If possible, comment on something, then pause and give him time to respond, since children take longer to answer than adults. Instead of saying, "How was the birthday party at school today?" try "I see there was a birthday party at school today. I'll bet that was fun!"
* **Converse while doing something together.** That gives you both something concrete to refer to. If he makes a mistake, it's easier to correct. For example, if you're playing cards and you ask him how many cards he has and he says four, you can gently correct him by saying, "Are you sure? I see three. Let's count them together."
* **Go out of the house.** Give your child language-rich experiences by going to the art museum or zoo. At the museum, you can talk about different paintings, the objects in them, the colors, the feelings they evoke. At the zoo, compare animals by color, size, and characteristics. At dinner, you can talk about your day and all the things you observed.
* **Variety matters.** To create a foundation for speaking, reading, spelling, and vocabulary, children need a wide variety of language experiences. Conversations around the dinner table, being read to, singing, reciting nursery rhymes and poems—all will enrich your child's language abilities. Letting your child speak to multiple people helps build his vocabulary faster. Saying the same thing a few different ways also strengthens his language abilities: "Give Billy the ball. Take it to Billy. Yay, you took the ball to Billy."

Games and Activities

Here are fun ways to help your child with vocabulary, comprehension, knowledge, similarities, and differences, all skills that are strengthened when you talk to your child about everything and anything. Younger children can play these games, but they may give limited and simpler answers. That's fine. As their verbal skills grow, they can give more detailed and complete responses.

"HOW MANY WAYS CAN YOU DESCRIBE A . . ." Take turns with your child describing something. When one player can't think of another synonym, use for, or key feature of the item, that person loses. Example: The object is a car.

Child: You drive it.
You: It has four wheels.
Child: It has a trunk.
You: It goes very fast.
Child: It takes you where you want to go.
You: I can't think of anything else. You win! **Age 2.5+.**

"I SPY" DESCRIPTIONS. Look at something in the room and describe it. First:

You: I spy with my little eye . . . something that keeps your feet warm. They're yellow and fuzzy.
Child: My slippers!
You: Very good. Now it's your turn.

Then:

Child: I spy with my little eye . . . something soft and white with two long ears and a cottontail.
You: Is it your stuffed rabbit?
Child: That's right. **Age 2.5+.**

"I'M THINKING OF SOMETHING . . ." You and your child take turns thinking of something and describing it until the other person guesses. First:

You: I'm thinking of something that's white, soft, on your bed, and you put your head on it.
Child: Pillow.
You: You're right! Now it's your turn.

Then:

> *Child:* I'm thinking of something that has four legs, fur, and barks.
> *You:* Gosh, I'm not sure. Can you give me another clue?
> *Child:* It likes to eat bones.
> *You:* A dog?
> *Child:* You're right! Good job. **Age 2.5+.**

ALIKE AND DIFFERENT. You and your child will take turns giving clues about how two things are alike and different:

> *You:* How is a lemon like an egg yolk?
> *Child:* You eat them. And they're both yellow.
> *You:* Good job. Now it's your turn.

Then:

> *Child:* How is a sweater different from a coat?
> *You:* A coat keeps you warmer than a sweater. You wear a sweater inside the house, but not a coat.
> *Child:* That's right! **Age 2.5+.**

MICROPHONE AND TAPE RECORDER. A fun way to help your child build his expressive language skills is to buy a toy microphone that amplifies his voice or a tape recorder. Take turns entertaining each other by singing songs, reciting nursery rhymes, and telling little stories and knock-knock jokes behind the mike or into the recorder. **Age 2+.**

In the next chapter, we'll talk about the enormous impact the ability to listen and respond will have on your child's success in testing and at school. We'll talk about ways you can build the skill at home.

11. Language and More

THE BIGGEST, MOST COMMON MISTAKE PARENTS MAKE:
NOT TEACHING THEIR CHILD TO LISTEN AND RESPOND

When your child starts school, he will be expected to listen to whatever the teacher is saying, answer her questions, and follow her directions. This is the model of every classroom in the world. When your child is tested, he will be expected to listen to the examiner's instructions, then complete the task asked of him. Some questions cannot be repeated, so it is important that your child pays attention to what is being said. For certain tests, such as the OLSAT, the ability to listen is more critical to a child's success than any other skill.

Learning to listen to the teacher or tester begins at home. You expect your child to listen when you ask him to get dressed for school, brush his teeth, or clean up his room. The ability to listen and respond appropriately will be key to your child's success within the family. Believe me, having a kid who doesn't listen takes much of the joy out of parenting. As tough as it is to teach your 2-, 3-, or 4-year-old to listen, it will be far tougher to teach the same lesson to your 12-, 13-, or 14-year-old.

Listening is different from hearing. Hearing is a passive process where your ears sense sound vibrations that are transmitted to your brain. Listening is active. It requires other abilities including processing (receptive) language, knowledge and comprehension of the subject, storing and retrieving information relevant to the communication (memory), and interpretation (thinking). Listening is learned over time. This is why Sam was so far behind when we finally fixed his hearing. In his early years, his inability to physically hear what was being said kept him from developing these other critical abilities.

Daily Life Lessons

INSIST THAT YOUR CHILD LISTEN AND RESPOND

The biggest, most common mistake parents make is not consistently insisting that their child listen and respond. When my kids were little, I was guilty of this. After a long day at work, you ask your child to do something, he resists, and it often doesn't seem worth the battle to get him to do what you ask. But the pay-off is enormous in life, testing, and school success (not to mention your personal sanity). The concept is simple. Don't take no for an answer. Here's how to integrate this kind of gentle "insistence" into your life.

GIVING A DIRECTIVE

Mommy: [gets down to her child's level] Honey, it's time to pick up your toys, so let's get started now. We'll do it together.

Child: [ignores his mother and keeps playing]

Mommy: [gets closer to child, makes eye contact, and speaks calmly] It's time to clean up your toys now. Let's start by picking up the blocks.

Child: No, want to play.

Mommy: [takes child's hands and gently but firmly guides him in picking up the first toy until he starts to help with cleanup.]

ASKING A QUESTION

Mommy: Why don't you tell Grandma what we did today?

Child: [puts his head down and doesn't answer]

Mommy: Can you tell Grandma about our day? [speaks calmly and patiently]

Child: [looks off at something else and doesn't respond]

Mommy: We went to the circus, didn't we? What did we do? Tell Grandma.

Child: Went to the circus.

A common mistake parents make is asking a question like this and when the child doesn't answer, the parent answers for him. That's fine if your child isn't speaking yet, but if he is, do not get into the habit of talking for him. Let me repeat this because it is so important. *If your child can speak for himself, don't talk for him!* If at first your child doesn't respond and you have to gently insist on an answer, you needn't be judgmental or impatient. Just urge him to speak for himself, even if his answers are short and simple. If you ask a question and let your child off the hook when he ignores you, he will learn he doesn't have to listen to you.

Here are ways to make it easier for your child to listen and respond:

* **Speak at Child Level.** Rather than addressing your child from the mountaintop, bring yourself to his level. He will listen more closely if you are kneeling by his side to tell him it is time to put his toys away.
* **Make Eye Contact.** If your child's gaze is wandering, he isn't paying attention.
* **Use Your Child's Name.** Stating your child's name helps to grab his attention. "Billy, it's time to pick up your toys."
* **Make Sure Your Child Can Hear.** Speaking slowly will make it easier for him to process what you are saying. Make sure the TV isn't on and you aren't shouting across a noisy room.
* **Prepare Your Child Verbally for Changes in Activity.** "Sarah, in five minutes it will be time to clean up your toys."
* **Don't Overrationalize or Overexplain.** When dealing with your child's behavior ("pick up your towel now"), use *less* language. When helping your child think about something ("What do you think dog Heaven is like? Let's try to imagine that together"), use *more*.
* **Don't Negotiate.** Children have to learn to do what their parents ask. They do not have to like it. Period. End of story. You can, however, mention the benefits of listening to you: "After you pick up your toys, we can watch *Arthur*."
* **Reinforce Your Message Visually.** It can help if you offer a visual cue when you speak to your child. You might start to put the crayons back in the box when you say, "It's time to pick up your art supplies." Or you could demonstrate what you want him to do to make sure he understands: "Let's set the table together. You put all the napkins out just like this."
* **Reinforce Your Message Physically.** If your child ignores your request, get close to him, take his hands gently, look him in the eye, and wait until you have his complete attention. Then reiterate your request—"It's time to pick up your toys"—as you lead him into doing what you asked.
* **Whisper or Sing.** If your child isn't listening, call him over so you can tell give him a secret message, and then whisper what you want him to do in his ear. You can also sing your directions: (to the tune of "London Bridge") "Joey needs to pick up his toys, pick up his toys, pick up his toys; Joey needs to pick up his toys so we can have our dinner." For some great cleanup and other transition songs, go to Preschoolrainbow.org/transition-rhymes.htm.

- ★ **Let Your Puppets Do the Talking.** If you have puppets or stuffed animals, talk through them using funny voices to make requests. "Hello, Sara, do you think you can put your toys in the box now? That would make me sooo happy!"
- ★ **Offer Two Choices, Both of Which Get the Job Done.** "It's time to pick up your toys. Shall we start with the blocks or the cars?"
- ★ **Be Realistic So Your Child Can Succeed.** If your 3-year-old drops a cup of orange juice on the floor, don't say, "Clean that up right now." Instead, hand him a paper towel and say, "Let's clean that up together. Here's a towel you can use."
- ★ **Make Listening Fun or Worthwhile.** Insisting that your child listen and respond doesn't mean you have to become Nazi-mom. Make it fun to respond. "It's time to get ready for bed. What do you say we make it a race to see who can get ready the fastest. Whoever wins can pick the first book!"
- ★ **Listening Ears.** Ask your child to stop and turn on his listening ears before you make a request.
- ★ **Demonstrate Good Listening.** When your child talks to you, show him that you are listening by making thoughtful responses and asking questions about what he says. Don't interrupt him, hurry him along, or pretend to listen when you really aren't. By watching how well you listen, your child will try to do the same.
- ★ **Don't Yell.** If you feel a scream coming on, put yourself in time-out. Psychologists say that the more you yell at your child, the more he will tune you out. Yelling doesn't work in the long run; it damages a child's sense of security and his self-esteem.
- ★ **Praise Him.** "You really listened well. Thank you." Children work for praise. It's such an easy reward to give in so many situations.

ALWAYS FOLLOW THROUGH ON CONSEQUENCES.

Don't let your child off the hook when he doesn't listen. Firmly and lovingly tell him again what you expect. Show him that when you warn him of consequences for not listening, you will follow through exactly as you say you will. Parent educator Barbara Coloroso says, "Children need parents who say what they mean, mean what they say, and do what they say they are going to do." She contends that it isn't the severity of consequences that motivates children, it's the certainty. Following through on consequences also helps your child learn cause and effect, an important cognitive concept that must be grasped before she can reason.

I know it isn't easy to follow through on consequences, but it is worth the effort. We have a watershed event in our home known as the "grape soda incident."

My husband and I took our 2-year-old daughter to a favorite restaurant one evening in Manhattan. We were all looking forward to dinner that night, and it took over an hour to walk there. Just before we arrived, Schuyler asked for grape soda. We told her no because it would spoil her appetite. Schuyler proceeded to throw the mother of all tantrums, treating the immediate world and us to ear-splitting shrieks for grape soda. We told her to stop and if she didn't, we would cancel our dinner. She screamed even louder, so we turned around and made the sixty-block trek home with her in her stroller howling, *"Grape soda! Grape soda!"* the entire time. People stared at us, clearly annoyed. At a stoplight one kind soul tapped me on the shoulder and said, "There's a kid who will never give up." At the time, I couldn't appreciate the silver lining behind the piercing shrieks that didn't subside until after we arrived home. It would have been much more pleasant to give Schuyler what she wanted, but once we told her the consequences of not listening, we were committed. Next time you're having your own "grape soda incident," hang tough. You're not doing your child any favors by giving in.

Games and Activities

There are all kinds of games and activities that will help your child strengthen listening and responding skills. Some can be incorporated into your regular playtime. Others are great to play while traveling, driving, or at bedtime. A quick aside: the first five games also build *gross-motor skills*. I've mentioned that IQ-type tests don't critique these skills, but they may be evaluated during a school interview or an assessment after your child starts kindergarten. To strengthen gross-motor skills, encourage your child to run, jump, gallop, hop, skip, dance, march, slide, tumble, throw a ball, kick, catch, bounce a ball, or ride a tricycle, Big Wheel, or scooter. A kindergarten teacher recently told me about assessing the gross-motor skills for a child in her class. She asked the little boy if he could stand on one foot. He stood on hers!

SIMON SAYS. The leader stands in the front and shouts commands like, "Simon says turn in a circle," "Simon says hop three times." The children must do what the leader says *if* she first says "Simon says," otherwise they are out. The last person standing wins. **Age 2+.**

RED LIGHT, GREEN LIGHT. The child stands a distance (12 feet or more) from the leader. The leader says, "Green light," and the kids move forward but must stop if they hear "Red light." Anyone moving when the leader says "Red light" goes back to the beginning. The first one to reach the leader wins. You can also play this by having your child lie on the floor and wiggle his arms and legs when you say "Green light," then stop wiggling when you say "Red light." **Age 2+.**

MOTHER MAY I? The leader stands on the opposite side of the room, giving commands to individual kids such as, "Jenny, take two steps forward [or turn three circles, or jump up and down four times]." She will say, "Mother may I?" If you say "yes," she can follow the command. If you say "no," she must stay where she is. If she doesn't listen and takes the steps, she is out of the game. The last player left in the game wins. **Age 2.5+.**

MARCO POLO. In the pool, a child closes her eyes and calls out "Marco." The other kids yell, "Polo." The child swims toward the voices and keeps calling "Marco" until she tags someone. That person becomes Marco. **Age 5+.**

FREEZE/DEFROST. Turn on music and get everyone dancing. Stop the music and yell "Freeze!" Everyone must stop in the position they are in. Then put the music on again and yell, "Defrost!" Everyone can go back to dancing. Kids and adults love this. **Age 3+.**

LISTENING BRAIN TEASERS. Make up a scenario and ask your child a question about it. This is more fun if you make the scenario silly instead of logical. **Age 3+.**

- ★ For younger children, keep it easy: "Sara's dog wore a bowl of fruit on his head. What did Sara's dog wear on his head?"
- ★ For older children, make it harder: "Sara's dog wore a purple hat on his head and a pink raincoat on his body. What did Sara's dog wear on his head?"
- ★ "Last night, I had a grass salad for an appetizer, fried ants for dinner, and bee ice cream for dessert. What did I have for dinner?"

CATEGORIES. Decide what the category will be. Let's say, things that have to do with winter.

You: Snow.
Child: Snow and ice.

You: Snow, ice, and skis.

Child: Snow, ice, skis, and cold [and so on].

If you make a mistake or can't think of response, you lose. **Age 3+.**

SING DIRECTIONS. Sing "If You're Happy and You Know It." This is a fun way for your child to listen to and follow instructions. **Age 1.5+.**

ONE-STEP, TWO-STEP, THREE-STEP DIRECTIONS. When your child is 2, ask him to complete simple tasks such as, "Bring me a spoon." By the time he is 3, he should be able to follow your two-step directions such as, "Bring me your bowl and then go wash your hands." When he is 4, he should be able to follow three-step directions such as, "Go to your room and get your red shoes. Then set them by the door." Practice giving your child directions one step at a time and then increasing the complexity of what you ask as he gets better at following multistep instructions. **Age 2+.**

WHAT'S WRONG WITH THIS STORY? When reading a favorite story to your child, change it and see if she notices. For example, when reading *Little Red Riding Hood*, let her encounter a bear instead of a wolf. She will probably correct you. Make a big deal about how silly you were to make that mistake. Change something else later in the story. **Age 2.5+.**

TALKING PUPPETS. Pick up a set of inexpensive finger puppets. I recommend shopping at Orientaltrading.com (a great site for party and craft supplies, too) where you can get a dozen finger puppets for as little as $3.99. You can also make puppets from old socks. This activity will require imagination on your part. Put a few puppets on your fingers and act out a short skit, then ask your child questions about it. Make your skits simple for younger kids. As they get older, the scenarios can be more complex and you might add information or math concepts. The objective here is to have your child practice listening and responding to something simple and then increasingly complex as she gets better at this. I particularly recommend this activity and Listening Brain Teasers if your child is taking the OLSAT. **Age 2.5+.**

SIMPLE

Daddy as puppy: Bark, bark, I'm a puppy and I love to dig up flowers. Then
        I eat them.

Daddy as kitten: Meow, I'm a kitty and I love to chase bugs. I eat them, too!

Daddy [wiggling the kitten]: Can you tell me what the kitty loves to do?

Daddy [wiggling the puppy]: What does the puppy love to do?

HARD

Daddy as puppy: Once upon a time, there was a dog named Diggy. It was his birthday. He wanted to have a swimming party. "Would you come to my party, Fuzzy?"

Daddy as kitten: "Meow, I'd love to! Let's ask Quacker to come, too. She's a duck and can teach us how to swim."

Daddy as duck: "Quack, quack! Yes, I'll come. I'll teach you both how to swim."

Daddy [wiggling the puppy]: Why did Diggy want to have a party?

Daddy [wiggling the duck]: What will Quacker teach Diggy and Fuzzy?

> In the next chapter, we'll go over all the basic concepts your child needs to know for testing and starting kindergarten, along with fun ways you can help her acquire this information and knowledge.

12. knowledge/Comprehension

> Was it not [in the first years of life] that I acquired all that now sustains
> me? And I gained so much and so quickly that during the rest of my life
> I did not acquire a hundredth part of it. From myself as a 5-year-old to
> myself as I am now there is only one step. The distance between myself
> as an infant and myself at five years is tremendous.
>
> *—Leo Tolstoy*

In the first five years of life, a child learns so much. She amasses a treasure trove of words and grammar. Beyond that, she acquires a fountain of information just by living in your home, accompanying you as you go about your day, attending preschool, having books read to her, flying a kite, building a sand castle, visiting the zoo or going to a circus—all the experiences and interactions that inform what she knows and understands about the world.

What Should My Child Know?

CONCEPT BOOKS

Pick up a copy of Richard Scarry's *Best First Book Ever!* If ever there was a crib sheet for testing, this is it. The comprehensive concept book covers all the basics: letters, numbers, colors, opposites, animals, and much more. If your child genuinely knows everything that is in this book by the time he is tested or starts kindergarten, he'll do great. I also recommend Scarry's *Best Word Book Ever.* It covers a bit more ground, sorting items in groupings: a page of fruit, a page of things found in a kitchen, a page of vehicles. These help children see what goes together in categories, something all standard tests cover. DK Publishing's *My First Word Book* is another excellent comprehensive concept book that uses real photographs. Some kids find the realistic, brightly colored pictures more engaging. They also publish individual concept books on topics such as animals, numbers, the body, and color.

If your child doesn't respond to Richard Scarry or the DK Publishing series, then pick up different books that cover the same concepts, but use characters she especially loves (Curious George, Sesame Street, Dora the Explorer). These usually concentrate on one important idea that your child will enjoy reading about. For example, Sesame Street has individual books about letters, shapes, numbers, bedtime, sizes and shapes, rhymes, opposites, animals, body parts, bedtime, bath time, the zoo, and more. If your child loves Disney characters, Arthur, Barney, Batman, Clifford, or Teletubbies, look for concept books featuring his favorites. He'll want you to read them to him over and over again. Also, check out the Little People flap books from Fisher Price. Two- and three-year-olds adore them.

Here is the basic information that children should be familiar with and that these concept books cover:

the alphabet
letters
colors
weather
parts of the body
the five senses
manners
going to school
home
shopping
helping with housework
the playground and toys
shopping at the supermarket
   (fruits and vegetables)
visiting the doctor and dentist
staying healthy
visiting the farm
a day in the country
inside the house
getting ready in the morning
bedtime
getting dressed
breakfast in the kitchen
mealtime
the baby

cars and trucks
the community
the workshop (tools)
the garden
the beach
the zoo
time
the circus
the city
the airport
trains
animals
insects
boats and ships
what to be when you grow up
making things grow
Mother Goose rhymes
numbers and counting
relativity
shapes
days of the week
months of the year
   (not necessarily in order)
seasons
holidays

BRAIN QUEST

Get a set of age-appropriate Brain Quest cards. These are decks of cards held together at the bottom by a grommet. Colorfully illustrated questions are on one side of each card; the answers are on the other. They are great for car or plane trips or waiting at the doctor's office. You'll find *My First Brain Quest, Brain Quest for Threes, Brain Quest Preschool,* and *Brain Quest Kindergarten.* These cover all the basic concepts a child should know by the time he enters kindergarten, and the questions are designed very much like IQ test questions. My kids could never get enough of these cards.

Hands-on Learning Is the Gold Standard

Letters, numbers, colors, and the other concepts mentioned are covered in computer software for children, on learning websites, in workbooks, on educational TV, and in games. Take advantage of these different media to vary the way you present material to your child. However, as instructive as these can be, the best way for your child to learn them is through *experience.*

Your child has already picked up much of this information quite naturally through his five senses. He learned about school by attending a preschool. He discovered what happens at the doctor by going for checkups. He mastered the supermarket when you took him and talked to him about what he was seeing, let him hold and smell the fruits and vegetables you chose, showed him what was in the meat and frozen food section. He has absorbed information about the home by helping you cook supper, clean the house, or fold laundry. He's discovered music and the sounds of nature by listening. To the extent you can bring these concepts to life by allowing your child to touch, feel, and experience them, that will be most effective way for him to truly grasp it. Remember, most children entering kindergarten are kinesthetic learners.

There is nothing like going to the beach, the zoo, the circus, the country, or to a city to teach a child what that experience is like. By visiting the beach, for example, he sees the sand, the ocean, the shells and fish that have washed up on shore, feels the crunchy sand beneath his feet, the hot sun on his face, and the cool shade under an umbrella. He hears the crashing of the waves, smells the sea air, feels the cold water against his body, tastes the saltwater, collects shells, builds a sand castle, and does much more. No book or DVD about going to the beach can match the experience of being there. If you are reading this book, my guess is that you make these kinds of experiences available to your child already.

Games and Activities

COLOR

TALK ABOUT COLOR IN DAILY CONVERSATIONS. "Would you like to eat a red apple?" "Can you pass me that yellow pencil?" **Age infant+.**

DECLARE A COLOR OF THE DAY OR WEEK. On red day, dress your child in red. When you are outside, see how many red things she can spot. Put a few drops of red food coloring in her bath. Serve red food for meals (apples, cherries, strawberries, tomatoes, et cetera). (Note: Do this for all concepts! Declare a number of the day, letter of the day, and so on.) **Age 2+.**

USE FOOD TO TEACH COLORS. Orange: carrots, sweet potatoes; yellow: bananas, eggs, cheese, corn muffin; green: salad, peas, broccoli; blue: blueberries, blue popsicles; white: pasta, mashed potatoes, vanilla ice cream, apple pieces; brown: chocolate, meat, potato skins. **Age infant+.**

MAKE A COLOR BOOK. Cut three pieces of cardboard. Glue magazine pictures showing all red items, blue items, and so on to each page. Cover the picture with clear Con-Tact paper or slide them into clear plastic sheet holders. Connect the pages by punching holes in the side of the cardboard and tying together with yarn. (Note: Do this activity for all concepts! Make number books, letter books, and so on.) **Age 2.5+.**

CREATE WITH COLOR. Give your child crayons, paints, markers, and paper to work with. Talk with her about the colors she chooses to work with. **Age 1+.**

WHAT COLOR AM I THINKING OF? Play a game where you list items of one color and let your child guess what you're thinking of: banana, the sun, butter. Yellow! Let her give you a list of items that are the same color and you guess what she's thinking of. **Age 2.5+.**

LETTER AND NUMBER RECOGNITION

SING THE "ALPHABET SONG" to your child from the time she is a baby. She won't understand what you are singing about at first, and she will think there is a single letter called "LMNOP," but as she gets older, she'll get it. **Age infant+.**

SING NUMBER SONGS AND RHYMES such as "One Potato, Two Potato," "One, Two, Buckle My Shoe" "Ten in a Bed," "Ten Little Indians." The words to these and other learning songs you'll remember from your own childhood can be found at Preschoolrainbow.org/transition-rhymes.htm. **Age infant+.**

READ ALPHABET BOOKS. AGES INFANT+. Here are some of my favorites:

> *Chicka Chicka Boom Boom*, John Archambault, Bill Martin Jr., Lois Ehlert
> (my number-one choice)
> *I Stink*, Kate McMullen
> *Alpha Bugs*, David Carter
> *Animalia Midi*, Graeme Base
> *Museum ABC*, Metropolitan Museum of Art
> *Alphabet City*, Stephen T. Johnson

READ NUMBER RECOGNITION BOOKS. AGE INFANT+. My favorites include:

> *My First Number Book*, DK Publishing
> *Ten Apples Up on Top!*, Dr. Seuss
> *How Many Bugs in a Box?*, David A. Carter

TEACH YOUR CHILD TO RECOGNIZE LETTERS, STARTING WITH HER NAME. Show her what her name looks like when spelled out in capitals and little letters. Pick the first letter and tell her the sound it makes. Make a game of looking for that letter on signs, cereal boxes, books—everywhere. Each day, focus on the next letter until you've spelled her whole name. Then go on to the letters in her daddy's or sister's name. When children go for school interviews, they are often shown an array of name tags and asked to pick their own. When we were faced with this, I realized the mistake I'd made naming my daughter Skyler, but spelling it the Dutch way: Schuyler. Teaching her to spell her name was tough. I fixed that with my second child, naming him Sam. **Age 2.5+.**

JUNK MAIL FUN. Give your child a piece of junk mail or an ad circular and a highlighter. Pick a letter. "Can you go through this and mark all the capital and lowercase *As* that you find?" With more than one child, give them each a piece of mail and make it a contest to see who can find the most.

FEEL THE LETTERS AND NUMBERS. Give your child access to an alphabet and number puzzle and magnetic letters and numbers to play with. **Age 1+.**

GET FOAM LETTERS and numbers for the bath. Every day, put one or two in the bath. Show him the letter and let him trace it with his hand. Play with the letters and numbers: "The *S* is coming to kisssss you. Sssssssssss." "The *T* is t-t-t-tickling your t-t-t-t-toe." "The 5 is coming to count your toes—1, 2, 3, 4, 5." **Age infant+.**

GO ON A "LETTER-EGG" HUNT. Write capital letters on Post-its. "Hide" them around a few rooms in your house. Send your child out to see how many letters he can find in three minutes. You can do this with shapes and colors as well. When he's older, put letters and numbers on the Post-its and tell him to bring back only the letters (or the numbers), but not both. **Age 2.5+.**

MAKE A PERSONAL ALPHABET POSTER. Take pictures of things in your child's world that start with various letters: family members, pets, your car, your house, your child's bed, et cetera. Make an alphabet poster together where *B* is your child's bed, *C* is your car, *D* is your family's dog, and so on. Hang the poster in his room. **Age 3+.**

MAKE COOKIES OR PANCAKES in the shapes of letters or numbers. **Ages 3+.**

LETTER SCULPTURES. Roll Sculpy, Fimo clay, or any substance that turns hard when you bake it into snakes. Help your child form letters and numbers out of each snake, then bake it. **Age 3+.**

PARTS OF THE BODY
SING "HEAD AND SHOULDERS, KNEES AND TOES," while pointing to each body part as you sing about it. **Age infant+.**

> *Head and shoulders, knees and toes, knees and toes*
> *Head and shoulders, knees and toes, knees and toes*
> *Eyes and ears and mouth and nose*
> *Head and shoulders, knees and toes, knees and toes.*

PLAY THE HOKEY POKEY

> *You put your left arm in, you take your left arm out*
> *You put your left arm in and you shake it all about*

You do the hokey pokey and you turn yourself around
That's what it's all about.

(Continue with other parts of the body). **Age 2+.**

PLAY SIMON SAYS (BODY PARTS). Play Simon Says but limit what Simon Says to actions around body parts. "Simon Says touch your nose." "Simon says pat your ears." "Simon says tickle your lips." "Scratch your knees." **Age 2.5+.**

DRAW A PERSON. As your child develops, her drawings will go from scribbles (age 2) to a representational attempt to make a person with a head sprouting vertical lines for legs and arms (age 3) to a more recognizable and complex person that may include a head, eyes, ears, mouth, nose, body, hands, fingers, legs, and toes. When she is coloring, encourage her to draw a picture of Mommy or Daddy or herself. **Age 3+.**

SEASONS

MAKE A SEASONS COLLAGE. take photos of the outside of your home in each season. At the end of the year, divide a poster into four squares and make a collage of your home during winter, spring, fall, and summer. **Age 3+.**

THE FIVE SENSES

Children use their senses to observe and investigate the world around them. Here is a song my children used to sing about the senses followed by activities you can do to bring them to life. **Age 2.5+.**

"FIVE SENSES" (sung to the tune of "Where Is Thumbkin?")

Fi-ive senses, fi-ive senses
We have five. We have five.
Seeing, hearing, touching,
Tasting, and smelling
We have five. We have five.

When you sing this song, point to your eyes when you sing "seeing," your ears when you sing "hearing," your fingers when you sing "touching," your mouth when you sing "tasting," and your nose when you sing "smelling."

SENSE OF TOUCH

WHAT DO YOU FEEL? Take an old pillowcase and place various familiar objects inside. Let your child reach inside and touch an object, feel it, and guess what it is. **Age 2.5+.**

SCRATCHY, BUMPY, SOFT. Pull together an assortment of textured items (cotton balls, velvet, sandpaper, bubble wrap, piece of wood, a marshmallow) and put them in the pillowcase. Ask your child to pull out something that feels soft, scratchy, bumpy, whatever. **Age 3+.**

SENSE OF SIGHT

WHAT DID YOU SEE? Put several objects out on the table and let your child look at them for thirty seconds. Then cover them up. Ask him what objects he saw. Next time, take away an object when you cover them up, then uncover them. Ask your child which object isn't there that was there before. This is a good memory-building game as well. **Age 3+.**

OUTDOOR INVESTIGATION. Give your child a magnifying glass. Take a field trip outdoors and investigate grass, weeds, bugs, rocks, leaves, twigs, and flowers. As your child describes what he is observing under the magnifying glass, take notes. Collect samples in baggies and bring them home. Later, your child can glue them to a piece of paper and you can write some of his observations down on the paper next to the samples. **Age 2.5+.**

SENSE OF TASTE

HAVE A TASTING. Have your child cover his eyes. Then have him bite into various foods you place in his mouth: a lump of sugar, a lemon wedge, a potato chip, a pickle. Let him guess what he tasted. Ask him to describe the flavor he tasted (sour, salty, sweet). **Age 2.5+.**

SENSE OF HEARING

TAKE A SILENCE HIKE. Before you go, brainstorm the sounds that you think you might hear. Make a list. Go outside for a walk and just listen. Then, talk about all the sounds you heard and whether your predictions were right. **Age 2.5+.**

WHERE IS THE SOUND? Have your child sit in the center of the room with his eyes closed. Then you tiptoe to another part of the room and make a sound:

clap your hands, whistle, clear your throat. When you make the sound, your child should point to where the sound came from. Switch places and let your child make the sound. Alternatively, while his eyes are closed, make a sound like the shaking of keys or a shuffling of cards. Can he guess what made the sound? **Age 2.5+.**

SENSE OF SMELL

WHAT'S THAT SMELL? Gather a variety of items from your home with various smells: perfume, soap, dog food, cinnamon, flowers. Have your child close his eyes and smell each thing. Can he guess what each is? **Age 3+.**

WEATHER

MAKE A WEATHER CHART FOR A MONTH. Using your calendar, mark down the predominant weather each day: sunny, partly cloudy, cloudy, raining. At the end of the month count up and compare the different kinds of weather days experienced. **Age 2.5+.**

TIME

TELLING TIME is a mathematical skill your child isn't likely to be ready to learn until kindergarten. Still, you can prepare him to learn this by making time a topic as you talk about everything and anything with your child. "These brownies take thirty minutes to cook. It is four o'clock now so they'll be ready at four-thirty." Show him your watch and explain how the second hand goes around every sixty seconds. Let him observe that and feel what a minute is like. When he watches a television program, tell him it takes thirty minutes.

> In the next chapter, we'll go over the memory skills your child will need for testing and kindergarten success and talk about how you can help build these through games and activities.

13. Memory: You Must Remember This...

KID-TESTED TECHNIQUES FOR STRENGTHENING MEMORY

For testing and kindergarten success, children need three kinds of memory: short-term memory to follow directions, working memory to manipulate information, and long-term memory to retrieve information learned in the past. Memory is fundamental to all higher-order thinking. Without it, you cannot think, reason, hypothesize, solve problems, or make decisions.

Life Lessons

YOUR PAST AND YOUR SHARED PAST. As you talk to your child about everything and anything, talk about your shared past experiences. Ask him questions to build his memory. "Remember when we went to visit Grandma last summer? That was so much fun. What city does she live in?" "You had the best birthday party last year. Do you remember the kind of party we had?" Show him old photo albums and talk about people in the pictures. See if he remembers who each person is when you go back to them again. Look at your own family photos and let your child tell you what he remembers about the time the pictures were taken.

ASK YOUR CHILD TO PARAPHRASE. To remember things, children must be able to take a long explanation they hear or read, or an experience they had and "shrink" it in their minds to an easy-to-remember size. Look for paraphrasing opportunities. When you give your child instructions, ask him to repeat what you said but in his own words. When you're about to read a book you've read before, ask him to tell you what it's about before you start. When something funny happens, ask him to tell Daddy the silly thing that happened to him today at school.

Games and Activities

I'M GOING TO GRANDMA'S HOUSE (SHORT TERM). This can be played with one or more children. Choose a category such as food, clothes, or furniture.

> *You:* I'm going to Grandma's house, and I'm bringing her a lamp.
> *Child:* I'm going to Grandma's house, and I'm bringing her a lamp and a couch.
> *You:* I'm going to Grandma's house, and I'm bringing her a lamp, a couch, and a bed [and so on].

If you make a mistake or can't think of a response, you're out. **Age 3+.**

WHAT DID I READ? (SHORT TERM). Open a book that your child hasn't memorized to a random page. Close your eyes and make a big deal of circling your pointer finger around and choosing a "random" sentence. Actually, the sentence won't be random. Choose a short sentence for a young child and a longer one for a child whose verbal skills are more advanced. Read the sentence. Ask your child to repeat it. **Age 3+.**

NUTTY NUMBERS (SHORT TERM). Give your child a string of numbers and ask him to repeat it. Start with two numbers and add more as your child gets better at this. When he masters this, give him a string of numbers and ask him to repeat them backward! Again, start with two and work your way up to longer strings. **Age 2.5+.**

PLAY TELEPHONE (SHORT TERM). Whisper a sentence in your child's ear and see if he can repeat it. Have him do the same for you. When you repeat what he says, get it wrong so he can catch you and correct you. Give your child the giggles by making your sentences funny. Start with short sentences and graduate to longer ones. **Age 3+.**

SILLY SAMMY OR SILLY SALLY (LONG TERM). Say something like, "Sammy was so silly that when he went to bed, he brushed his teeth with soap and washed his hands with toothpaste. What is silly about that?" "Silly Sammy is so silly he wears a frying pan for a hat and gloves for shoes. What's silly about that?" This game not only builds memory, it strengthens children's understanding of their world as well. For every "wrong," the child realizes what is "right," for every absurdity, his grasp of reality becomes stronger. **Age 2.5+.**

ALL ABOUT ME (LONG TERM). Help your child learn important information such as his first and last names, his parents' names, his address, phone number, and birthday. Make up a little rhyme he can memorize: "I live on Third Avenue and my favorite dinner is beef stew. The number on my door is 321 and my favorite dessert is a honey bun." Or set it to a tune like "Mary Had a Little Lamb," "I live at 3-2-1, 3-2-1, 3-2-1, I live at 3-2-1 Third Av-en-oo-oo; I live in New York City, New York City, New York City, I live in New York, New York, 1-0-0-2-1." I just saw a report on TV about a little boy named Alex who called 911 after his mother fell down the stairs. Luckily, his mother had taught him to sing their address, which he did for the dispatcher, who immediately sent help. **Age 3+.**

WHAT WAS YOUR DAY LIKE? Encourage your child to talk about his day and his feelings. Make a bedtime ritual out of sharing "the best thing that happened to me today" (or the funniest, worst, or scariest). **Age 3+.**

FAMILY CONCENTRATION (SHORT TERM). Take photos of family members, pets, your home, and other familiar things. Get two sets developed. Laminate the photos or glue them to heavy stock. Start with four or five photos and their matches. Lay them facedown on the table. Have your child turn one over and then another. You do the same. Whenever two matches are chosen, that player takes those cards. Play until all matches are located. Whoever has the most matches wins! Later, add more photos to the game. **Age 2.5+.**

MONKEY SEE, MONKEY DO (SHORT TERM). Play a game with your child where you take turns tapping your nose, ears, mouth, and cheeks in a special order and ask each other to copy what you did in the same order. When your child does the tapping, make a mistake and let him catch you. **Age 2.5+.**

WHAT'S MISSING? (LONG TERM). Look for activity workbooks with exercises involving pictures of common items with parts missing (e.g., a bike without a wheel, a chair with three legs) where the child is asked what is missing from the picture. For young kids, look for *What's Missing Baby Daisy?: A Book About Missing Parts* from Disney and *Big Bird Beep Book: What's Missing*, or search "what's missing" in an online bookstore. **Age 2.5+.**

WHAT'S WRONG? (LONG TERM). Look for workbooks with exercises involving pictures where things are wrong: a child drinking from a tennis shoe, a car driving on the ocean. Three books full of pictures like this are Anna Pomaska's *What's Wrong with This Picture*, Ellen Booth Church's *What's Wrong* for preschool to 3, and Rachel Lipman's *What's Wrong with This Picture? Around Town*. These are also found in *Highlights* magazine, a fabulous magazine for your child. They have a special preschool version called *High Five* for children ages 2 to 6. This inexpensive publication ($1.97 per issue) is full of fun activities supporting intellectual development and testing preparation. Go to Highlights.com. **Age 3+.**

PLAY A SHELL GAME. Set out three upside-down paper cups. Let your child watch as you put a cookie under one. Move the cups around and see if your child can keep his attention on the cup covering the cookie. Ask, "Where's the cookie?" If he guesses right, let him eat it. **Age 2.5+.**

MEMORY PATTERNS (SHORT TERM). Create a pattern using seashells, buttons, change, Froot Loops, or other manipulatives. Show it to your child. Then cover it up and see if your child can re-create it from memory. **Age 3+.**

XYLOPHONE (SHORT TERM). Using a toy xylophone, tap three bars with a mallet and have your child tap the same three bars. As he masters three bars, move up to four and five or more. Have your child tap bars for you to follow. Make a mistake and see if she corrects you. **Age 3+.**

> In the next chapter, we'll review the basic mathematics skills your child needs to have by the time she is tested for or starts kindergarten and ways you can make sure she has picked up these critical abilities.

14. Mathematics

NATURAL WAYS TO BRING OUT YOUR CHILD'S INNER MATH GEEK

Many young children are able to recite numbers from 1 to 10 or recognize the symbol for each number even though they don't understand what the numbers mean. These are verbal and spatial skills, similar to reciting and recognizing the alphabet. It has nothing to do with being able to calculate or reason mathematically. Just as it was more important for children to learn preliteracy skills than to recognize words on flash cards, it is more important for children to learn the underlying concepts of mathematics than to identify numbers. What does *more than* mean? What does *bigger than* look like? What does *three* really look and feel like? Still, children are sometimes asked to identify numbers in a school interview or on certain intelligence tests. Many tests evaluate math skills through simple addition and subtraction word problems and counting questions.

How Children Learn Math

Math skills unfold sequentially in young children. Just as babies must babble before they can talk, children must master several simpler math principles that build sequentially before they can add and subtract. By age 3, a child can comprehend basic principles of counting. She knows that each M&M in a pile is assigned one number, that numbers occur in order, that the last number counted is the total number of M&Ms, that you count M&Ms the same way you count Cheerios, blocks, marbles, and anything else, and that M&Ms can be counted in any order—left to right or right to left (which is different from reading words and sentences, which must always be decoded from left to right). They learn that anything can be counted: tangibles like pennies, fingers, toes, and people, and intangibles like days of the week, months of the year, and hours in the day.

Our brains are wired to learn both language and math. The best way to help your child master these concepts is to allow her to discover them for herself through play. Children learn to talk by being surrounded by language every day, soaking it in and unconsciously absorbing the rules of grammar. This is how children internalize basic mathematical concepts such as pattern, sequence, ordering, spatial relations, sorting, comparing, classifying, and one-to-one correspondence. Many questions on intelligence tests are designed to assess a child's understanding of these ideas.

* **Pattern and sequence** is the logical, predictable way things reoccur. A child notices that he wakes up in the morning, has breakfast, attends preschool, goes to the park, has dinner, takes a bath, plays with Mommy, and goes to bed. This helps him predict and anticipate what might happen next. When he hears a story, he knows that it has a beginning, a middle, and an end. He sees that the days of the week and months of the year appear in a predictable order. He learns the language of sequencing (*before, after, last, next, yesterday, today, tomorrow*).

* **Ordering** is the organization of things by size. A child stacks blocks from the largest on the bottom to the smallest on top. He nests cups with the smallest on the inside and the largest on the outside. At school, the teacher asks the children to arrange themselves in line from shortest in front to tallest in back. He learns that numbers are ordered from small to large.

* **Sorting** is the organization of objects and ideas by like attributes (size, shape, feel, color, texture). A child arranges socks by color and silverware by forks, spoons, and knives. He puts his books on the bookshelf, his blocks in the toy box, and his cars in the Fisher-Price play garage. Sets, or collections of like objects, are fundamental to mathematics. Understanding sorting helps children understand sets.

* **Classifying** is the placing of like objects together and naming them as a group or set. A child groups his plastic animals into two piles and calls one group "farm animals" and the other "wild animals." A child understands that cherries, apples, and pears are fruit while lettuce, peppers, and onions are vegetables.

* **Comparing** is the identification of specific attributes in objects or ideas and evaluation about how they are similar or different. A child compares the differences (or similarities) between apples and oranges, plants and trees, girls and boys, joy and sadness.

* **One-to-one correspondence** is giving each object being counted one count. A child looks at three blocks and touches each one, counting 1, 2, 3. He knows what three means. Before children can understand that three blocks are the same as the symbol 3 and the word *three*, they must start by counting concrete objects (manipulatives).
* **Spatial Relations** are explored in depth in the next chapter. Basically, spatial relations describes the physical relationships of objects and people. Children learn about geometric shapes (*square, triangle*), size (*large, small, tall, short*), distance (*far, near, high, low*), position (*right, left, above, below*), order (*largest, smallest*), quantity (*few, many*), volume (*full, empty*), directionality (*up, down, under, over*), and time (*long, short, quick, slow*).
* These basic concepts are integral to mathematics, but also to other aspects of intelligence that we've discussed. Spatial relations are fundamental to nonverbal skills. Sequences, sorting, and comparing are essential to language and cognitive abilities. A verbal question on an intelligence test might be, "Tomatoes, cherries, and fire engines are all what?" (Red). A math task on an intelligence test might require the child to sort red buttons and white buttons into groups.

Daily Life Lessons

Here are ways you can help your child discover mathematical concepts through your daily interactions.

TALKING. When you talk to your child about everything and anything, integrate math language into your dialog.

* When running errands: "What shall we do first? Second? Third?"
* "You have school in two more days."
* "Dinner will be in five minutes."
* "Look, it's eleven o'clock, time for your nap."
* "Do you want a whole cookie or half a cookie?"

COUNTING. When you are talking about everything and anything with your child, make a habit out of counting things.

* "How many eyes do you have?" "How many toes do you have?"
* "You don't like your spinach? How about taking five more bites. One, two, three, four, five."

* "Let's button up your jacket. I've buttoned the first button, now I just have to do the second and third."
* "Let's count the days until vacation, shall we?"

ADDITION AND SUBTRACTION. When you are talking about everything and anything with your child, talk about adding and subtracting.

* "It's cold so I'm going to put two blankets on you. Do you want to be even warmer? I'll add one more and then you'll have three."
* "Here are four Hershey Kisses. Do you mind if I eat one? Then you'll have three left."
* "I'll give you two cinnamon crackers and three apple slices. How many snacks will you have?"

SORT IN DAILY LIFE. When you can, help your child put items into groups.

* "Let's sort the clothes by darks and lights."
* "Why don't we put all your shoes in pairs and set them on this shelf."
* "It's cleanup time. Let's put the big toys in the closet, the medium-sized toys in the bookcase, and the small toys in the toy box."
* "Here's my change from today. Will you put the pennies in the penny jar, the nickels in the nickel jar, the dimes in the dime jar, and the quarters in the quarter jar for me?"

CLASSIFYING: ORGANIZE YOUR PANTRY TOGETHER. Put the soup cans, vegetable cans, and fruit cans together. Put cereals in one area and condiments, spices, oils, and vinegars in another.

ENVIRONMENTAL PATTERNS. Look around and see what patterns you and your child can find. For example, patterns in a rug, tiles, bricks, a stone wall, fabrics, weavings, wicker baskets, ripples in a pond, the skin of a snake.

PLANNING SEQUENCES. When you are doing something with your child or going somewhere special (e.g., going on vacation, baking a cake), talk about the sequence of steps you have to take. For example, "Before we scramble these eggs, we'll need to take the eggs and butter out of the fridge. Then we'll get a bowl and a pan out of the cupboard. After that, we'll need to put the pan on the stove and heat it . . ."

SEQUENCES IN DAILY LIFE. When you can, help your child create and think about sequences in his own life.

- ★ **Make a chart of your child's schedule and post it.** "At 8:00 you wake up and make your bed. At 8:30 you have breakfast. At 9:00 you brush your teeth. At 9:30 you go to school."
- ★ **Food.** "We eat salad first, our meal second, and dessert third."

ORDERING IN DAILY LIFE. Help your child put items in size order.

- ★ "Let's line up these cookie jars from biggest to smallest."
- ★ "Why don't we put the smaller pots inside the bigger pots so we'll have more room in the cabinet?"
- ★ There are stacking and nesting toys you can buy where rings are stacked on a stick from largest to smallest or where smaller items fit inside larger ones (cylinders, cups, Russian nesting dolls).
- ★ Put a spool of thread on one side of the room and your child's largest toy on the other side. Gather several of your child's toys and stuffed animals. Place them in order from smallest (near the spool) to the largest.

COMPARE EVERYTHING! Whenever you can, ask your child to compare two things: pepperoni pizza versus cheese pizza, his two favorite books, two kinds of birthday parties, the price of two boxes of cereal at the store, sizes of sweaters, whatever!

COMPARISON PHOTOS. If you have a small chair for a child (we used a tiny white rocking chair), take a photo of your toddler in the chair. Every six months, take a new picture of her in the chair. Glue the photos next to each other on a poster board and let your child compare how much she's grown. Also, take your child's school pictures from nursery school on and hang them in order down a long hallway. We did this, and my kids loved to compare their growth from year to year.

BOOKS. Read aloud books that teach mathematics:

> *Anno's Counting Book,* Mitsumasa Anno (numbers, counting)
> *1, 2, 3 to the Zoo,* Eric Carle (counting)
> *10 Little Rubber Ducks,* Eric Carle (order)
> *12 Ways to Get to 11,* Eve Merriam (addition and subtraction)
> *Five Creatures,* Emily Jenkins (sets)
> *My Grandmother's Clock,* Geraldine McCaughrean (time)
> *I Spy Little Numbers,* Jean Marzollo and Walter Wick (recognition)
> *My First Opposites Board Book,* DK Publishing (comparison)

DIALOGIC MATH. When reading aloud to your child, ask math questions such as, "How many pigs are in this picture?" "How many spiders are on the wall?" "Which billy goat is the biggest?" "Which animal has the most teeth?"

FOOD FRACTIONS. When making lunch, cut your child's sandwich in half. Cut a small pizza into quarters. Give your child a square of cheese and show him how to fold it in half, then in quarters. Then invite him to eat it!

Games and Activities

COOK AND BAKE TOGETHER. Help your child measure out various ingredients so he can start to learn the difference between a teaspoon and a tablespoon, a cup and a quarter cup. **Age 2+.**

ARCHEOLOGICAL DIG. Get a plastic dish tub and fill it halfway with rice. Hide miniature plastic toys (e.g., animals, people), coins, seashells, rocks, marbles, or other small trinkets inside the rice. Put plastic measuring cups and a funnel on top. Give the tub to your child and let her play. She will transfer rice from cup to cup, learning about measuring, comparing capacity, and volume. She'll dig up the manipulatives and sort them, count them, then rebury them. **Age 2.5+.**

WAR. Divide a deck of cards by the number of players. Everyone puts their cards in a stack and turns one over at the same time. Whoever has the highest card (including aces and face cards) gets to keep the cards from that round. Whoever has the most cards at the end wins. **Age 3+.**

HIGHER/LOWER. Play this once your child knows numbers. "I'm thinking of a number between one and ten. Can you guess?" As your child guesses, tell him "bigger" or "smaller" (or "higher" and "lower") until he gets it. **Age 3+.**

PRACTICE PATTERNING

PATTERN BEADING. Pick up a set of colored cubes, large stringing beads, or colored buttons. For young children, keep patterns very simple (ABAB or AABBAABB) and make them harder as your child masters the skill. Or start a pattern yourself and let your child guess what comes next: "Blue, red, yellow, blue, red . . . what's next?" **Age 2.5+.**

M&MEMORY PATTERNS. Create a pattern with M&Ms and then mess it up. See if your child can re-create the pattern from memory. If he can, he gets to eat it. **Age 3+.**

SNACK PATTERNS. With your child, make him a snack but set it out in a pattern on his plate. Or when you are having people over for a party, get various kinds of cookies or crackers and cheese. Have your child set them on the tray in a pattern. **Age 2.5+.**

BODY PATTERNS. Demonstrate a body movement pattern and see if your child can copy you. If he can, see if he can do it twice in a row. For example: clap, clap, jump, jump, and turn a circle. Movements can include hopping, jumping, snapping, marching, stomping, eye blinks, and making silly faces. **Age 3+.**

PRACTICE SORTING

SORTABLE ITEMS. Fill paper cups or a cupcake pan with colored paper clips, beads, buttons, change, jewels, Goldfish, Gummi Worms, seashells, pasta, nuts, beans, whatever you can think of (watch out for choking hazards). Have your child sort the items by color, shape, size, type. These are also good for patterning. **Age 2.5+.**

MAKE PAIRS. Take your shoes out of the closet. Mix them up. Make a game out of putting them back into matching pairs. **Age 2.5+.**

PAINT CHIPS. Go to the hardware store and collect an assortment of paint chips. Have your child sort them by color. Then, within a color family, have him order them from lightest to darkest. **Age 3+.**

TOY SORT. Look for opportunities to sort the toys your child already has. Sam had a collection of Batman and superhero action figures. We would put all his Batman figures together, Jokers, Riddlers, and so on. He also loved Beanie Babies, so we would sort them by color and type of animal. Schuyler enjoyed sorting her Barbie and Polly Pocket outfits by color and types of clothing. **Age 2.5+.**

PRACTICE COMPARING

GROWTH CHART. Keep a growth chart in your child's room, marking his height every six months. Each time you measure him, compare how tall he is now to how tall he was last time you measured. **Age 1+.**

WATER PLAY. Give your child plastic measuring cups to play with in the bath. **Age 1+.**

VERBAL ANALOGIES. Play a verbal analogy game with your child. These are based on the relationship between the first two items being the same as the relationship between the second two. If you can figure out the relationship between the first pair, you will be able to guess the missing item. Visual matrix questions work this way as well. **Age 4+.**

★ Things that go together: "Peas are to carrots as salt is to [pepper]."
★ Opposites: "Big is to small as tall is to [short]."
★ Synonyms: "Big is to large as unhappy is to [sad]."
★ Classifications: "Blue is to color as banana is to [fruit]."
★ Object and characteristic: "Sky is to blue as grass is to [green]."
★ Object and location: "Car is to garage as tub is to [bathroom]."
★ Object and function: "Pencil is to write as shovel is to [dig]."
★ Problem and solution: "Itch is to scratch as hungry is to [eat]."

PRACTICE CLASSIFYING

START A COLLECTION. Help your child start a collection of something that interests him. A collection of seashells, dinosaur figures, or bugs can be divided into categories that your child can classify. For example, "These bugs can fly and these can't." **Age 3+.**

PLAY THE *$20,000 PYRAMID*. Take turns naming things that go together and keep naming them until your child guesses the category. For example: "Pens, pencils, crayons—" "Things you write with!" "Dogs, cats, guinea pigs—" "Animals that are pets!" **Age 3+.**

PRACTICE ONE-TO-ONE CORRESPONDENCE

COUNTING. Encourage your child to count objects. Put out three items. Ask him how many there are. Have him touch each object as he counts it aloud. Teach him that the last number counted is the answer to "How many [objects] are there?" Increase the number of items as his skill improves. At first, help him touch each object as he counts. Later, he will learn to do it visually. **Age 2.5+.**

ZERO. Draw a big zero on a piece of white paper. Put several small items inside and have your child count them. Take the items out and ask, "How many are there now?" When your child says none, explain to her that zero is the number that means there are no objects. **Age 3+.**

COUNT 'N COMPARE. At mealtime, line up five Cheerios and have your child count them aloud. Line up five Goldfish directly across from each Cheerio and have your child count *them* aloud. Ask him if the number of Cheerios and Goldfish are the *same* or *different.* Take two Goldfish away and ask if there are more Goldfish or Cheerios. Try lining up and counting five cookies across from five Cheerios. Does your child still think they're the same? You can make a game of this with blocks and other small toys. **Age 3+.**

SECRET MESSAGE. This is fun with more than one child. Fill a bowl with small items (beads, coins, shells) and set it across the room. Write a number on a small slip of paper and fold it up. Call your child over and whisper, "I'm going to give you a secret message. Don't tell Daddy or Wendy or Ted. When you see the secret number on the paper, go get that many items from the bowl." When your child brings the items back, count them and say aloud, "You had the number seven, didn't you!" Kids love this. **Age 3+.**

POST-IT MATCHING. Set out five Post-its (if your child is 2.5) and ten (if she's 3+). Write the numbers 1 through 5 or 1 through 10 on the Post-its. Give her a jar of pennies (or other small items). See if she can put one penny by the 1, two pennies by the 2, and so on. Alternatively, you can make piles of coins in different amounts. See if she can match the pile of three with the 3, et cetera.

HIDE-AND-SEEK COUNTING. Hide something in a room that your child would love to find. Give him circuitous directions (stopping each time as he follows them) until he finds what you've hidden: "Take two steps forward. Turn to the couch. Take three steps backward. Hop two times to the chair. Look under the chair. What do you see?" **Age 3+.**

PLAY DOMINOES. They make bigger and more colorful ones for children, but the matching of dots is excellent practice for counting and recognizing numbers. **Age 3+.**

PRACTICE ADDITION AND SUBTRACTION
ADD 'N SUBTRACT MINDBENDERS. Make a game out of addition and subtraction questions. When your child first begins, start very simply with numbers from 1 through 5 and let her use her fingers to count out the problem. Example: "Two boys, two girls. How many children?" Have your child hold up two fingers on each hand and count each one to figure out the solution. Or "Four birds. Two flew away. How many are left?" Have your child hold up four fingers, then take two away and count what is left. **Age 4+.**

Here are some more:

★ "Three apples. Two oranges. How many pieces of fruit?"
★ "One short tree. Two tall trees. How many trees in all?"
★ "Two chicks in the first nest. Four chicks in the second nest. How many chicks in all?"
★ "Three jellyfish. One goldfish. How many fish in all?"
★ "Four cats. Two dogs. How many pets?"
★ "Five swans. Three are on land. The rest are in the lake. How many swans in the lake?"
★ "Six puppies. Two are brown. The rest are black. How many are black?"

A BEAR TALE. Put five Teddy Grahams in front of your child. Tell an addition and subtraction story like this: "Look, there are five bears playing in the woods when along comes their two cousin bears." [Put two more Teddy Grahams out.] "How many do we have now? Seven, that's right! The seven bears went for a swim in the pond when three of them decided to go to the picnic grounds to find food." [Take away three.] "Now how many do we have? Four, yes we do! The four bears that were left remembered they were invited to a birthday party, so they got out of the pond and hiked over to their friend's den. There were four more bears there." [Add four more.] "Now how many do we have?" You can do this with Gummi Bears, animal crackers, and Goldfish. **Age 3.5+.**

PLAY STORE. Put together a selection of cereal boxes, canned food, and other small grocery items. Put a Post-it on each item with a price under ten cents. If you have a toy cash register and shopping cart, enlist these in the game. Give your child a clear baggie filled with nickels, dimes, and pennies. Talk to her about what each coin is worth. Take turns being the shopper and the shop owner. Start by having the shopper buy one item and have her pay for it with exact change. Later have your child buy more than one item and pay for that (addition). When her math skills are stronger, let her be the shop owner. Make a purchase that requires her to give you change (subtraction). **Age 4.5+.**

In the next chapter, we will talk about visual-spatial skills. While these are an aspect of mathematical reasoning, we will explore them separately. These skills are so important to school success that they are covered on any test your child might take.

15. Visual-Spatial Reasoning

HOW THIS LITTLE-UNDERSTOOD ABILITY IMPACTS YOUR CHILD'S
SCHOOL SUCCESS—AND WHAT YOU CAN DO TO BUILD IT

Visual-spatial intelligence is the ability to process any kind of spatial information: that is, everything you see such as people, places, objects, symbols, and so on. It isn't so much about vision as it is about how the brain receives information through the eyes and then organizes it in the mind. Children need to be able to interpret and comprehend visual-spatial information (e.g., discriminate letter shapes, read; interpret maps, charts, and tables; identify shapes). They must be able to create their own visual-spatial drawings (e.g., write words, draw pictures, organize a page, make maps and charts).

Young children who have visual-spatial disabilities often don't like to color, draw pictures, do puzzles, or play with blocks or other toys involving construction. They tend to have poor organization skills, keep their notebooks and rooms messy, and have a bad sense of direction. Often they cannot learn left from right or how to read a clock. Some have trouble reading facial expressions and body language from people and thus have difficulty making friends.

Daily Life Lessons

Here are ways you can help your child strengthen her visual-spatial skills.

SHAPE WALK. When you are out walking or riding in the car, see how many shapes your child can spot in the world. Car tires are circles. Windows are square or rectangular. A roof might look like a triangle. What else can your child find?

BUILD RELATIVITY INTO YOUR DAILY CONVERSATIONS. When you are talking about everything and anything, bring relativity into the discussion. Which building is the tallest on our block? Which is the shortest? Can you find a big car? A small car? At the grocery store, which cucumber is the longest? In our family, who is the tallest? The shortest? Who is the heaviest? When you cut a piece of cake, ask if she wants a small, medium, or large piece. When you are in the kitchen, point out which jars are empty and full, which person took more or less of a serving of vegetables, which items are on the high shelf and which on the low shelf. Cut a piece of pie into two equal pieces, showing her what *equal* means.

Games and Activities

MASTER SHAPES

SHAPE PUZZLES AND BLOCKS. You might recall that the ability to recognize and draw triangles, circles, and squares is the basis for writing and recognizing letters and numbers. To help your child learn shapes, get her puzzles that feature shapes and different-shaped blocks. **Age 1+.**

THE ORIGINAL COLORFORMS SET or COLOR MAGIC STICKER PLAY BOOK. These sets include hundreds of brightly colored stickers that come in circles, squares, rectangles, triangles, wedges, and ovals that can be arranged to create people, cars, airplanes, houses, animals—whatever the imagination can cook up. They easily peel away from the laminated surface and can be used over and over. As children work with these stickers, they see all the geometry that exists in the world around them. Buy them at Amazon.com and other toy stores. **Age 3.5+.**

SHAPE PICNIC. Have a picnic with foods of different shapes: Doritos (triangles), crackers (square and rectangle), bologna (round). Help your child use a cookie cutter to make shapes with cheese, cookies, and sandwiches. **Age 1.5+.**

TRACE A SHAPE. Cut out a variety of shapes from a piece of poster board. Have your child hold the shape on a piece of construction paper, then trace it with a pencil or crayon. She will have made a beautiful shape! Now have her cut it out. **Age 3+.**

COPY MY PATTERN. Many intelligence tests include a task where the examiner creates a design from pattern tiles, blocks, or three-dimensional objects and the child is asked to copy the design. This is a particularly important subtest as it allows the examiner to assess not only a child's spatial and fine-motor abilities, but also his problem-solving skills. Does he plan ahead or jump right in? Does he use trial and error? Does he learn from his mistakes? Does he get frustrated with difficult tasks? How well does he concentrate? Can he sustain his attention and remain focused under pressure? How fast does he complete the task (processing speed)?

Get a set of pattern blocks (also called parquetry blocks). These are brightly colored tiles in various shapes that can be combined to make beautiful patterns and designs. You can also do this activity using the Original Colorform Set, Unifix, or linking cubes, or by making your own pattern squares from Post-it notes (see below). Using the tiles or pattern blocks, make a design and have your child copy it. Start with something very simple and progress to more complex patterns as he masters the skill. Let your child make a design and you copy it. Make a mistake and see if he notices. **Age 3+.**

★ To find linking cubes and pattern blocks, check out Lakeshorelearning.com, Etacuisenaire.com, and Wonderbrains.com.

★ Thinkfun makes a series of puzzles that are somewhat similar to the materials testers use for block design tasks. Go to www.Thinkfun.com and check out Block by Block, Shape by Shape, Square by Square, Izzi, Brick by Brick, and Top This! MightyMind makes a product like this as well.

MAKE YOUR OWN "PATTERN BLOCKS" USING POST-IT NOTES

- Choose two brightly colored square Post-it notepads. I like using pink and orange three-inch squares.
- Use a glue stick and glue twelve pink and twelve orange squares on a piece of cardboard.
- When the glue has dried, cut out all twenty-four squares. Keep the edges straight.
- Take four pink and four orange squares and cut them diagonally into triangles. Keep the edges straight.
- Take four pink and four orange squares and cut them in half into rectangles. Keep the edges straight.
- Now you'll have square, rectangle, and triangle "pattern blocks."

UNFRAMED AND FRAMED PUZZLES. On some tests, children are given pieces of an image without a frame in which to put it together. This might be an animal, face, car, house, that sort of thing. When Sam was little, I would go to Toys 'R Us where they had giant birthday cards on sturdy stock with beautiful color pictures of characters that were popular, like the Power Rangers, Shrek, and Batman. I would cut out the figure and then cut it into four or five pieces. These became his borderless puzzles. Because he was interested in the characters, he always wanted to put them together. You can also cut the front of your child's favorite cereal box into a puzzle. But before tackling unframed puzzles, have your child work with framed puzzles. At first, they should be simple knob puzzles with few pieces, followed by knobless puzzles where the pieces fit only one same-shaped hole. Next try 6- to 12-piece nonjigsaw tray puzzles. As he becomes more adept, he can handle puzzles with more pieces and unframed puzzles. Visit Growingtreetoys.com for some wonderful puzzles. **Age 2+.**

MEASUREMENT. You don't need yardsticks and tape measures to teach young children principles of measurement. Instead, show your child how to use her shoe to measure how many "shoes tall" her friend is. Or she can use string, blocks, and her hands to measure something. **Age 2+.**

HIDDEN PICTURES. *Highlights* magazine always features pictures where items are hidden within a larger picture: a fish is inside a carpet design, a dog's collar is a watch, a woman's hat is a squirrel. You can find these online at Highlights kids.com. *Highlights* offers concept books featuring pages of hidden pictures. Go to Highlights.com. The *I Spy* and *Where's Waldo?* books are also great for finding hidden pictures. For free *I Spy* and *Where's Waldo?* games online, go to Scholastic.com/ispy and Findwaldo.com. **Age 3+.**

BLOCKS. Blocks help children understand spatial relations. Children ages 1.5 to 3 years old can work with larger blocks. After age 3, try to get a set of unit blocks. They come in several sizes and shapes, but are all based on the proportions 1:2:4. You can put two rectangles together and they will be the same size as a larger square. Two triangles can be combined to make a square. Through block play, your child learns about depth, width, height, length, weight, volume, shape, symmetry, balance, patterns, counting, sorting, grouping, part-whole relationships, fractions, adding, dividing, subtracting, and more. As you observe your child playing with blocks, here are some things you can do:

* After he builds a block tower, help him count the number of blocks he used.
* Help him re-create the same structure using different-size blocks.
* Talk about the different shapes he used.
* Make patterns using different-shaped blocks.
* Talk with him about balance. How high can the tower go before it falls down? If it does fall down, ask him to think about what he can do differently so it doesn't fall next time.
* Use relativity language when talking about his block creations; *on top of, next to, beneath, higher, lower.*
* Ask him what he plans to build before he starts.
* Or just step back and let him play with blocks.

GLOBE. Have a globe in your home that you build into the conversation. Show your child where you live, or where her grandparents or other people she knows from out of town live. When you travel, show her on the globe where you are going. Point out the land and the water. You can discuss the different kinds of transportation one could use to get to each place and how long it would take. Talk about the animals in the different countries, as well as cultures, foods, terrain, and weather. **Age 2.5+.**

> In the next chapter, we'll talk about everything you can do to help your child develop thinking abilities.

16. Cognitive Skills

WHAT IT REALLY TAKES TO RAISE A BABY EINSTEIN (HINT: IT'S NOT ON A DVD)

Let's face it, learning to recognize the color blue or the number 8 isn't likely to get a kid excited. Do you know what gets a 5-year-old excited? Infinity. "How big is infinity?" "If it's always raining somewhere on earth, do all the raindrops in the world add up to infinity?" Forget infinity, "How was I four yesterday and five today?" "Did I grow a year in just one day?" "Why can't I run away from my shadow?" According to Amusingfacts.com, the average 4-year-old asks 400 questions a day. After Sam's hearing was fixed, he talked nonstop and mostly he asked questions: "If dinosaurs don't exist, why are there so many pictures of them?" "If I stand in the rain, will I grow faster?" "Mommy, when you were little, were you a girl or a boy?" "Would I be able to hear music on Venus?" "Where do stars go when I can't see them?" "How will Grampa find his friends in heaven?" I remember wondering, *Will this child ever stop talking?* The answer is yes, when he becomes a teenager. So enjoy your little inquisitor while you have him.

A preschooler's main job in life is to ask questions brought on by a relentless desire to make sense of his world. "What do bees talk about in their hives?" "Do ants elect a president?" As parents, there is nothing more delightful than rediscovering life's wonders through our children's eyes. When a child experiences something new and unexpected, he must find a way to make sense of it. "Mommy planted seeds and grew tomatoes. I planted a steak bone but didn't grow a cow. Why not?"

There is so much to learn, and it is our responsibility to help our kids uncover the secrets of life on earth. Children ponder mysteries that haven't crossed our minds in thirty (or forty) years, like "How do they get the little people inside the TV?" or "If people come from apes, where's my tail?" While their questions get tiresome at times, they give us a peek into our kids' busy brains, telling us what they are thinking about and interested in. The sheer playing around with ideas is the most exciting part of the preschool years.

> If a child is to keep alive his inborn sense of wonder, he needs the companionship of at least one adult who can share it, rediscovering with him the joy, excitement, and mystery of the world we live in.
>
> —Rachel Carson

Intelligence tests measure a child's thinking or cognitive skills. When a child combines aspects of cognitive skills to evaluate what they see, hear, and read, and then make decisions, reach conclusions, or solve problems based on analysis of information, they are using *higher-order thinking*. Kids naturally use these skills, often getting it wrong, but only because they are just beginning to understand the laws and rules governing the world. This is demonstrated by the fanciful observations reflecting children's unique viewpoints and quoted in Russian author Korney Chukovsky's 1928 book, *From Two to Five*:

* **Observing and asking questions.** Children watch, listen, and read to get the basic information to begin their exploration: "I like snow better than sun. I can build a fort out of the snow, but what can I make out of the sun?"
* **Sorting, classifying, comparing for conceptual thinking.** Once information has been gathered, children must sort it into groupings and classifications. As they notice patterns and similarities and differences, they begin to conceptualize: "The ostrich is a giraffe-bird."
* **Reasoning.** Based on information children gather, classify, and compare, they start to make sense of concepts or form opinions. A little boy just saw his grandmother remove her dentures: "Now take out your eyes, Granny!"
* **Hypothesizing.** After facts have been gathered, classified, and compared, children use reasoning skills to predict what might happen next: "Mother, who gave birth to me. You? I knew it. If Daddy had given birth to me I would have had a mustache."
* **Problem Solving.** With experience, children eventually realize that situations can be changed. Using creative thinking, they generate ideas, look for alternatives, and

try to see beyond the obvious to solve a problem. George cut a worm in half with his toy spade. "Why did you do that?" he was asked. "The worm was lonesome. Now there are two of them."

★ **Critical Thinking.** Children consider different sides of an issue or possible solutions. They weigh the pros and cons and form an opinion. A mother complains at her son's endless questions: "If you don't answer my questions, I'll remain stupid. If you do answer them, Mommy, I'll get smarter and smarter."

★ **Decision Making.** After examining and evaluating all sides of an issue or the options on the table, the child makes the best choice she can: "Mother, all people will die, right? But someone will have to place somewhere the last urn with the ashes of the last dead person. I would like to be that person! All right?"

Observe the tiny preschooler using *higher-order thinking*: A little girl *plans* to paint a blue sky on a large piece of paper. After painting for a few minutes, she *observes* that her brush is so small that it will take too long to paint the sky. *Hmmm, this is a problem.* She *reasons* that painting with her hands would cover the paper more quickly, so she pours the paint on her palms, but before she touches the paper, she *evaluates* this approach and decides it's too messy. While washing her hands, she *observes* a sponge by the sink. *Maybe a sponge would work like a big brush*, she *hypothesizes*. *Yes, I'll give it a try*, she *decides*. This time, by sponging the paint on the picture, she makes a satisfactory sky and her *problem is solved*.

We live in a world where there is no shortage of information. In school, students are bombarded with data and facts. But success in school (and life) requires much more than the ability to memorize. These days, teachers let students bring crib notes into tests because facts aren't as important as the ability to sort them, evaluate them, and come to conclusions based on analysis. Students who use high-order thinking grow up to be more creative, flexible, and persistent because they know how to generate, critique, and choose from an assortment of ideas. They aren't flustered when they hit a dead end—they know how to seek out alternatives. As a parent, you can foster your child's higher-order thinking skills through your daily interactions and special activities.

Daily Life Lessons

As you talk to your child about everything and anything, use these techniques to encourage him to think for himself:

PROMOTE QUESTIONS. When your child asks you those *who, what, where, when,* and *why* questions, support him, give him answers that will encourage his desire to explore deeper, engage in conversation on the topic, and expand the discussion. Keep a question book handy. If your child asks a question that you don't know how to answer, say, "Let's write it down." Later, research the question by going online, looking at books, or asking an expert.

DON'T SOLVE PROBLEMS FOR YOUR CHILD. Too often when a child doesn't know what to do, we tell him. By doing that, we've taken away an opportunity for him to use his own problem-solving skills. If a child is constantly directed on how to do things, he will look to adults for the answers rather than try for himself. Express confidence in his ability to solve the problem and help him if he struggles, but let him do it. You'll be teaching him to take initiative and risks, two vital skills for school and life success.

PRACTICE SOLVING REAL-LIFE PROBLEMS. When the ball rolls under the couch, ask your child how he would suggest retrieving it. When she can't get herself dressed in time for school, ask her to think of things she could do differently to be ready faster. Every day there are countless moments where your child can practice problem solving.

ENCOURAGE EXPERIMENTATION. Teach your child that there is rarely one correct way to solve a problem. If she tries an unusual approach to a project or a problem, applaud her: "Good thinking!" "I like what you're doing." If her solution doesn't work, praise her for her effort: "Look at all the different ways you're trying to put that puzzle together. Keep at it. You'll get it."

ASK THOUGHT-PROVOKING QUESTIONS. Stimulate your child's thinking by asking:

> Open-ended questions: "Why do you think the little boy in the picture is crying?"
> Questions with many answers: "What colors can the sky be?"
> "What if" questions: "What would happen if a child were the president?"
> "What different ways" questions: "Tell me all the different ways you could use a shoebox"
> "Why" questions: "Why did you decide to use that block here?"

"How" questions: "How do you think that little girl felt when she realized she was on the wrong bus?"

BE A THINKING ROLE MODEL. Narrate your own thought processes as you solve problems and let your child help: "I was going to make pancakes this morning, but we're out of milk. I could make eggs instead, or we could go to the store and get milk, or maybe we could go to McDonald's. What do you think?" When you are making a big purchase or planning a vacation, involve your child in the research you do to teach her how important it is to get the facts before making a decision.

SHOW THAT IT'S OKAY TO MAKE MISTAKES. Let your child see you make mistakes so he'll know it's okay. What matters is that we try and then learn from what doesn't work: "Look, I cooked the popcorn too long and it burned. Let me make another bag and not cook it so long."

GIVE YOUR CHILD A VOICE. Making choices helps your child become comfortable with decision making. For example, let her choose between two pairs of pants to wear, whether to have chicken or fish for dinner, which book to read or board game to play.

USE MOVIES AND BOOKS TO PONDER OTHER SOLUTIONS. In many books, movies, and TV shows, the plot centers around a character with a problem to solve. Talk about how the character solved his problem and come up with other ways he might have resolved it.

TEACH A PROBLEM-SOLVING MODEL. Imagine that your two children are fighting over who gets to use the computer (hard to imagine, I know).

1. Instead of acting as King Solomon, sit them down and ask them to *brainstorm different solutions*. Brainstorming encourages creativity and flexibility in thinking. Have them think of as many ideas for computer-sharing rules as they can. Write down all the ideas, no matter how silly or unfeasible (sometimes these inspire other brilliant ideas).
2. Talk over the ideas and together *choose two* that seem fair to everyone.
3. Put each idea on top of a page and together *evaluate the pros and cons*.

4. After looking at all sides, *ask each child his opinion on which option is best and why*. If the children don't agree, ask nuanced questions to get them thinking and guide them in making a decision you can all live with.

Through this model, you are teaching your children that there is always more than one answer to a problem, but if you explore different possibilities, you can make thoughtful decisions backed by good reasons.

HELP YOUR CHILD BECOME ADAPTABLE. If, after using the problem-solving model, the decision you made doesn't work, show your child that you can go back, reevaluate, and try something else. The ability to roll with change is critical to succeeding in our dynamic world.

HELP YOUR CHILD MAKE CONNECTIONS. Encourage your child to look for connections. For example, when you are watching a TV show, ask if he can relate the situation dramatized to something that happened in his life.

HAVE STIMULATING DINNER TABLE OR BEDTIME CONVERSATIONS. As your child gets older and can handle more high-order thinking, initiate discussions about issues or current events that will allow him to express his opinion, think critically, and work with abstract concepts. For example, "If you were the president of the United States, what is the first thing you'd do?"

ASK HER OPINION. Anytime you are having a discussion or disagreement within the family, ask your child what she thinks and why.

MAKE PLAY A PRIORITY
Earlier, we said that play is as important for the development of your child's mind and spirit as anything else she does. Here's what you can do to support your child's play.

PROVIDE OPEN-ENDED MATERIALS FOR FREE PLAY. When choosing toys for play, avoid fancy electronic toys that direct what your child can do with them. Instead look for open-ended toys and materials that can be used many different ways. Open-ended materials inspire creativity, pretend play, decision making, and social interaction. When a child plays with Lincoln Logs, for example, he will have to think about what he's doing and plan what he'll build in his mind before he starts. One day he might make a log cabin and the next day a horse farm. Consider getting some of these open-ended materials: Play-Doh, crayons, chalk, paper, glitter, glue, cotton balls, scissors, blocks, Duplos, Legos, Playmobil toys, blocks, balls, and puppets.

Things around the house can be used for play as well. Pillows, cushions, and blankets make wonderful forts. Books, toys, and empty food containers can be set up to make a store. Kitchen chairs can be transformed into a bus. Paper cups can be turned into cell phones. Paper plates can become masks. Brown paper bags and socks can be used for puppets. Boxes can be transformed into tunnels. Pots, pans, and plastic containers and cans filled with rice, beans, and pennies can become instruments.

ENCOURAGE PRETEND PLAY. When children initiate fantasy play and enact events from their life or imagination, they get to experience a feeling of control and work out emotional issues. A child may pretend to be a superhero fighting off a villain who represents his worst nightmare. He develops resourcefulness by generating different means of attack and eventually finds a way to handle his fear. Making up stories, generating alternate scenarios, and role playing gives children practice in solving divergent problems, the kind with multiple solutions. Kids who engage in fantasy play grow up to become better problem solvers.

To facilitate fantasy play, create a dress-up corner by filling a drawer or trunk with costumes and props that can spice up a child's fantasy. It doesn't have to be expensive. A daddy shirt, tie, high heels, purse, old Halloween costumes, a tablecloth cape, a toy stethoscope, a broken cell phone, toy food, eyeglasses, hats, and old jewelry work just fine. Goodwill, Salvation Army, used clothing stores, and tag sales always have funky clothing and props for low prices.

LET GO OF CONTROL. When your child is digging holes to China or making mud pies, give him time and space to experiment, explore, think, and try out his ideas. You are not the director. He is. Adults who constantly exert control over children quash their creative spirits. When your child has built a city with roads using blocks, this is not the time to ask him to sort his Matchbox cars by color. Instead, ask him to tell you about what he built and what he plans to do next. The value of play is the play itself, not what is produced. As long as your child is engaged and having fun, that's all that matters.

MAKE PLAY DATES AND GO TO THE PARK. These are so important for teaching kids social skills: cooperation, taking turns, sharing, compromising and problem solving.

LET YOUR CHILD DO NOTHING. Give your child time to goof off, get bored, reflect, ponder, find ways to amuse himself, and daydream. William Gates Sr. tells a story of his wife finding young Bill dawdling in the basement. She said, "Bill, what are you doing?" He said, "I'm thinking, Mom. Don't you ever just think?" William Sr. and his wife looked at each other and said, "You know, I'm not sure we do."

> David Elkind, author of *The Hurried Child*, says that those "most likely to succeed in tomorrow's knowledge economy won't be the weary souls who have been drilled since birth to master memorization, but rather the creative people who can solve problems and think independently."

Games and Activities

Most of the activities and games we've talked about already will support your child's cognitive development. Here are a few more:

HIGHLIGHTS MAGAZINE (AND *HIGHLIGHTS HIGH FIVE*). I can't recommend this publication enough as it contains activities that stimulate your child's thinking. My favorite section for this is called BrainPlay. It's full of questions that go from easy to hard. The child is encouraged to start at the beginning and see how far he can go thinking of answers. Here are sample questions:

> What do we clean with shampoo? With soap? With toothpaste? With detergent?
> "My muscles are sore." said Caleb. "What could have caused that?"
> Which of these can we live without? Water, sleep, food, computers, houses?
> If pets were in charge of households, how would things be different?
> What is the difference between the way you walk on a sidewalk when it's dry compared to when it's icy? **Age 3+.**

PICK UP SOME KID TALK: CONVERSATION CARDS. This is a great tool to get children talking and thinking. Each card gives an interesting piece of information such as, "Ice cream cones were created in 1904 at the St. Louis World's Fair, when an ice cream seller ran out of dishes and put the ice cream into a rolled waffle." Then it poses a question: "If you could invent or combine any foods, what would you make? What would you call it?" Go to Funiqtoys .com. **Age 3+.**

THE CRITICAL THINKING COMPANY puts out some good workbooks that build reasoning skills. Take a look at *Building Thinking Skills Beginning* and *Can You Find Me Pre-K, Mind Benders Beginning 1*, and *Thinker Doodles: Clues and Choose Beginning*. Go to Criticalthinking.com. **Age 3+.**

THINKING BRAIN TEASERS. Ask your child an inferential question to which he would know the answer. Inferential questions make you think beyond just the information that is supplied.

> Bobby gathered his toothbrush, pajamas, and favorite stuffed bear. Is he going to bed or to a party?
> Daddy put on his coat, mittens, and hat. What season is it?
> When reading a book to your child, ask inferential questions about the pictures or content. For example, look at the expression on this tiger's face. What do you think he's feeling? Who do you think was more afraid when they ran into each other—Goldilocks or the three bears? Why? **Age 3+.**

TRUE/FALSE BRAIN TEASERS. This is a good game for the car or while waiting at the doctor's office. Ask your child true/false questions to which he would know the answers. **Age 2.5+.**

> True or false? We are riding in a blue car.
> True or false? You have two eyes, two ears, and two noses.
> True or false? The summer is cold and the winter is hot.

JOKES AND RIDDLES. A great deal of research finds a close relationship between humor and creativity. Both require you to look at things from an unusual and unexpected perspective. For example, what do you call a train that sneezes? Ah-choo-choo train! Pick up some age-appropriate joke and riddle books for your child. I recommend *What Do You Hear When Cows Sing?* by Marco Maestro and *My First Book of Knock Knock Jokes*, by Tad Hills.

"TEACH ME EVERYTHING YOU KNOW ABOUT . . ." Pick a topic and ask your child to teach you everything he knows about dinosaurs, cars, superheroes, chocolate, or anything that really interests him. Write down what he says so you can read it back to him. Ask him questions. Make a second list of things he wishes he knew about the subject. Read the list back to him. Talk about all the ways you might find the answers. Teach him that there are many resources he can turn to for help with his investigations. Work together on getting the answers he wants. **Age 3+.**

5 REASONS WHY. Take turns asking each other questions and giving five reasons explaining your answer. For example: "What do you like better, chocolate ice cream or apple pie?" "Which would you rather do, go to the circus or the zoo?" "Who would you rather meet in person, Batman or Superman?" **Age 3+.**

DIALOGIC PICTURES. Collect funny or thought-provoking photographs from magazines and newspapers. From time to time, take a few out and ask your child what he thinks just happened in the picture. If he needs help, ask questions to provoke his thinking. **Age 3+.**

WATCH THE CLOUDS AND THE STARS. Get out in nature. Let your child pick up sticks, play in water, or chase frogs. Lay in the grass with your child and look up at the clouds. What do you see? A cloud that looks like a mouse? A heart? A grandpa? At night, watch the stars. Do you see patterns? How long do you think it would take to reach a star in a spaceship? Do you think there is life on those stars? A wonderful book about imagining shapes in clouds is *It Looked Like Spilt Milk*, by Charles G. Shaw. **Age 1+.**

> In the next chapter, we'll go over fine-motor skills, which are required to carry out many of the tasks included on tests and are vital to school success.

17. Fine-Motor Skills

SECRETS OCCUPATIONAL THERAPISTS USE TO GET CHILDREN'S FINGERS
TO DO THE WALKING

While fine-motor skills themselves are not specifically evaluated on most intelligence tests, many of the activities that are assessed demand these skills to carry them out. You'll recall that *fine-motor skills* are those requiring use of the small muscles in a child's hand. They are needed for cutting with scissors, doing puzzles, manipulating buttons, coins, beads, and blocks, tying shoes, zipping and unzipping, and more. *Graphomotor skills* involve the use of hand and finger muscle movements necessary to write with a pencil or crayon. Interestingly, a child can have good fine-motor skills and poor graphomotor skills, and vice versa.

HOLDING A PENCIL

When your child first begins to write or color, have him use fat pencils, crayons, or markers. He will grasp it in his fist and move his entire hand to draw or color. This is called an *immature pencil grip*. Later, in school, teachers will want him to grasp his pencil with equal pressure between his thumb, the side of his middle finger, and the tip of his index finger. This is called the *tripod, pincer*, or *mature pencil grip*. When your child is assessed for kindergarten, the tester will note in her summary if he is using a mature or immature pencil grasp.

Your toddler first colors with an immature grip. An occupational therapist (OT) once told me that when he is three or four, a good way to get him to begin to hold the color with a mature grasp is to break your colors or pencils in half. He'll have no choice but to hold the crayon with a pincer grip because it will be too small to fit in his fist. Another trick is to get him to paint with a cotton swab. He will naturally manipulate it with three fingers. Here are some other tools that can help:

* **Colorful rubber pencil grips.** There are many types of these available. Ideally, you would talk to an OT for help picking the right one for your child. The wrong one can lead to a problematic grip.
* **Tri-Write crayons.** If you don't want to break your crayons in half, occupational therapists use a product called **Tri-Write crayons,** which are small pyramid-shaped crayons that also force a pincer grip and help children learn a mature pencil grasp. These and other tools to help with fine-motor skills are available at Toysforautism.com. Crayola makes washable triangular crayons that also guide toddler's fingers into the pincer grip.
* **Easels and chalkboards.** When possible, children should practice writing, drawing, and painting on stable vertical surfaces. This incorporates arm and shoulder movement and positions the wrist to develop good thumb movements. If your child is having trouble holding and controlling a pencil, writing on an easel should make it easier.
* **Lite-Brite** cubes, where kids plug colored pegs into holes to make pictures, really help with the pincer grip.

If your child is struggling with the pincer grip, don't make yourself crazy. Children's fine-motor skills have to do with the development of the frontal lobe of the brain. That area isn't expected to support graphomotor skills until age 6 or 7. However, the area is more developed in some youngsters ages 4 or 5. If your child hasn't gotten it yet, he may just need more time for his frontal lobe to mature.

Daily Life Lessons

ENCOURAGE INDEPENDENCE

Toddlers are famous for saying "Me do it!" and parents should take advantage of their desire for independence. Encourage your child to learn to dress himself, button his own buttons, zip his zippers, brush his teeth, comb his hair, and tie his shoelaces. Set up his closet and dresser so his clothes are within reach, his bathroom so he can get his own toothbrush and toothpaste. Arrange his room so that toys, games, and art supplies are close to the ground. You can buy those kid-friendly shelves that are found in preschool classrooms at Kaplanco.com. In the kitchen, let him spread the peanut butter on his sandwich, stir the cake mix, pour rice into the pot, or milk into the cereal with a measuring cup that has a spout. Store snacks within his reach so he can get his own box of raisins or apple slices. Let him help you load plates and silverware into the dishwasher, put food away after grocery shopping, and fold washcloths after you do laundry.

HANDLE CHANGE. Put a piggy bank in your child's room and give her change to put in the slot. When you park at a meter, let her put in the change.

TURN PAGES. When you read together, let her turn the pages.

CRAFT SUPPLIES. Make sure you have plenty of craft supplies available for your child to use at home: construction paper, crayons, markers, pencils, paint, brushes with sponges, glue, modeling clay, colored foam, scissors, stamps, yarn, felt, jewels, and glitter. Encourage your child to draw, color, tear paper, glue, and create to her heart's content. Crafts projects exercise not only the small muscles in children's hands, but also the imagination.

SMALL FOOD. Picking up small foods one at a time such as Cheerios and Gold-fish is a good way to practice fine-motor skills.

COMPUTERS. Working on the computer is excellent exercise for little fingers and wrists.

Games and Activities

Many of the activities that I've recommended already are wonderful for building fine-motor skills. Some examples include: sorting and classifying with manipulatives, playing board games and dominoes, working with large blocks for young children, smaller blocks for older kids, playing with linking cubes and parquetry blocks, stringing beads, making patterns with food, and playing with puzzles. Here are a few more:

CUTTING. When cutting with blunt scissors, have your child cut fringe from paper, cut along curved and angled lines, cut various shapes, cut out newspaper coupons, and cut clay. There is an inexpensive book you can buy called *Scissor Skill Patterns* that offers a variety of activities for fine-motor development practice. Kumon also offers excellent first-step workbooks that help children cut paper, fold, trace, sticker, and paste. Have him cut shapes and then glue what he cuts onto a piece of construction paper. **Age 2.5+.**

PLAY-DOH AND DOUGH. Occupational therapists use "Cando Theraputty" to help kids build fine-motor skills. You can use any brand or make your own. Whether your child plays with it, squeezes it, rolls it into snakes or balls, cuts it, pounds it or molds it, he will be strengthening his small hand muscles. Take three cans worth of Play-Doh and hide small manipulatives or toys in it and let your child dig them out. At Lakeshorelearning.com, you can get dough in various scents. Play-Doh Model Magic is more resistant dough that you can mold and leave out and it dries hard. If you go to Testingforkindergarten.com, there is a Play-Doh recipe. **Age 2+.**

PRACTICE DRAWING SHAPES. Draw a circle, square, or triangle and have your child copy it. Make it more fun by using a Magna Doodle, eraser board, Buddha board, or let your child use her finger to draw shapes in the air. **Age 3+.**

* If your child is having trouble with shapes, draw examples with a yellow marker or highlighter and have her draw over them with a dark crayon.
* **Triangle drawing trick.** Triangles are usually the hardest shape for a young child to learn to draw. You can show her how to put three dots on a page and connect them. That will make a triangle.
* Make cardboard stencils that your child can use to trace shapes.
* If you draw pictures of people together, there will usually be lots of circles and ovals. When this type of task appears on a test, your child is given extra credit if there is more detail. So as your child's drawings become more sophisticated, encourage her to add all the hands, fingers, ears, and hair. If she draws a basic house picture, there is often a square (house and window), rectangle (door), triangle (roof), circle (sun), and curlicues (smoke from chimney).

PRACTICE WRITING LETTERS

* Begin with capital letters, because they are easier to master. They require only four strokes: big and little lines, big and little curves. Workbooks, where children trace letters for practice, are a great place to start, and then move on to tablet paper. **Age 3+.**
* Let your child practice writing her name with paper and pencil, shaving cream, chalk on the sidewalk, her finger in sand or flour or with finger paints or even in

the air. Write her name on paper using a yellow highlighter and let her trace it until she can write it herself.

★ If your child is having trouble mastering letters, check out Handwriting Without Tears at Hwtears.com. **Age 4+.**

CONNECT THE DOTS. After your child can identify numbers 1 through 10 and letters of the alphabet, give him connect-the-dots puzzles. If you Google "pre-school activities connect the dots," dozens of free sites will appear where you can print these out. **Age 3+.**

MAGNA DOODLE AND ETCH-A-SKETCH are fun tools that require wrist and finger dexterity. **Age 3+.**

CONSTRUCTION TOYS. Lincoln Logs, Erector sets (easy play bucket), Legos, Duplo blocks, Tinker Toys (junior edition), and other building toys support fine-motor skills and imaginations. **Age 3+.**

BLUNT TWEEZERS. Using tweezers, have your child pick up paper clips one at a time from a bowl and move them to another bowl. See how many she can pick up in sixty seconds. Do this also with cornflakes, marshmallows, and Cheerios. **Age 3.5+.**

POURING. Get two small pitchers and a plastic cup. Fill one pitcher with rice. Have your child practice pouring rice from pitcher to pitcher. Later, put water in a pitcher and let her pour it into the cup. **Age 2.5+.**

SPRAY BOTTLE. Give your child a spray bottle filled with water and help her go around the yard, spraying your plants. Or put food coloring in the water and let her go outside and spray the snow! Squeezing the trigger of a spray bottle is good exercise for small hands. **Age 2.5+.**

ONE-HAND SORTING. Give your child a mixture of a few small objects (buttons, beads, coins) to hold in one hand. Have him sort and place each item into different cups one at a time using his thumb and index finger. **Age 3.5+.**

HEADS OR TAILS. Line up an assortment of coins, all heads up. See how many your child can turn over with his fingers in thirty seconds. With more than one child, make it a race. **Age 3+.**

SPONGE MATH. In the bathtub, give your child a cup and a sponge. Ask him to predict how many times he'll have to squeeze water into the cup before it fills up. Have him dip the sponge in water, then squeeze the liquid completely into the cup. Count how many squeezes it takes. **Age 3+.**

FOLDING PAPER. Give your child an origami square and teach him how to fold it diagonally into a triangle. Show him how to fold one in half into a rectangle. For more, go to Origami-instructions.com. The Kumon workbook *Let's Fold* offers super-basic origami projects. **Age 3+.**

TIE A KNOT OR A BOW. There are many fun ways to teach a child to tie his shoes. Check out *Red Lace, Yellow Lace*, by Mark Casey, Judith Herbst, and Jenny Stanley. SpongeBob has a fun episode on tying shoes as well. For a variety of ways to teach a child to tie his shoe, google "how to tie a shoelace." **Age 4+.**

PAPER CLIP NECKLACE. Make a chain from colored paper clips. **Age 4+.**

CARD GAMES. There are all kinds of age-appropriate card games for preschoolers, all requiring finger dexterity to play. Go Fish, Hearts, and Old Maid (yes, it still exists!) immediately come to mind. **Age 3.5+.**

> In the next chapter, we'll venture beyond the world of testing to explore what children need for life success.

18. Beyond Testing Success

THE 5 MUST-HAVE SKILLS EVERY CHILD NEEDS TO SUCCEED IN LIFE

Let me begin by saying that the qualities I'm talking about in this chapter are *not* specific to testing success (although they will help). They *are* critical to life success. I started this book by telling you that I am not a psychologist. I am a mother who dug into the research and turned herself into enough of an expert to help her own son. I've shared everything I learned about how to help your child succeed on intelligence tests and (more important) to get off on the right foot in kindergarten. If you raise your child with lots of language, play, books, music, and interesting experiences, she's likely to have a solid IQ, but once she gets past 120 (high-average), that won't matter much. British psychologist Liam Hudson says that you are as likely to win a Nobel Prize with a 120 IQ as a 200 IQ.

In 1921, Lewis Terman, who created the Stanford-Binet test, reviewed the records of more than 250,000 California students, identifying 1,500 of the best and brightest with IQs of 140 to 200. He meticulously monitored their progress through adulthood. By the late 1950s, only one had made a lasting impact on society: Jess Oppenheimer, who created the sitcom *I Love Lucy*. Many had good jobs, but some were considered failures. Terman ultimately concluded, "Intellect and achievement are far from correlated."

Rena F. Subotnik, author of *Genius Revisited: High IQ Children Grown Up*, says, "We know that most children we select for gifted programs do not turn out to be outstanding adult performers or thinkers. We also know that many gifted adults were not identified as gifted children in school." Albert Einstein and Carl Jung come to mind. Subotnik conducted a study of students attending Hunter College Elementary between 1948 and 1960. They had an average IQ of 157 and had attended the finest gifted program in the country. "Contrary to the expectations associated with the label of 'genius,'" the study noted, "they tended to hold modest goals for themselves." Her study concluded that for success later in life, "nonintellectual factors" probably matter more.

What are these nonintellectual factors? I would be remiss if I talked about what a child needs to do well at testing and school without also underlining the character traits needed for life success. Social skills, empathy, motivation, self-reliance, adaptability, creativity, common sense, morals—they all matter.

As I studied this subject, five interconnected qualities kept popping up as being key to excelling in adulthood. They are curiosity, a devotion to your passion, persistence, a tolerance for failure, and self-control. As you go about raising your child, keep these in mind and do whatever you can to foster them. Your son or daughter won't pick these up in one or two lessons. They require time to take root. All you can do is plant the seeds and tend to them as your child grows.

Curiosity

William Gates Sr. believes that Bill Gates's defining quality is his insatiable curiosity. As a boy, he read the entire *Encyclopedia Britannica*. In fact, he read everything he could get his hands on and constantly asked questions. His parents encouraged that and made it fair game to talk about anything in their family's lives around the dinner table.

Eleanor Roosevelt once said, "I think, at a child's birth, if a mother could ask a fairy godmother to endow it with the most useful gift, that gift should be curiosity." Nurturing your child's curiosity will help him develop a love of learning. How can you do this? You can help him explore all that captivates him without fear of failure. Notice what sparks his interest and provide the tools to dig into it further. Give him access to books, read to him, take him to museums, the planetarium, field trips. Encourage your child to go in whatever direction his mind wants to take him. We don't get to choose what captivates our children, we can only be attentive to it and then support it.

> Don't force your kids into sports. I never was. To this day, my dad has never asked me to play golf. I asked him. It's the child's desire to play that matters, not the parent's desire to have the child play. Fun. Keep it fun.
>
> —Tiger Woods

Devotion to Passion

In *Talent Is Overrated*, Geoff Colvin talks about the "ten-year rule." All the research has shown that in fields from sports to academia to athletics to arts, no one becomes great without at least ten years of hard preparation. In his book *Outliers: The Story of Success*, Malcolm Gladwell calls this the 10,000-Hour Rule. He says it takes 10,000 hours of practice—twenty hours a week for ten years—to become successful in any field.

The private school Bill Gates attended owned an early computer. He became so fascinated by it that he'd sneak out at night and spend hours upon hours playing with it, studying it, and finally running programs. By the time he started high school, he had put in over 10,000 hours. Before they came to America the Beatles had performed live together 1,200 times, often doing eight-hour sets. That doesn't even count the intense and prolonged days they put into their rehearsals. By Steven Spielberg's sixteenth birthday, he had made three films: a Western, a World War II flying movie, and a science fiction adventure. He would fake sick to stay home from school so he could edit his films. In his early teens, Walter Cronkite was already a copy boy and cub reporter at the *Houston Post*. Interestingly, Bill Gates, Steven Spielberg, and Walter Cronkite all dropped out of college because they couldn't wait to get started in their fields of interest. Thomas Edison summed this idea up when he said, "Genius is one percent inspiration and ninety-nine percent perspiration."

If you look at any list of qualities of giftedness in a child, you'll see "works independently and concentrates for long periods on things that interest him." A gifted child who is fascinated by dinosaurs will have joyfully logged so many hours of study by the time he enters kindergarten that he is a virtual encyclopedia on the subject. When Sam turned 6, he became obsessed by baseball. Of course, we signed him up for Little League, and my husband practiced throwing and catching with him every evening. We watched movies about baseball, read books about it, and went to college games—everything we could do to feed his voracious appetite. At 7, he could quote statistics and answer any baseball question on ESPN's *Stump the Schwab*!

Dr. Mel Levine, a top learning expert, talks about a parent's responsibility to foster their child's strengths, knacks, talents, and affinities. "A mind grows through the pursuit of deep interests, the following of its inclinations. An affinity can bring on expertise. I would like to see every kid become an expert on something, accumulating more knowledge and insight on particular topics than anyone else in the immediate vicinity."

Persistence vs. Smarts Mind-set

In 1998, Stanford University psychology professor Carol Dweck performed an experiment where she gave two evenly matched groups of elementary students the same IQ test. When one group did well, they were told that they must have worked hard to get the result. The other group was told they must be very smart to have done so well. Over time, Dweck found that the children who were told that they were smart fell apart when they hit challenges, gave up easily when faced with tasks they didn't think they could do, and lost confidence in their abilities. Children who were praised for working hard were more likely to seek out challenges, persist in the face of difficulty, and handle setbacks more easily. What does this mean for parents? Do not praise your child for being smart. Instead, praise her for trying, for her strategy, her persistence, her efforts, her concentration, her choices, for not giving up. Your praise should be specific and genuine. Check out Dweck's book, *Mindset*, for more on this study and how to praise your child's process over her intellect.

Dweck says that intelligence is not fixed; it can be changed as long as we believe we can improve ourselves. If we think our abilities are limited by our natural intelligence, then they will be. She stresses the importance of raising children to value learning over good grades because competency can be developed with practice. As a parent, you should encourage your child to take on challenges that stretch her capabilities, work hard to improve, and confront and correct her deficiencies. When a child makes a mistake, she should be praised for trying, not criticized for getting it wrong.

Tolerance for Failure

In his *Talent Is Overrated*, Geoff Colvin argues that the idea of natural talent is a myth and the path to great performance is a concept called "deliberate practice." The essence of this is the willingness to continually stretch yourself just beyond your current abilities, practicing repeatedly what you have not mastered in response to feedback given to you by a coach or teacher. He talks about Tiger Woods, whose father put a putter in his hand at 7 months. Tiger practiced regularly from the age of 2 and studied with professional teachers from the age of 4. The reason Tiger can hit a ball from a sand trap into the hole is because he has practiced making that shot thousands upon thousands of times. Thomas Edison tried more than ten thousand times before he created the first successful lightbulb. Michael Jordan says that failure is the key to his success: "I have missed more than nine thousand shots in my career. I have lost almost three hundred games. On twenty-six occasions I have been entrusted to take the game-winning shot . . . and missed. And I have failed over and over again in my life. And that is why I succeed." What do Walt Disney and Bill Gates have in common? They both started businesses that failed before they achieved remarkable success. Albert Einstein's explanation for his successful discoveries was, "[N]ot that I'm so smart, it's just that I stay with problems longer."

Think about this. It isn't fun to practice something you're not good at over and over again. But that's the only way a person can go from good to great. Enroll your child in piano, tennis, or any activity that interests him so that he can experience what it is to practice scales or hit balls and see improvement in his technique. If you find that your child is frustrated by something he is attempting to master, try to isolate the aspects of his performance that are tripping him up, get him instruction on how to do it right, and encourage him to practice the hard part until he masters it.

Self-control

In the late 1960s, Stanford professor of psychology Walter Mischel conducted experiments in which he offered 4-year-olds a choice. They could either have a marshmallow right away, or, if they could wait while he stepped out for a few minutes, two marshmallows when he returned. Low delayers resisted the treat for an average of three minutes while high delayers could wait fifteen minutes until Mischel came back in the room. Michel followed these children for many years and discovered the following differences.

Low delayers were more likely than high delayers to:
- ★ have behavioral problems in school and at home,
- ★ struggle in stressful situations,
- ★ have trouble paying attention,
- ★ have difficulty maintaining friendships,
- ★ get lower SAT scores,

- ★ have significantly higher body mass as adults,
- ★ have problems with drugs.

High delayers:
- ★ had SAT scores that were on average 210 points higher than low delayers,
- ★ were better adjusted and more dependable adults.

Doesn't this make sense? Aren't we all beholden to our self-control? Even if you have a high IQ, you still have to forgo going to the mall or watching TV to do your homework. If you want a big career, you have to work long and hard. We've seen that it takes ten years or ten thousand hours of practice to become great at anything. To save money for retirement means giving up vacations, expensive handbags, designer shoes, or whatever else we'd love to have right now.

Mischel found that while the low delayer stared at the marshmallow until he could resist it no longer, high delayers distracted themselves, often playing with toys or singing while waiting for the researcher to return. Mischel said that the key to self-control was to avoid thinking about the reward in the first place. This is important information for parents. We can teach our children to distract themselves when they can't have what they want immediately.

Since Mischel's experiment, Dr. Roy Baumeister, a psychologist at Florida State University, has performed further research in self-control (also called willpower, patience, or delayed gratification). He found that the trait of self-control is like a muscle that can be strengthened by consistently working it out in small bites. Building up self-control in one aspect of life (such as exercising, improving your posture, or flossing every day) will increase one's overall ability to self-regulate in *all* other areas of life. Studies have shown that the discipline of a regular workout program leads to decreased smoking, alcohol, caffeine, and junk-food consumption. What does this research mean to parents? We must teach our kids to wait for rewards in a variety of situations so that they acquire the "master virtue" (as Baumeister calls it) of self-control or become high delayers (as Mischel described it).

Daily Life Lessons

Here are some ways to help your child work out her patience muscles and improve her odds of personal achievement.

DON'T RUSH TO HELP YOUR CHILD EVERY TIME SHE ASKS. Tell her, "I can't do it now, but I can after I finish the dishes." Don't get her hooked on immediate gratification. Kids must learn to tolerate frustration.

SUGGEST WAYS TO DISTRACT HERSELF WHILE SHE WAITS. "Why don't you play with your Barbies until we can start making the cookies?"

MAKE WAITING CONCRETE by connecting how long she'll have to wait with your completion of an activity ("when I finish making dinner") or use a timer and tell her you'll do what she asks when the bell rings.

MAKE WAITING WORTHWHILE. Follow through with whatever you promised so your child sees that if she waits, there is a reward.

MARTIAL ARTS are excellent for improving focus, concentration, self-control, confidence, and patience.

CARING FOR A PET will teach patience and self-control.

DO PROJECTS AND ACTIVITIES TOGETHER THAT TAKE TIME FOR A PAYOFF. Planting flowers from seeds, baking cookies, and fishing all require waiting for the reward.

READ CHAPTER BOOKS as soon as your child is ready (age 4 or 5). This way, he'll learn to wait for the next installment. The *Fudge* series by Judy Blume are wonderful first chapter books.

HAVE SCHEDULES for TV time, snack time, playground time, plans for the day. Schedules help kids learn to wait for things.

BOARD GAMES teach children to be patient and wait their turn. Games like hide and seek teach kids to wait while the other children hide and while you're hoping not to be found.

SUGGEST WAYS TO EXTEND A FAVORITE ACTIVITY. If your child draws a picture, encourage her to add glitter or colored glue. If she builds a town with blocks, propose that she bring out her Polly Pockets and take them to the zoo.

BE A ROLE MODEL FOR SELF-CONTROL. When you get upset, yelling, threatening, and spanking won't help your child learn to control his own emotions when he is upset.

PRAISE your child for his patience.

These qualities can hardly be separated from one another, and yet each is needed to do well in life. First, a child has to be *curious* about something—let's say singing—and curious enough to want to explore it and learn more. She becomes *devoted to her interest*. No one has to push her to practice. She does it for love. Mom praises her willingness to work at her passion. The child *persists*, rehearsing in front of the bathroom mirror every day, participating in school talent shows, going to performance camp in the summer. Mom arranges for a singing teacher who stretches her beyond her abilities, inspiring her to practice what she has not mastered. *She tolerates failure* each time she doesn't get it right until she finally does. It is going to take years before she is good enough to become professional, but she is willing to wait because she has *self-control*.

Are these 5 qualities enough to ensure success? While ten thousand hours of practice is critical, Malcolm Gladwell argues in *Outliers* that factors such as luck, culture, heritage, upbringing, and timing also play a key role in achievement. He says that it isn't the intellectually gifted who succeed; it is those "who have been given opportunities and have the strength and presence of mind to seize them." That may be true, but you can't go wrong if you instill these 5 critical qualities in your child.

> In the next chapter, we'll talk about how to build all the Activities and Life Lessons we've discussed into your daily routine, whether your child will be tested in the near future or more than a year from now.

19. How to Get Started

ACTIVITY PLANS EVEN THE BUSIEST PARENTS CAN MANAGE

Special Time, Special Box

When Sam tested so poorly on his first WPPSI, I had just over a year to work with him. Here is what I did. I made a special treasure chest just for him. It was a box covered with gray and black paper and brightly colored pictures of Batman and his archenemies. Sam loved Batman so much that he would beg me to bring out the box so we could play. He was always willing to do any activity that came from the Batman Box. I filled it with materials that I felt were most closely connected with tasks he would be asked to do on his test. Some were Batman related, others weren't. Every night, we had a special 30- to 45-minute Mommy-Sam playtime. We "played" longer than I'm suggesting you do learning activities with your child, but that was because Sam had a lot of catching up to do. Each activity was educational, designed to help him grow developmentally. But to him, it was pure fun.

The lesson I learned from this is that children will do anything that involves something they love. If your child has a favorite character or is obsessed with cars, dinosaurs, Pokémon, princesses, or Polly Pockets, incorporate them into the material that you use during your special time together.

Assess Strengths and Weaknesses

Once I understood the skills Sam would need for the test (language, knowledge/comprehension, memory, mathematics, visual-spatial, cognitive, and fine-motor skills), I tried different activities with him in each area to get an informal assessment of his strengths and weaknesses. In his case, language, knowledge/comprehension, and fine-motor skills were soft spots. The first two made sense to me since he hadn't been hearing well for some time. The third surprised me, but an occupational therapist explained that lots of kids who have hearing problems also have fine- and gross-motor difficulties. I never understood why, but it didn't really matter. His motor skills were weak and we needed to shore them up. In the next section, I've included an informal assessment you can use to get a sense of where your child is with each ability. Later, when you're doing activities together, put extra emphasis on the areas where he seems weakest (while always keeping it fun). If you use this assessment and find that your child is having trouble with language skills (for example), don't assume he has a language or speech disability. Only a trained psychologist or speech pathologist can determine that.

An Informal Ability Assessment

Do these activities with your child over the course of a few days and make note of what he does well and where you think he needs more practice:

LANGUAGE
1. Play "I'm Thinking of Something..." page 105.
2. Do Listening Brain Teasers, page 112, or Talking Puppets, page 113.
3. Read a very simple story to your child and see if she can tell it back to you (stories from Storysmarts.com are ideal).

KNOWLEDGE/COMPREHENSION
4. Using a comprehensive concept book like Richard Scarry's *Best First Book Ever!* as your guide, get a sense of how much your child knows about letters, colors, numbers, body parts, weather, and all the basic information children are typically introduced to by kindergarten.

MEMORY
5. Play Nutty Numbers, page 125.
6. Do Pattern Beading, page 134, or M&Memory Patterns, page 134.

MATHEMATICS
7. See how many Cheerios your child can count.
8. Can your child sort M&Ms by color?
9. Do the Add 'n Subtract Mindbenders, page 137.

VISUAL-SPATIAL REASONING

10. Give your child a piece of paper and a pencil. Can he copy a straight line, a cross, a circle, a square, and a triangle?

11. Play Copy My Pattern, page 141.

COGNITIVE SKILLS

12. Do BrainPlay questions from *Highlights* magazine together, page 151. If you don't have access to the magazine, go to Testingforkindergarten.com and click "Questions to make your child think" for other questions you can use.

FINE-MOTOR SKILLS

13. Give your child a piece of paper and a pencil. Can he write his name?

14. What kind of pencil grip does your child have?

15. Give her a square piece of paper. Can she fold it diagonally into a triangle?

If Your Child Will Not Be Tested for More Than a Year

Follow the **long-term activity schedule** below and introduce activities listed in appendix II little by little over the course of the year. If your child has a test coming up soon, follow the "Express Prep Schedule on page 174.

Long-Term Activity Schedule

WEEK 1: Take note of your child's strengths and weaknesses in areas of verbal, cognitive, memory, mathematics, performance, and fine-motor skills. Review where he is with each *milestone* in chapter 6. Perform the *simple assessment* of your child's abilities.

WEEK 2: Reread chapter 7. Pick up a few *learning tools* that you think your child may enjoy working with: CDs, DVDs, computer software, workbooks, games. Check out some of the free interactive websites and workbook pages mentioned and try them with your child. See how well she does and if she enjoys them.

WEEK 3: Reread chapter 10. This week, make a conscious effort *to talk with your child* about everything and anything in the course of daily life. If your child is already talking, are you having Ping-Pong conversations? If not, be conscious of listening and expanding on what your child says and helping her make connections. Even if she isn't talking yet, you can still respond to her vocalizations and expressions. You can narrate your life and she will absorb much of what you say.

WEEK 4: Reread chapter 7 on *reading aloud* to your child. Watch the video located at Readingrockets.org/shows/roots. Start using dialogic and active reading techniques. Pick up some wordless picture books and let your child read them to you if he's already talking. If not, you can read them to him. Order a bundle of six stories from Storysmarts .com and see how your child does. Keep talking about everything and anything.

WEEK 5: Reread chapter 11. This week, focus on *teaching your child to listen*. When you direct him, are you making sure he responds? When you ask him a question, are you letting him answer? Are you using some of the tools to help your child listen like saying his name, not overrationalizing, and reinforcing your message visually and physically? Are you following through on consequences? Keep talking and reading aloud.

WEEK 6: Reread chapter 9 on *introducing music into your child's life*. Make sure that you are playing all kinds of music at home for your child to hear. Are you singing together and getting him to move to the beat? Is your child able to make sounds with bells, shakers, pots, and wooden spoons? Consider signing him up for an age-appropriate music class or instrument lessons. Keep talking, reading aloud, and teaching listening.

WEEK 7: Reread chapter 12 on *knowledge and comprehension*. Review the basic information a child should be familiar with by the time he starts school. By knowing this, you'll remember to include it when you're talking to him about everything (chapter 10). Do you have concept books you can read together using the dialogic technique? Each day this week, choose one activity from this chapter and do it together. Keep talking, reading aloud, teaching listening, and enjoying music.

WEEK 8: Reread chapter 13 on *building memory*. Each day this week, pick one memory game or activity to try with your child. Keep talking, reading aloud, teaching listening, and enjoying music.

WEEK 9: Reread chapter 14 on *mathematics*. Go back to the milestones and remind yourself where your child's math understanding is so you can start there. Make a special effort to introduce math into your conversations. Do one activity a day from this chapter. Keep talking, reading aloud, teaching listening, and enjoying music.

WEEK 10: Reread chapter 15 on *visual-spatial reasoning.* If you don't have a set of pattern blocks, make your own using Post-it notes. Whether you have parquetry blocks or any of the other materials suggested in the chapter, try making designs and having your child copy what you make. Get an idea of how simple or complex you can go with her. Do puzzles together and assess how complex a puzzle your child can complete. Each day, try an activity in this chapter to get a sense of where she is with visual-spatial skills. Keep talking, reading aloud, teaching listening, and enjoying music.

WEEK 11: Reread chapter 16 on *how to raise a thinking child.* This week, notice whether you are using techniques that encourage independent thinking such as asking *what if* questions, letting your child solve her own problems, and encouraging experimentation? Is your home set up for play? Do you have open-ended toys, art materials, and costumes? If not, look around the house and find things you can use or visit Goodwill to pick up fun costumes and props for fantasy play. If you haven't subscribed to *Highlights* magazine (or *Highlights High Five*), look into it this week. Keep talking, reading aloud, teaching listening, and enjoying music.

WEEK 12: Reread chapter 17 on *building fine-motor skills.* This week, take note of where your child is with her fine-motor skills. How does she hold a pencil or crayon? If she's 3 years old and using an immature grip, try breaking your crayons in half so she'll use her fingers to hold them. How well does she cut with scissors? Let your child flex her fine-motor skills naturally by buttoning her own buttons, combing her hair, eating raisins, and helping you fold laundry. Try one activity a day from this chapter. If you haven't started using workbooks yet, this would be a good week to try one. Keep talking, reading aloud, teaching listening, and enjoying music.

WEEK 13: Reread chapter 18 on *skills to succeed at life.* This week, think about how you can become more conscious of supporting your child's curiosity and helping him learn patience. Notice what activity or subject captures his passion, be it dinosaurs, dance, gymnastics, music, or sports. What are you doing to help him cultivate this interest? Are you reading books on the subject? Is he taking some kind of lessons so he can experience what it's like to get better with practice? Keep talking, reading aloud, teaching listening, and enjoying music.

WEEK 14: By now, having done activities for each ability with your child, you should have a good feel for her strengths and weaknesses and have found some new activities she likes. This week, and for every week that follows, *choose a theme of the week* (a letter, color, number, or concept). During the week, do three to four activities designed to help your child master the week's theme. Besides these, choose one activity a day from appendix II and do it for 10 to 15 minutes. Pick the ones you think your child will especially enjoy, but also pay attention to her areas of weakness and help her learn to tolerate boredom. That seems manageable, right? Don't do it alone; enlist your spouse and caregiver in taking charge of some activities. In weeks 15 through 18, you'll see examples of how you might set up a week of activities.

WEEK 15: This week, we celebrate the letter A. When *declaring a special week*, do activities around the celebrated letter (number/color/concept) such as making a letter book by cutting out pictures of things beginning with A, looking for *A*s in books you read and on signs outside, writing *A*s and *a*s in chalk on the sidewalk, putting an *A* on your child's pancakes in whipped cream—your imagination is the limit.

Monday:	Play the Hokey Pokey to learn body parts, page 120.
Tuesday:	Bake cookies together (math skills) in the shape of *A* (to support our theme).
Wednesday:	Boredom toleration activity for child who avoids puzzles and blocks: For spatial reasoning, using pattern blocks, make patterns and have your child copy them, page 141.
Thursday:	To support thinking, play 5 Reasons Why, page 153.
Friday:	Go to Nickjr.com and play a counting game, page 75.
Saturday:	Play Talking Puppets to build listening skills, page 113.
Sunday:	Play Brain Quest cards for general skill building, page 117.

Keep talking, reading aloud, teaching listening, and enjoying music.

WEEK 16: This week, we celebrate *shapes*. We'll make a shape book, practice drawing shapes with chalk in the sidewalk, and have a shape picnic, page 140.

Monday:	Play "I Spy" Descriptions for language, page 105.
Tuesday:	Play Simon Says to build listening skills, page 111.
Wednesday:	Read a Story Smarts book for preliteracy skills, page 92.
Thursday:	Let your child practice writing her name, page 119.
Friday:	Play Silly Sally or Silly Sammy for memory skills, page 125.
Saturday:	To strengthen math skills, play dominoes, page 137.
Sunday:	Boredom toleration activity for child who avoids puzzles: do puzzles, page 142.

Keep talking, reading aloud, teaching listening, and enjoying music.

WEEK 17: This week, we celebrate the color green. We'll wear something green every day; eat salad, avocados, and green Gummi Bears; put green food coloring in the bathtub; and watch a DVD about colors.

Monday: Sing songs into the microphone for language and music, page 106.

Tuesday: Play "Teach Me Everything You Know About..." for thinking skills, page 153.

Wednesday: Play Family Concentration to build memory, page 126.

Thursday: Make a paper clip necklace for fine-motor skills, page 159.

Friday: Plant flowers to build patience and strengthen sequencing skills, page 166.

Saturday: Visit the beach, a city, or the zoo for knowledge, page 117.

Sunday: Play Robot Voice for preliteracy skills, page 91.

Keep talking, reading aloud, teaching listening, and enjoying music.

WEEK 18: This week, and every week after, *choose a theme for the week*, pick a few supporting activities, and select one activity a day to build a different skill. Keep talking, reading aloud, teaching listening, and enjoying music.

If Your Child Will Be Tested in Less Than a Year

For parents with limited time to prepare a child for an intelligence test, the twenty suggestions below will give you the biggest bang for your buck. All are age-appropriate for kids soon to be tested for kindergarten. Caveat: If your child's informal assessment shows he is particularly weak in verbal skills or visual-spatial abilities (for example), you should practice more activities from those sections in the book. Here are the twenty most important activities I recommend if your time is limited:

Express Prep Schedule

1. **Talk** to your child all the time about everything! Chapter 8.
2. Strengthen **listening and responding** abilities. Chapter 9.
   * Do the **Talking Puppets activity**, page 113.
   * Work with books from **Story Smarts**, by Marion Blank, PhD, and Laura Berlin, PhD, at Storysmarts.com, page 92.
3. **Read aloud** to your child using the *dialogic technique*. Choose books your child will love. Chapter 10.

4. **Free play.** Give your child plenty of time for play. Make sure you have open-ended toys and materials for art and fantasy play. Chapter 16.
5. **Build knowledge.** Pick up a copy of Richard Scarry's *Best First Book Ever!* or DK Publishing's *My First Word Book.* Use this as your guide to what your child should know by the time he tests for kindergarten. To help your child master the basic concepts these books cover, sample some of the media discussed in chapter 7: *educational DVDs, software, free interactive websites, and workbooks.* Teach these basic concepts using the medium to which your child responds best. Also reinforce these concepts through hands-on experiences like going to the grocery store or visiting the zoo.
6. **Play How Many Ways Can You Describe a . . .** page 105.
7. **Play Categories,** page 112.
8. **Play I'm Thinking of Something,** page 105.
9. **Play The $20,000 Pyramid,** page 136.
10. **Play Verbal Analogies,** page 135.
11. **Play 5 Reasons Why,** page 153.
12. **Use Brain Quest Cards,** page 117.
13. **Play with unframed and framed puzzles,** page 142.
14. **Build Math sensibility.** Chapter 14. Build mathematics into your daily interactions at home. By this I mean, make a practice of counting everything out ("You want five Cheerios? Here they are. One, two, three, four, five"), make relative comparisons whenever you can (bigger, smaller, taller, shorter), demonstrate addition and subtraction in mundane actions like giving your child more Cheerios ("You had five Cheerios and we're adding three more. Let's count what you have now. You have eight Cheerios"), or taking away one blanket ("Are you too hot with three blankets? Okay, we'll take one away and now you'll have two blankets").
15. **Use Manipulatives.** Use manipulatives to count, sort, create patterns, and make adding and subtracting concrete. Chapter 14.
16. **Play Copy My Pattern,** page 141.
17. **Read *Highlights* magazine** (or *Highlights High Five*). Chapter 13. Have fun with the jokes, riddles, stories, and doing various activities, especially hidden pictures and BrainPlay.
18. **Practice Fine-motor Skills.** Chapter 17. Give your child plenty of practice drawing basic shapes, letters, and people with pencil, chalk, and crayons. Make sure your child can execute simple fine-motor actions such as cutting shapes with blunt scissors, folding paper, tying a simple knot, and writing his name.
19. **Play Nutty Numbers** for verbal memory, page 125. **Play Family Concentration** and **What's Missing** for visual memory, page 126.
20. **Use workbooks,** page 75. Workbooks offered by Thinkingtolearn.com and the Brain Quest workbooks are good for test preparation.

TEST-SPECIFIC PREPARATION

If your child will be taking one of the more common tests described in this book, look it over and see if there is anything particular you might want to practice with her. For example, the Stanford-Binet has a visual absurdities subtest, so you would want your child to work with the one of the What's Wrong books suggested on page 127. The Stanford-Binet also evaluates verbal absurdities, so you would want to play the game "Silly Sally" or "Silly Sammy" that is described on page 125 with her. The WPPSI has a Picture Completion subtest, so you would want her to work with one of the What's Missing books suggested on page 126. If your child is taking the OLSAT, be sure to do the practice test that is currently available at: http://schools.nyc.gov/Documents/Offices/GT/LevADOE.pdf.

In the event that the NYC schools change the test they give for TAG programs (this happens regularly), you can still check their website to see if they put up a practice test for a different assessment instrument. Go to: Schools.nyc .gov/Academics/GiftedandTalented.

Free Daily Practice Test Questions

If you'd like to receive daily IQ test prep questions for children ages 3 to 5 (they should take about a minute), go to Testingforkindergarten.com and subscribe.

Part III

What These Tests Really Mean

HOW YOUR CHILD'S TEST SCORES WILL AFFECT THE OPTIONS AVAILABLE TO HER

In this section of the book, you will learn:

★ How to know if your child is gifted.

★ Where to learn about the best talented and gifted (TAG) programs in your community.

★ How to get your child into a competitive TAG program or magnet school.

★ Strategies to improve your child's chances of getting into a top private school.

★ Why your child's assessment in public kindergarten can limit or expand opportunities for her entire education—and what you can do about it!

★ How tests are used to assess developmental delays and learning disabilities.

★ What to do if your child has delays: how to benefit from government-funded services, including doctors, teachers, therapists, and even private special-needs school.

20. Your Best Public School Options

GIFTED PROGRAMS, MAGNET AND CHARTER SCHOOLS

The Gifted Child

I hope I'm not bursting your bubble, but chances are good that your child isn't a genius. He's probably not even gifted. Remember the bell curve we talked about earlier? Well, most of us (me, you, our kids included) fall somewhere in the middle. Don't cry. We can still live happy and productive lives.

To identify giftedness in children (and conversely, learning disabilities), a good educational psychologist will rely on more than just a test score. She will interview the parents to get a detailed picture of the child's history, ask them to complete questionnaires and checklists that would help identify giftedness, and talk to them in depth about why they think their child may be gifted. She will gather similar information from the child's preschool and other teachers. Using all of this information, along with her clinical judgment, she will be able to give a detailed assessment of a child's cognitive, academic, and social-emotional abilities.

> **THE GIFTED CHILD**
>
> Children who are gifted tend to have many of the following characteristics, although not necessarily all of them:
>
> - progresses rapidly through developmental milestones (e.g., instead of knowing 300 words at age 3, knows 1,000)
> - learns quickly, easily, and with great depth
> - experiences development that may be uneven, excelling more in one area than another

- has high verbal abilities including an extensive vocabulary
- has a great storehouse of information and knowledge
- may teach himself to read early
- prefers factual books to fiction or fairy tales
- highly curious, seeks information and knowledge for its own sake
- always asking *how*, *why*, and *what if*
- highly observant with an eye for detail
- has an excellent memory
- shows reasoning, logical thinking, and creativity in academics and play
- is an original thinker, combining information and ideas in unexpected ways
- loves to experiment and solve problems
- generates many ideas and solutions to problems
- demonstrates an unusual facility for numbers, calculates in her head
- readily grasps underlying principles and can make valid generalizations
- works independently and concentrates for long periods on things that interest him
- demonstrates leadership, initiative, and perseverance
- is good with numbers, puzzles, blocks
- may collect things
- has a good sense of humor, loves riddles and verbal humor
- prefers older companions
- may struggle with easy material while thriving on complexity
- is emotionally sensitive
- is highly energetic

When my children were little, I was sure they were gifted until I learned more about kids who were the real deal. Let me introduce you to a few young brainiacs whom I don't know personally but have read about in newspapers that profiled them because they are so extraordinary. When we talk about genuinely gifted children, this is what we're talking about:

- ★ At 2, Georgia Brown, after seeing the musical *Beauty and the Beast,* told her parents, "I didn't like Gaston [the villain]. He was mean and arrogant."
- ★ Before he was 2, Jonathan Estrada was shaping all fifty states out of cheese slices and indicating where the state capital was with a bite mark (he made Utah and Rhode Island on David Letterman's show).
- ★ Chyrese Exline didn't utter a word until she was almost 2. But when she did, she spoke perfectly and already knew her colors and letters, and could read.

* Terry Tao mastered all elementary school math while still in kindergarten. At 7, he could discuss Boolean algebra, abelian groups, and other advanced math concepts. Frankly, I don't even know what those are.

Terry's father, Dr. Billy Tao, an Australian pediatrician who raised three profoundly gifted sons, talked about ordinary smarts versus extraordinary genius in a *Weekend Australian* article. "There is a difference between genius and people who are just bright. The genius will look at things, try things, do things totally unexpectedly. It's higher-order thinking. Genius is beyond talent. It's something very original, very hard to fathom." I would say that shaping cheese slices into states and biting out the capitals at age 2 qualifies, wouldn't you?

Being Gifted Isn't Always a Gift

So your child isn't technically gifted. It's not the end of the world. In fact, some would say it is a gift for a child *not* to be gifted. There *is* a downside, you know.

In a study of 282 geniuses, including Voltaire, Lincoln, Descartes, and Michelangelo, researchers Keith Simonton and Anna Song found that superior intelligence was linked to inferior physical health during youth. The philosopher Descartes, for example, was so sickly as a child that his parents let him sleep until noon. Later he said that those mornings were when he came up with his best ideas. Perhaps being sickly as a kid helps build intellectual development, but who wants their child to suffer poor health?

Children with exceptionally high IQs are different from other kids and have trouble fitting in, often getting picked on. Children make fun of them, calling them "dweebs," "nerds," and "Herbs." We live in a society that values beauty and brawn over brains. The current trend, fueled by resource limitations, is to educate gifted students in regular classrooms, which may magnify the social issues.

Finding the right school situation for a highly gifted child can be daunting. Consider a 5-year-old who reads like a 10-year-old, plays chess like a 15-year-old, has mastered algebra, but shares her toys like a 3-year-old. Do you homeschool her? Accelerate her a few grades? Put her in kindergarten but place her in higher-grade classes for reading and math? With the wrong placement, children like this may get bored and act out in class or give up altogether.

In this country there are as many school-age kids with IQs above 145 as below 55. Yet our schools spend $8 billion a year on remedial programs and $800 million on gifted education. Savvy parents with bright but not technically gifted children manage to get their kids a slice of that $800-million pie, while only 20 percent of kids evaluated as truly gifted find their way into them. Personally, I don't envy any parent of a highly gifted child trying to find the appropriate learning environment. It's as complicated as finding the right classroom for a learning disabled child. If your little one hasn't emerged as an Einstein by age 4, it's okay. Even Einstein didn't even emerge as an Einstein by that age.

TAG Programs Vary But Are Always in Demand

Earlier I mentioned a California study showing that children in gifted programs make 36.7 percent more progress each year than kids in regular classrooms. Since these are often the best public education alternatives, competition can be fierce. Gifted programs vary widely from city to city. Let me give you the lay of the land and tell you how to go about finding what's available in your community, along with some tips on how to get your child in.

Under the Individuals with Disabilities Education Act (IDEA), every state requires that schools provide special education for students diagnosed with physical, mental, or learning disabilities. That is not so for gifted students. Many states, but not all, require that gifted children be identified; some states, but not all, mandate that they be served. Where state law requires the creation of gifted programs, details such as what defines "giftedness" and how qualified students will be educated are left up to the local districts. States that don't mandate the creation of gifted programs may still have discretionary funds that can be used for that purpose. For this reason, there is a hodgepodge of offerings across the country, no agreed-upon definition of "giftedness," and often befuddling admissions criteria that leave many deserving children out in the cold.

Gifted programs are usually referred to as TAG (talented and gifted) or GATE (gifted and talented education) programs. With a limited number of public TAG programs in each district, many deserving children are turned away. Last year, 5,800 children applied for 28 spots in a Chicago gifted kindergarten class. At Hunter College Elementary, one of the oldest schools for gifted students, thousands of students took the entrance exam for 48 kindergarten spots. In Manhattan, applications to the city's gifted programs tripled in 2007. Lately, the competition for places has gotten even tougher for a number of reasons:

* ★ **The economy.** With the economic downturn, families who would otherwise have sent their children to private schools are seeking the best options that public schools have to offer: TAG programs.
* ★ **Better education.** Gifted programs have long served as a middle-class haven from overcrowded or underperforming public schools.
* ★ **Public focus on bottom 25 percent.** Public school teachers used to teach to the needs of children in the 50th percentile. Ever since the passage of the federal No Child Left Behind (NCLB) Act, teachers are shifting their focus to the bottom 25th percentile. A University of Chicago study recently concluded that NCLB pushes teachers to ignore high-ability students through its exclusive focus on bringing struggling students to minimum proficiency.

Types of Programs and Accommodations

Budget considerations have a lot to do with the depth and breadth of public gifted programs everywhere. As districts face financial hard times, gifted programs, often seen as a luxury, are the first to be trimmed, gutted, or cut out. Within a given district, there may be:

1. Magnet schools that serve only gifted children
2. Schools-within-a-school model, where a separate gifted school operates inside a regular school's facility
3. Self-contained gifted classrooms within a regular school
4. Pull-out classes for gifted students taught by specially trained teachers (who often split their time among many schools in a district)
5. Accelerated groupings within regular classrooms, where the teacher offers alternative assignments or independent or group projects for higher-performing students
6. Before- or after-school enrichment programs.

For children who are highly gifted (145+ IQ), but whose school districts don't offer an appropriate program, schools may provide:

1. Independent projects
2. Online replacement curricula (with remote access to teacher) that children can do independently
3. Multiple-age ability groupings

4. Entire grade skipping
5. Specific class grade skipping.

Some cities have private TAG schools, such as Ricks Center for Gifted Children in Denver, Colorado, and the Rocky Mountain School for the Gifted in Boulder, Colorado. Other programs, like Hunter College Elementary, are affiliated with teachers colleges as opposed to public school districts. In cities with multiple programs, some are more coveted than others. In New York City, for example, the Lab School and the Anderson Program (both public), and Hunter College Elementary (college affiliated) are considered the crème de la crème of gifted programs. These have higher minimum cutoff scores than the less-coveted gifted programs. To be considered, children must score in the 97th or 98th percentile (moderately gifted) versus 90th percentile (high average) for the city's other TAG programs. The Davidson Academy in Reno, Nevada, one of the country's top public gifted programs, requires IQ scores of 145 (highly gifted) or above to be considered for admission.

If after testing in the top 2 to 3 percent and a thorough assessment, an educational psychologist pronounces your child intellectually gifted, you are going to have to work very hard to find an appropriately challenging program to meet his needs. With many TAG programs opening up to serve a wider range of intelligence, fewer programs exist to educate children with extremely high academic ability. I would suggest that you talk to the psychologist who tested your child or find an expert in gifted children who can map out a course of learning and recommend local programs that might work for someone with his intellectual profile. Two websites that offer extremely helpful advice to parents facing this challenge are Davidsongifted.org and Hoagiesgifted.org. An excellent book on understanding profound giftedness is *Gifted Children: Myths and Realities*, by Ellen Winner.

QUALIFICATIONS FOR GIFTEDNESS VARY

The research is solid that children scoring in the 97th percentile and above and those scoring in the 3rd percentile and below need specially trained teachers. That said, programs with cutoffs at the 97th percentile and above are becoming fewer and farther between. Offering what some see as an "elite" education to children who already have the advantage of a high IQ doesn't sit well politically in some circles.

Many people feel that testing children for admission to gifted programs is unfair given the evidence that intelligence tests are biased against children from disadvantaged homes who have not had the same life experiences and preschool education as children from middle-class and affluent families. To equalize access, districts are casting a wider net by expanding their definition of giftedness or giving more credit to bright children from diverse or economically disadvantaged backgrounds. Here are some ways they are going about it:

★ Hernando County, Florida. Students with an IQ of 120 (high average) qualify for gifted status if they come from a low socioeconomic level or if English isn't their first language.

★ Denver, Colorado. To qualify for gifted status, educators consider a student's test scores along with teacher assessments and nominations. They get extra points if English is their second language or if they receive federal meal benefits. Conceivably, a student scoring in the 75th percentile (average) on an IQ test could be considered for a gifted program.

★ Raleigh, North Carolina. Offers gifted and talented magnet schools, but that doesn't mean the students are *academically* gifted. Here schools are "seeking to find the gifts and talents of every student."

★ Districts are offering magnet programs for creatively gifted children in areas of music, art, and performance (such as the Special Music School in New York City) in addition to programs for the intellectually gifted.

★ Districts are broadening their definition of "gifted" to include lower-scoring students who can be characterized as "bright," "high-achieving," "high ability," or "talented" and considering factors besides test scores for admission. Some districts have abandoned the "gifted" label altogether because it they find it condemning to children who are left out.

WHAT DOES THIS MEAN FOR YOU?

With so many gifted programs expanding their criteria for entry, your child may qualify for a TAG or enrichment program (or whatever your district calls it) even if he doesn't score in the top 2 percent to 3 percent on his IQ test. These tend to offer the highest quality curricula within districts and are worth exploring.

TIPS FOR GETTING YOUR CHILD INTO A TAG PROGRAM

★ **Do your research.** Gifted programs vary so much from city to city and district to district that it is incumbent upon you to dig deeply and identify the best programs for which your child may qualify. Researching programs isn't easy. Public TAG programs are constantly being revamped, rules for admissions may change, and administrators with the right answers can be hard to find.

★ **Use online resources.** By Googling "gifted and talented programs in [your city]," you should get a list of the choices available. Or visit the National Association for Gifted and Talented Children's website (nagc.org), where you will find a list of state associations for gifted programs. Someone at your state association should be able to direct you to your local options. Another excellent resource is the Gifted Development Center in Denver, Colorado. You can visit their website at Gifted development.com.

★ **Start early.** The application process for the most selective schools usually starts in September of the year *before* your child would enter a program. Most schools have limited open house and tour dates, so you want to sign up for these and get them on your calendar. Call the school and find out how to apply and any application deadlines that you need to meet. Make sure your child meets the birthday cutoff.

★ **Talk to parents, teachers, and guidance counselors.** Talk to other parents in your community who may have had experience with local TAG programs, along with teachers at your child's preschool. If you call the school for which you are zoned and ask to speak to the guidance counselor, she should be able to give you information about gifted programs for which your child might be eligible. Be a little careful here, however. Sometimes school officials aren't as helpful as they could be because they are concerned about losing children, which means losing public funding, and especially losing children who do well on tests and have involved parents.

★ **Check your district's website.** Your school district's website should also have a section for gifted programs. Explore it to see what is available, the requirements for application, and criteria for acceptance. If a test is mandated, the website should tell you which test and how to sign up. Often there are application deadlines, so check this out as soon as possible.

★ **Consider applying outside your zone.** TAG programs are usually magnet schools, and these tend to allow application outside your zone. Applying outside your zone will give you more options to consider. Check your local rules.

★ **The application process will vary.** Most academic TAG programs use IQ and readiness tests for qualification. The list of instruments relied upon is extensive, but the intellectual skills these tests appraise are almost always the same seven abilities we have been talking about. Most schools will consider only children who make their cutoff score. In some districts, the score alone is enough to guarantee a place. In others, the child may be invited for interviews and further evaluation. Parents and preschool teachers may also be asked to complete questionnaires about the child's interests, developmental history, and qualities of giftedness, which will be considered in the admissions decision.

★ **Don't be modest.** If you are asked to complete a parent questionnaire giving examples of your child's abstract reasoning and analytical abilities, interests, talents, curiosity, self-motivation, persistence, verbal skills, memory, and self-direction, don't be modest. Include stories that will bring your child to life on paper. (See page 195 for an example of how to do this.) If your application asks for a parent statement, explain anything special your child brings to the school (e.g., diversity), why he is a good fit for that particular program, and why you, as parents, would be assets to the school (e.g., volunteering, fund-raising). With some schools that won't make a bit of difference, but with others, it will.

★ **Tell your child what to expect.** If the school requires follow-up testing or a school visit, ask someone at the school to tell you exactly what will happen. Let your child know what to expect so he won't be surprised. You probably won't be told what will happen inside the testing room since that's usually a big secret. However, they should tell you generally what the visit will be like, how long it will last, and the kinds of things your child will be doing.

★ **Set your child up for a good visit.** If your child has trouble separating from you, let your husband or babysitter take him. Bring something to read or do with him while you are waiting. Let him know that he is going to visit a school you are considering for him, but reassure him that he won't be going there for a long time (otherwise, he'll worry about having to leave his beloved preschool now). Tell your child to listen to the teacher and do what she says, have fun, and consider if he might like to go to this school in the future. Try not to show any stress. It's out of your hands now. You can't control what your 4-year-old does behind closed doors.

Charter and Magnet Schools

In most cities, parents have options to enroll their children in charter and magnet schools in addition to their local public school. *Charter schools* are created by private groups (companies, parents, teachers, community groups, or nonprofit organizations) who submit and get a charter approved to run their own school. They receive public money (except for their facilities) and offer unique learning environments. They are small and approved to operate for a limited period of time, usually three to five years, after which their charter can be renewed if they meet their goals. Because they are managed separately from the district, they are freer to innovate, try different instructional practices, lengthen the school day or school year, dismiss underperforming teachers, and experiment with merit pay. Charter schools tend not to have competitive admissions criteria, but they are often in demand so they will have lotteries or first-come, first-served policies.

Magnet schools are public schools offering specialized and theme-based curricula, such as programs that focus on leadership, writing, international studies, language, creative arts, and museums, for example. They may offer a particular teaching method such as Montessori or one based on Howard Gardner's Multiple Intelligence theory, or they may serve children with special talents. TAG schools are almost always magnet programs. One magnet school in Wake County, North Carolina, offers a gifted program that is based on the belief that "every child has gifts and talents to nurture." There is no test for entry, and they offer classes that would spark the passions of many kids, such as Kitchen Chemistry, New Wings to Rocket Boosters, Theater Games, and Architectural Design.

About one-third of magnet schools have competitive entry requirements. These may take the form of intelligence, creativity, or learning style tests, or an interview or audition. Other magnet schools use lotteries, first-come, first-served applications, or percentage set-asides (a certain percentage of the students must come from the neighborhood) for admissions.

TIPS FOR GETTING YOUR CHILD INTO A MAGNET OR CHARTER SCHOOL

★ **Do your research.** Magnet and charter programs vary from city to city and district to district. Do a Google search of "magnet or charter schools in [your city]." Most of the programs in your area will come up. Since these schools are part of public school districts, a search of your local school district's website will also have information on magnet and charter schools to consider. Two good sources for more information are Magnet.edu and Uscharterschools.org.

★ **Start in September, a year before your child will enroll.** Most schools have limited spaces for open house and tour dates, so you want to sign up for these and get them on your calendar. Call the schools that interest you and find out how to apply and any application deadlines that you will need to meet. Make sure your child meets the birthday cutoff.

* **Learn how they make admissions decisions.** Lottery? First-come, first-served? Percentage set-asides? Waiting lists? If you have additional children, do they offer a sibling preference?
* **For magnet schools, learn about admissions criteria.** If your child has to test, audition, or interview, make arrangements for that. Ask how the school evaluates applicants and makes admissions decisions.
* **Talk to people in the know.** Your nursery school director, teachers, and parents in your neighborhood may be able to give you firsthand information about local magnet and charter schools.
* **Consider the fit.** Think about your own child and how she learns best. A school that sounds great on paper may not be a great fit for your child.
* **Consider diversity.** Most magnet and charter schools are committed to making their program available to students from a wide variety of ethnic backgrounds and income levels. What is the demographic and socioeconomic makeup of the school you're considering?
* **Who do you know?** If you happen to know someone who works at the school where you're trying to get your child admitted, ask them if they can help. It is not unheard-of for administrators to pull strings to get their friend's children admitted to their schools. I know you're shocked to hear this. I was once considering an in-demand public school for Schuyler. The registrar told me, "Sorry, the application deadline has passed," and she wasn't willing to take our application. Just then, I saw a friend who (to my surprise) was a guidance counselor there. She took me aside and said, "No problem. If you want Schuyler to go here, she's in. I'll take care of it." Ultimately, we did not choose this school, but if we'd wanted it, the fix was in. It's unfair, but it happens.

For What to Look For and Questions to Ask When Touring a TAG, Magnet, or Charter School, see pages 196 and 197.

Have a "Safety" Public School

This is enormously important whether you are trying for a TAG program, magnet, charter, or private school. You never know what's going to happen as you go through the admissions process. In every city, there are excellent public schools that would work for your child, if only for one year while you come up with a better option. In some cases you must live in the zone to get in. Other districts have lotteries to determine who can apply. And others will consider variances, allowing you to apply outside your zone. As you explore gifted, magnet, and charter programs, identify a public school that your child absolutely can attend. Many will require that you apply by a certain date to be guaranteed a place, and you don't want to miss that opportunity should your other school options fall through.

> In the next chapter, we'll talk about how to increase your child's chances of getting into a competitive private school.

21. Getting Past the Velvet Rope

PRIVATE SCHOOL ADMISSIONS

To go private or not to go private? That is the question. Every year parents must decide whether 'tis nobler to suffer the slings and arrows of outrageous tuition or take their chances in the public school system. When I had my business, clients deciding between public and private kindergarten would ask which I'd recommend. While some people would disagree, my view was if money is no object, choose private. The facilities are almost always better, the classes are smaller, more subjects are offered, teachers aren't required to teach to standardized tests, the curriculum is more flexible, and the "extras" are unequaled. However, if money is an object (and for most of us it is), go with the very best public school you can. Do your research and get your child into an excellent gifted, magnet, charter, or regular public school at least through fifth or sixth grade. You can rethink your decision for middle and high school, but you will have saved well over $100,000 in after-tax dollars (more in some markets). Besides, public schools do have advantages. They are free, their student bodies are more diverse, and their teachers are usually paid more than private school teachers so they often attract more experienced staff.

Let's say money is no object for you or maybe it is, but you're willing to do whatever it takes to put your child in private school. If you live in a competitive market, get ready for a wild ride. Every year, normally sane parents lose touch with the voice of reason as they hear rumors of "fifty applicants for every spot" or "two hundred families didn't get in anywhere." As the stomach churns, a few mothers and fathers turn into those embarrassing caricatures you read about, like the father who engaged an acting coach to help his "blah" 4-year-old interview better or the parents who showed up at their daughter's interview with a PowerPoint presentation on all that their daughter and family would bring to the school if accepted.

It is important to understand that if your child doesn't get into the school of your choice, it may have nothing to do with him or your family. Schools often have too many applications for a limited number of spaces. After making room for siblings, legacies, and diversity candidates, the remaining spaces have to be divided to equalize the number of boys and girls in a class. The odds can be daunting. If your child does get into private school, chances are it's a good match. As difficult as the application process can be, it works. While parents may be displeased about not getting their first-choice school, they are often astonished at how right the final outcome turns out to be.

Unlike TAG programs, the process for applying to private kindergartens tends to be similar across the country. It usually begins in September a year before your child would actually start school. Find out the date when you can call for an application or whether you can get one online. There are schools that give out a limited number of apps, so don't dawdle. In competitive markets, schools have been known to stop taking applications before the announced cutoff. If the school you want is in demand, apply early.

In some cities, you *do* have to put children on wait lists years earlier just to be eligible to apply when they're old enough, so you should talk to other parents and call the schools that you think may interest you early on. Even if you have no idea what you'll want when your child is ready, put yourself on the list so at least you'll have the option.

While my focus here is on getting into kindergarten, the process to apply for other grades is only slightly different. Here is what most schools require:

1. An application (which may include essay questions for parents)
2. Parent tours
3. Parent interviews
4. Child interviews
5. Test scores
6. Nursery school report
7. Letters of recommendation (not all schools require these)

Admissions directors may also consider your family's religion if the school has a religious component, siblings and legacies, diversity of the child and parents, and first-choice letters. Unofficially, some schools consider the family's donor potential, their social circles and accomplishments (e.g., extra points for being a movie star or mayor, or owning a restaurant where next year's gala event can be held). I'm pretty sure the Obama girls tested well when they applied to Sidwell Friends, but I assure you they got extra points because their father was about to become president.

In some cities, during the application process, your nursery school director will offer you counsel and even advocate for your child in the end. In those cases, remember that she has thirty children to place, so she may not always be giving you impartial advice where your interest conflicts with another family's (e.g., you both have the same first-choice school and they have room for only one kid from your child's class). If you are homeschooling your child or if he goes to a nursery program where the director doesn't help with placement, you'll have to be your child's advocate through the process. In larger markets, you can hire a school advisor who will assist you (just as I used to advise families). They can be an enormous help behind the scenes because they've seen it all. Caveat: If you've just moved to a city and you're using an advisor, you can be open about it. If you're not new to the city, keep the fact that you have an advisor to yourself. In those circumstances, it's usually not looked on favorably by admissions directors.

It's About Fit: How to Decide Where to Apply

The number of schools you'll want to apply to varies by city. In competitive markets like Manhattan, LA, or San Francisco, parents apply to as many as ten schools. In cities like Dallas or Denver, where fewer families choose private schools, you need apply to only a handful.

Consider what you want in a kindergarten and lower school.

- ★ Do you want a coed or single-sex school? If your city has single-sex schools, I suggest you visit one. I've seen many families who were adamantly against them change their mind after touring.
- ★ Do you want a school with a religious component?
- ★ Does location matter? Busing can be expensive.
- ★ Do you want a program that goes all the way through high school?
- ★ Do you want your child to wear a uniform?
- ★ Will you need financial aid? Does this school offer it?

People always used to ask me, "What's the best school in Manhattan?" The truth is, the best school is the one that is the right fit for your child and family. Schuyler struggled with learning issues. Many people considered Dalton or Spence the "best" schools in the city. For Schuyler, they would have been terrible. Finding the right fit for your child's unique character and learning style will lead to a positive school experience. How do you determine fit? Ask yourself . . .

* In what kind of environment would my child thrive? Traditional and structured? Progressive and creative? Small or large?
* Has she shown an interest in the arts, athletics, dance, or music? Does one school have a great program in her area of interest?
* Is there a particular school culture where *you'd* feel more comfortable? Each school has its own personality that should fit your family's like a puzzle piece. These are the people whose children will become your child's friends, and their values and lifestyles will affect who your child becomes. You will make friends with these children's parents when volunteering in the classroom or for fund-raisers. Are you most comfortable in an upscale, elitist environment? Down-to-earth progressive? Multicultural? Social? Artistic? Traditional? Conservative? Liberal?
* Are there values you seek in a school? Community-service oriented? Intellectual? Nurturing? Competitive? Academic excellence? Athletics? Commitment to diversity?
* When you visit the school, how "at home" do you feel? Listen to your gut. In NYC, everyone used to tell me that Spence was the "best" girl's school. It is situated in the privileged world of the Upper East Side in a gorgeous mansion and, yes, it is a fabulous program. But I'm downtown through and through. I knew when I toured that I would feel out of place there, and it wasn't the environment where I wanted my daughter to grow up. I'm sure that if any of the Spence parents there had toured the progressive, no-dress-code downtown school that we did choose, they would have felt as out of place as I did in their school.

Don't apply only to the prestigious programs. Schools have reputations that are often based on park bench gossip and outdated information. Schools you've heard other people snub their noses at could be the perfect fit. Schools you hear are a direct pipeline to Harvard may not be that at all and may be the worst possible fit for your child. Judge each school for yourself.

Have a "Safety" Public School

I said this to families considering competitive public programs and I'll say it you: In every city, there are excellent public, magnet, and charter schools that would work for your child. As you explore private schools, research your local public school options and find one that your child can definitely attend.

Your College Essay Flashback: The Application

If there are essay questions, here are some hints on handling these:

* Keep your answers short, maybe half a page per question. You can type your answer on a separate sheet of paper.
* Make sure you answer the question(s) they ask.
* Your goal is to leave an emotional impression with the director, to convey the qualities that make your child special, and to demonstrate how those attributes translate into a good match for the school. After the director reads your essays, you want her to feel that this child and family would be an asset to her program.
* Hit the school's hot buttons. If it is known for its athletic program, talk about your child's interest in sports. If it has a strong music department, mention that your child has played violin since she was 2 (she has, hasn't she?).
* Back up your points with short personal stories that will bring your child to life on the page. For example:

Wing is passionate about cars. He'll draw them, play with them, set up pretend car washes for them and he knows the name of every make of car on the road. Last summer, Wing spent one month in Korea, and by the end of the month, he knew the names of all the Korean cars, too. He has a keen memory not only for cars but for everything he sees and hears. Recently, we went to a restaurant that we had visited once before as a family, about a year and a half ago. He lit up when we went inside and reminded us of the last time we ate there, the family we had been with, and even what my mother had been wearing. He has always had a great memory for music. At 16 months, he began humming the melodies of classical music he would hear. Today, he knows many classical songs that he can hum perfectly. When Wing was around 3, we noticed that tears would come to his eyes whenever he heard a sad aria. It is touching that a boy as young as Wing can so deeply appreciate music. Wing now takes violin lessons so he can make music himself.

★ If you are having trouble getting started, pretend you are writing a letter to a friend who doesn't know your child and answer the questions in the application. The words and stories will come more easily.

★ If there are several essays, examine the impact your series of answers will make as a group.

★ Check for misspellings and grammatical errors.

A Peek Behind the Curtain: School Tours

★ Tours are a must. A school may sound perfect by reputation, but when you arrive, your instinct may tell you it's not a good fit. The most important question to ask is, "Can I imagine my child learning and being happy in this environment?"

★ Be on your best behavior. Even if a parent is leading the tour, she will probably report back to the admissions director on the parents she met.

★ Don't take notes. Turn off your cell phone.

★ Don't ask questions that might insult the tour guide. For example, avoid asking if the school has a drug problem or if there have been any drive-by shootings. You laugh, but I've had parents ask these questions when I led tours of my children's schools.

★ When you're touring, don't monopolize the group with your questions. Since so many things to look for and questions to ask are the same whether you are touring a private or public school, I have combined the list below for both sets of parents:

WHAT TO LOOK FOR WHEN YOU TOUR A SCHOOL

★ How welcoming is the school toward parents?

★ Do you like the atmosphere? Is it warm and nurturing? Formal and structured?

★ Is the building well maintained and clean? Are bathrooms clean? Is the school orderly and neat?

★ Does it have all the facilities that are important to you? A gym? A pool? Outdoor space? Dance studio? Art room? Theater? Computer labs? Playground?

★ How big are the classes?

★ How do students behave as they move through the hallways or play outside?

- ★ Are the children engaged and interested? Do they seem courteous, happy, and disciplined?
- ★ Are teachers warm and enthusiastic?
- ★ Are the classrooms light, cheerful, and filled with interesting materials?
- ★ What is the work on display like? Does the artwork allow for individual creativity or is everyone making the same-shaped bowl? Are the children already writing?
- ★ Is there a cafeteria? Does the teacher stay with the little ones at lunch? How nutritionally balanced is the food? Is it good?
- ★ Is the student body diverse? Are the teachers diverse?
- ★ What are the parents like at drop-off? Are they working parents or stay-at-home moms? If you work and they don't, would you feel comfortable?
- ★ How safe do you feel? Do they have good security?
- ★ Do students wear uniforms? If not, are you comfortable with the dress code?
- ★ What is your gut reaction to this school? Can you see your child being happy there?

QUESTIONS TO ASK WHILE TOURING OR MEETING WITH SCHOOL PERSONNEL

- ★ **Private school.** What is the mission or educational philosophy of this school?
- ★ **TAG program.** How does your school approach gifted education? How is it different from the curriculum offered in general classrooms?
- ★ **Magnet school.** How is the school's magnet theme incorporated into the school environment?
- ★ **Charter school.** Can you tell me more about your charter? How is this school different from a typical public school? Can I get a copy of your latest performance report?
- ★ **Private, TAG, magnet school.** How do you evaluate children for admission? If there is a test, which one is it and how to do I arrange for my child to take it? Are there follow-up interviews?
- ★ **Public school.** How do your students' test scores compare to those of other schools? Have scores been rising or falling in the past few years?
- ★ **Private school.** How do your students perform on standardized tests? (You probably can't get comparisons between local private schools on these.)
- ★ **Private school:** What is your endowment? How do you raise money? Do you give scholarships?
- ★ **Public school:** Do you raise money for special programs or equipment?
- ★ **All schools:** What are the administration's highest priorities?

* How long has the principal or school head been in her job? How does she interact with the students?
* Is there a strong sense of community here?
* What are the highlights of your school's curriculum in math, reading, science, and social studies?
* How do you integrate art, technology, music, and creativity into your core curriculum?
* How do you address different ability levels in reading and math? If kids are grouped by ability, how frequently are they reassessed and moved to different ability levels?
* Do you offer physical education? Visual arts? Music? Language? How often?
* What is a daily schedule like?
* Do you have a special philosophy for learning and teaching? How is it put into practice in the classroom?
* How much homework is given? When does it begin? How long are students supposed to spend on homework each night?
* Do families here tend to use tutors?
* How many children per class? Are there assistant teachers?
* How do you encourage and monitor a student's progress?
* Do kids work in small groups or spend most of their time in full-class instruction?
* How experienced are the teachers? What is the turnover rate? What kinds of professional development opportunities do they have?
* How often do you have parent-teacher conferences?
* (For K-12 programs) Where do your graduates go to college?
* Do children do community service? What kind?
* Are there programs for learning-disabled or gifted students?
* Is there an after-school enrichment program? What is it like? What does it cost?
* Is there child care before or after school? What does it cost?
* Is transportation available? Is there a cost?
* How do you keep the students secure? How safe is the neighborhood?
* What would happen if there were an emergency? Can you tell me about the plans you have in place?
* Can you talk about the diversity of the school? Is there a commitment to strengthening it?
* In the current economy, what kind of cutbacks have you had to make?
* How involved are parents in school? What types of volunteer opportunities do you offer?

- ★ Are there any events coming up that we could attend that would help us get a feeling for the school and community (e.g., a play, holiday show, spring fair)? If yes, you should definitely go to get a better feel for the school.

Just Be Yourself: Parent Interviews

- ★ Parent interviews vary from short and sweet to long and in-depth. Usually directors interview one set of parents at a time, but sometimes they will conduct group meetings.
- ★ Both parents should attend if at all possible. Both should speak.
- ★ Be positive. Be yourself. Be concise.
- ★ Don't call the director by her first name unless she introduces herself that way and you've noticed that the staff calls each other by their first names.
- ★ As with the tour, be on time and turn off your cell phone.
- ★ Do not name-drop, go over the director's head by calling her boss, or talk about how much money you would donate if accepted.
- ★ Dress appropriately to the school. Don't overdo it with jewelry or obvious designer accessories.
- ★ Schedule interviews for the schools you most want toward the end of the process. You'll be more practiced and the director will remember you.
- ★ Your job is to make the director like you. Period. I remember an interview we had at our first-choice school for Schuyler. The assistant director (also a coach) interviewed us. He and my husband talked about the school track team the entire time, which threw me. But they accepted Schuyler. If your interview feels more like an engaging conversation than a formal exchange, you've done well.
- ★ Your child can still be accepted if the assistant director interviews you. If you want to increase your chances of meeting with the director, ask for her by name when you schedule the appointment.
- ★ Think of this as a job interview. Give the director a good firm handshake and make eye contact. Demonstrate that you know your child well. When you interview, act as though each school were your first choice, and you will more easily show your sense of humor, enthusiasm, warmth, intelligence, and interest. Your goal is to be offered a space. You can always say no.
- ★ As with a job interview, be prepared. Read the catalog or website so you don't ask questions that are obvious (e.g., "Is this an all-girls school?"). Don't give generic answers that could just as easily have come from any other parent. The director will ask you, "Why our school?" Think ahead of time about the two or three

aspects of their program that are most attractive to you and how your particular child will benefit from them. Expect to be asked: "Tell me about your child." For this, prepare a few memorable stories that will help the director know your child and remember your family.

★ If you have a situation that might be perceived negatively, strategize ahead of time how to talk about it. For example, if your child has a learning disability, should you mention it? If you're in the middle of a difficult divorce and your soon-to-be ex isn't with you, what do you say? Talk to your nursery school director about handling these sensitive subjects.

★ Have a few thoughtful questions ready. Besides the questions suggested in the last section, here are a few that you'd ask only the admissions director:

    ★ Do you want parents to send you a first-choice letter? How important are these to you?

    ★ Can you put me in touch with other parents who have children in the school so I can learn more from their point of view?

"I'll Be Late for Work Today; My 4-Year-Old Has a Very Important Meeting": The Child's Interview

★ Try not to take your child out of nursery school for an interview. Ideally, take him first thing in the morning before school.

★ The parent your child separates most easily from should take him.

★ Keep any anxiety you are feeling separate from your child.

★ Bring a book to read to him while you're waiting for the visit to start.

★ Find out ahead of time what the interview will be like and tell him so there are no surprises. Some schools interview a child one-on-one. Others will put him in small groups and observe him playing, doing a project, or demonstrating certain abilities. When he arrives, some directors will shake his hand (you might want to practice this). They will notice if he recognizes his name tag when it is set among other children's tags. They will observe how he interacts with other kids, if he follows directions, listens and participates, that sort of thing. They may read a story to the children and ask the kids questions about it. Often kids are asked personal questions like, "When is your birthday?" "What is your address?" "Do you know your phone number?" Your child may be directed to draw shapes or a picture of himself; cut with scissors; write his name; count objects from 1 to 10; name numbers, letters, and shapes; create sets of *more*, *less*, or *equal* using manipulatives; sort objects; do puzzles; make patterns with beads; fold paper a certain way; build a block tower.

★ During your child's interview, teachers will observe him, checklist in hand, and note how he performs in various areas such as:

  ★ Level of attention. Does he work to completion or jump around?

  ★ How clear is his speech? Quality of vocabulary?

  ★ Cooperation level. Does he listen to the teacher? Does he seek interaction with teachers and peers? How well does he interact with other children? Is he shy, friendly, aggressive?

  ★ How well developed are his fine-motor skills?

  ★ Depending what testlike activities the child is asked to do, the teacher will assess his success.

  ★ On a scale of 1 to 5, do you recommend this child?

★ Dress your child the way students in the school dress. If it is an informal, progressive school, play clothes are fine. If it is a uniform school, something more formal is appropriate.

★ Don't make a big deal out of the visit with your child. Tell him one day prior. Say something like, "Before school tomorrow, we're going to visit one of the big boy schools I told you about. When we're there, you'll meet the teacher and some other kids, you'll work in the classroom, play, have a snack, so it should be fun. While you're there, think about whether this is a kindergarten you'd like to go to next year. After your visit, I'll be waiting for you."

★ If your child is reluctant to go, promise him that if he goes and does his very best, you'll take him to his favorite ice cream shop afterward (or some other little reward that will motivate him).

★ If he won't separate or has a bad interview, you might ask your nursery school director to call and explain that his behavior was an aberration (which, of course, it was). She may be able to arrange another visit or have the admissions director come observe him in his current classroom.

★ Expect at least one disastrous interview. Don't worry—you'll laugh about it at his wedding.

Yes, Virginia, There Is a Dossier: The Nursery School Report

Most likely, your nursery school will be asked to complete an extensive questionnaire about your child to determine if he has the skills the ongoing school will expect him to have before acceptance. The questionnaire may cover:

* Intrapersonal skills: goes to bathroom on her own, feeds and dresses self, tolerates frustration, separates well from parents.
* Interpersonal skills: follows rules, works cooperatively with other children, listens to teacher, shares, takes turns, engages in classroom conversations, follows directions, has good manners, asks adults for help, displays curiosity.
* Gross-motor skills: moves spontaneously to music, demonstrates basic movements (walk, run, jump, hop, slide, gallop, skip), walks on balance beam, moves body into different positions as directed (over, under, in front of, behind).
* Fine-motor skills: quality of pencil grip, cuts with scissors, stacks objects, dressing skills (snap, buckle, button, zip).
* Cognitive and visual-spatial: matches, names, and sorts basic colors and shapes into groups; duplicates 3D block designs; identifies positions of objects (over, under, behind).
* Language: recognizes, names, and describes pictures; describes simple experiences and events; summarizes a basic story.
* Knowledge: knows letters, colors, numbers, shapes.
* Mathematics: counts, matches sets, estimates, extends patterns.

The questionnaire may also inquire as to how involved you are as parents, whether you donated your time and money to the school, and if you paid your bills on time. There is also room for your child's teacher to write a full, descriptive report addressing your child's social and intellectual skills, personality, behavior, and whatever else the teacher feels is important to understanding her as a prospective student. You will not see this report. The only thing you can do to influence it is to be the most cooperative, generous, easy-to-work-with parent you can possibly be when your child is in nursery school.

Letters of Recommendation

Letters of recommendation should be provided only if the school asks for them. Here are a few tips for writing these:

★ Provide only as many letters of recommendation as the school requests.

★ Have someone who really knows you and your child write the letter. The purpose is to help the admissions director get a broader and deeper understanding of your family and child.

★ If you know other parents or trustees at the school who can speak in a letter about your child, your family, and how well you would fit the community, that is helpful.

★ Don't arrange for famous people who really don't know you or your child to write the letter. It is a waste.

★ Never ask a friend of a friend who is a trustee or alumnus to recommend your child. Unless they know you, you have no idea what they will say.

★ Whether or not the school requests letters of recommendation, you can ask another parent, teacher, or trustee who knows you well to drop in on the admissions director and make a personal recommendation. Be sure that the director thinks highly of the person you ask to speak for you. If you are a family of means who will donate, this person can communicate that message on your behalf. If you bring it up yourself, it will appear crass. Caveat: Don't ask someone connected to the school to go to bat for you unless the school is your first choice. If your child is accepted and you turn the school down, they'll be angry with you.

★ Don't go overboard by asking too many people to advocate on your behalf. You'll come off as aggressive and annoy the admissions director.

I Like You; I Really Like You: First-Choice Letters

In the last stage of the admissions process, about two weeks before decisions are due, you can send a letter to your favorite school saying in essence, "You are our first choice. If you accept our child, we will take the spot." Some schools consider these and others don't. When you interview, ask each admissions director if she wants first-choice letters. If you aren't sure, talk to your nursery school director. A few tips on these include:

★ Don't send a first-choice letter to more than one school. Duh, right! But people do it. Admissions directors talk and they find out!

- If you send one and the school accepts your child, you have a moral (but not a legal) obligation to send her there.
- If you have a definite first-choice school, you can ask your nursery school head to call the director and assess your child's chances of getting in. If she finds out they aren't even considering your child, she'll tell you and you won't waste a first-choice letter. If they do show interest, send the letter.

The Final Decision: Trading Children Like Stocks and Bonds

Toward the end of the process, in the most competitive markets, kindergarten admissions directors may call your nursery school director and say something to the effect of, "We're considering these four families of yours but have only one spot to offer. Which family do you think would be the best fit? Would they say yes to us if we offered a spot?" This can get very tricky. If your director knows it's the first choice of three of the families and your second choice, she's unlikely to recommend your child even though you like the school very much and would take it if you didn't get your first choice. Let's say it *is* your first choice, but the director knows that your second choice school *really* wants your child and is going to offer him a place. She's unlikely to recommend your family to the director who is calling, since in her mind your child already has a spot and she has thirty other kids to place.

If you do have a first choice, tell your nursery school director, but let her know the other schools you also like and would absolutely consider if offered a place. Ask your director (very nicely peppered with lots of "pleases") not to do anything to dissuade your non-first-choice schools from offering your child a place if they express interest. If you've been a model nursery school family, there is a chance she will respect your request. If you've been a pain in the butt, don't count on it.

Acceptances, Rejections, Wait Lists

- **If your child gets your first-choice school:** Congratulations! Call any other school that accepted him and let them know he won't be coming.
- **If your child is wait-listed at your first choice and gets accepted at other schools:** Decide which of the other schools you would choose if the first choice

doesn't come through. Then call the schools you wouldn't accept and let them know to take you off their wait lists so other kids can be admitted. Call your first choice and tell them you are still interested and would take a spot if one opened up. Try to get a sense of how likely it is that your child will get in. Your nursery school director can do that for you if you're not able to get the information. Check back with the admissions director every few days to see if the picture is clearing and what your child's chances are. There will be a deadline by which you must accept or reject the offer from the school that said yes. If the deadline comes and you haven't been offered a place in your first-choice school, you'll have to sign a contract and make a deposit to your second-choice school or you'll lose that option.

★ **If your child gets wait-listed everywhere:** Call each school that wait-listed your child and let them know that you would take a spot there if accepted. Check back with them periodically. Let's say a school that's not your favorite offers you a place. They'll send you a contract and you'll have a few days before it's due. Keep checking with the other schools to see if another place opened up. Your first goal is to get your child a place that is acceptable to you and, second, to get your child the best place you can. When the deadline is upon you, you'll have to choose from whichever schools made offers.

★ **If your child doesn't get in anywhere:** This happens to families every year, but don't despair. You have a few options:

   ★ Choose your local public school and reapply for private first grade (or kindergarten if your child is on the young side) next year.
   ★ Wait until the dust settles. When it is closer to the start of school, call the programs you were most interested in (or maybe some to which you never applied) and see if space has opened up. People move unexpectedly and spaces magically appear at the finest schools.
   ★ Don't take this personally, by the way. In a highly competitive environment, the most adorable, bright children from amazing families get shut out. You will find a good school for your child.

★ **If there is a timing problem:** In New York City, all of the private schools send out their acceptances on the same day, which makes it easy to commit because they all have the same deadline. However, the public gifted and talented programs send out their acceptances much later. In other cities, private schools do not necessarily mail acceptances on the same day, but they do tend to make their decisions before the public schools.

Let's say your child gets into a private school, but you'd rather see her go to your local TAG program if accepted. First, check the private school's contract. They are all different, but most require a *nonrefundable deposit* to hold a space. Go ahead and make the deposit. In most cases (but not all), there is *first deadline* by which you'll owe half the tuition if you don't tell the private school that your child isn't going to attend. Then there is a *second deadline* by which you'll owe the entire tuition if you don't give notice that your child isn't coming. If all goes well, you'll find out that your child was accepted to the TAG program before that first deadline and lose only your initial deposit. That will hurt but may be worth it since your child will get a free public school education at an excellent school. If the public school doesn't tell you until after the first or second deadline, you'll have to decide if it's worth paying the tuition to take advantage of that free TAG spot.

In the next chapter, we'll talk about how public schools use testing for ability grouping and why it is important to keep your child out of the slow group!

22. How Public Schools Use Testing

THE DOWN-AND-DIRTY DISH ON ABILITY TRACKING

Ability Tracking

Oh, how we love to laugh at those misguided private school parents who believe that their child must get into certain top nursery programs or they'll never get into the A-list private schools, which will inevitably keep them out of Harvard. Public school parents have different concerns. Whether they call it "tracking" or give it a more acceptable label, most public schools engage in some form of ability placement, where students are grouped together by slow, average, and advanced skill levels and instructed differently depending on the group to which they are assigned. Students may be assigned to a self-contained classroom based on competence (i.e., a TAG program) or they may be in a homogeneous classroom and placed in special groups for subjects such as math and reading. Students do better academically if they are learning alongside equal or more able pupils. It is in your child's best interest to get placed in the highest possible grouping for her capability.

> **CHILDREN SHOULD BE READY FOR KINDERGARTEN ON DAY ONE**
> Kids are evaluated for ability groupings via informal assessments as soon as they start kindergarten. This makes it critical for public school parents to get their children as ready for school as they can possibly be. To give your child the best chance to excel in the classroom, make sure she has the verbal and performance skills every kindergartener should have by the time she's evaluated.

The rationale behind tracking is that ability groupings allow teachers to increase the pace and provide higher-level instruction for brighter students and teach at a slower pace with more repetition and a simpler curriculum to low-achieving students. The high achievers benefit by not being slowed down by their less-able peers, and the lower achievers don't feel the pressure of having to keep up with students who catch on more easily. Private schools avoid tracking by not accepting less-able students and by sending children who come to need extra help to a reading or math specialist and then bringing them back into the regular classroom when help is no longer needed (often after their parents have gotten them tutored). Private-school students who can't keep up in the long run are often "counseled out" and replaced by better-performing students. Public schools can't do this.

Tracking is a controversial issue in education for a number of reasons:

- ★ **Inaccurate placement.** Because readiness tests are often done in groups, they are limited in what they measure, and since a child's test performance can be impacted by so many factors, researchers say that children are placed in inappropriate groupings up to half the time.
- ★ **Inability to move.** In many schools there is little movement from lower to higher tracks as children's skills improve.
- ★ **Placement becomes self-fulfilling.** Once tracked, teachers often perceive children based on their labels, seeing low-tracked kids as slow in all areas of their learning and high-tracked kids as bright all around. This is fine for kids who are put in the accelerated track, but can be devastating for children who are labeled "slow learners." Research shows that teachers have reduced expectations for low-tracked students, so these labels become self-fulfilling prophecies.
- ★ **Different quality education.** Tracking forces teachers to use different curricula and classroom styles. Teachers in the lower tracks often focus on behavior and discipline and use more rote techniques like drills and worksheets. Teachers in higher tracks emphasize academic achievement and provide deeper, richer content.
- ★ **Impact can be long-term.** Students tracked in slow groups get easier lessons and assignments as early as kindergarten, are surrounded by less-able peers, and by the end of the year aren't prepared to handle harder curricula. So the next year, they are once again placed in the slow group and the cycle continues. After several years of lower-quality instruction surrounded by weaker peers, the student is at an extreme disadvantage. On the flip side, high-level placement expands a student's chances for greater opportunities throughout her education.

* **Impacts self-esteem.** Students placed in higher-level classes have better self-esteem and higher personal expectations regarding what they can achieve. Dr. Marion Blank, director of the A Light on Literacy program at Columbia University, has spent a lifetime working with children who have reading difficulties. She says, "It is disabling and devastating for the children to be placed in the lowest-ability groups. They know where they stand. Most believe that they can't compete with their classmates. Their self-confidence suffers. Often, they give up." Super-chef Jamie Oliver, who had learning disabilities as a child, often recounts a story of being pulled out of his regular classroom for a special reading and writing track as the other kids taunted him, singing the phrase "special needs" to the tune of "Let It Be."
* **Bias.** Because tests are often limited by language and cultural biases, children from low-income or minority homes and from homes where English isn't the first language get lower scores. Some see ability groupings as an attempt to put white students in higher tracks and minority students in lower tracks.

What Does This Mean for Parents?

We can all agree that placing children into ability groupings is unfair. But if that is the policy of the school your child will attend, your choice is to make sure your child doesn't get hurt by the practice or apply him to a private school that doesn't track children.

If you understand what educators expect of children given the highest placement—all the verbal and performance skills we have been talking about in this book—and you help your child acquire these abilities, he is more likely to be placed in advanced groups that will ultimately afford him superior teachers, an accelerated curriculum, greater encouragement, a self-fulfilling prophecy on the positive side, better self-esteem, and a wider range of opportunities for his entire education. By working with your child so he has what he needs to be placed in the advanced group, you will give him this automatic advantage.

But let's face it: no matter how hard you work with your child, he may have areas of weakness that you can't help him overcome. There's that pesky bell curve to consider, and most of our kids fall in the middle. With Schuyler's spatial issues, I'm not sure I ever could have gotten her ready to handle placement in an advanced math group. If your child isn't initially tracked in a higher group, you'll want to stay involved and help him improve his skills so that he can be moved. It is important to understand how tracking works at your child's school so you can make sure he is put in the right group for his ability. Here are some actions you can take:

* When you go to parent-teacher conferences, ask about your school's tracking policy. Since the word "tracking" is out of fashion, she may say they don't do it. Dig deeper to find out how they teach children with different abilities. They may engage in the practice and call it by a nicer name.
* If the teacher tells you how well your child is doing, that doesn't mean he's doing well in the appropriate ability group. He could be working in a group that is too easy for him. Find out where he has been placed.
* Learn how placement decisions are made. Is it based on testing? Informal assessments? Classroom observation? Academic performance?
* Ask how students in the same grade are instructed differently. Often kids placed in lower-track classes learn a simplified version of what is taught in the higher track. Make sure your child is learning everything he needs to be ready for the next grade.
* Learn how performance expectations change from one track to another.
* Find out if your child can move between groups if her skills improve. If the answer is yes, ask how her skills will be measured and what she must achieve in order to move.
* If your child is placed in the slowest or middle reading group, get her started on the inexpensive online program at Readingkingdom.com. In my opinion, this is the best resource today for struggling readers.
* If your child is placed in the slowest or middle math group, two effective and inexpensive sources of help are Time4learning.com and Kumon.com. You can also go to Internet4classrooms.com (pre-K resources/mathematics) for free online activities to build early math skills. If your child is in the slowest or middle writing group, go to Hwtears.com for help.
* Monitor your child's progress. If she's not learning what she needs to in school, get her extra help. Make sure the teacher reassigns her if she shows positive growth.

Bottom Line: Stay on top of your child's placement and make sure she is getting the instruction that is appropriate for her and not being shortchanged.

If your child's school does track children, there are ways it can be done that are better than others. Ideally, their groupings will be fluid and temporary. Students should be reevaluated regularly and promoted to more challenging curricula as their abilities improve. To support children's self-esteem, it is important that they be made to understand that everyone has different strengths, and while one child might do well in math, reading may be hard for him. Students should know that if they work hard and improve, they can move.

If these aren't the policies in place, talk to your child's teacher and school principal. Express your concerns and lobby for change. If you feel your school's tracking policy is discriminating against minority students and you want to challenge that, you can file a complaint with the U.S. Department of Education's Office of Civil Rights.

Next are examples of informal assessments a kindergarten teacher might use in the first weeks of class to determine whether to place your child in the beginner, intermediate, or advanced reading/writing/math groups. She would observe him and complete each of the checklists below:

Informal Assessment

Name of student: _____

Reading Behaviors (Y—yes, M—most times, S—sometimes, N—no)
_____ Shows an interest in books
_____ Desires to be read to frequently
_____ Follows the direction of print (holds book correctly, left to right, top to bottom)
_____ Reads pictures
_____ Distinguishes between pictures and print
_____ Recognizes speech print relationship
_____ Recognizes that print carries meaning
_____ Understands and applies knowledge of letter sounds (N—none, F—few, S—some, M—most, A—all)
_____ Hears and repeats initial sounds of words
_____ Identifies word that doesn't rhyme among 3-word choice
_____ Knows letters in name
_____ Reads print from the environment
_____ Distinguishes letters from numbers
_____ Identifies upper-case letters (N—none, F—few, H—half, M—most, A—all)
_____ Identifies lower-case letters (N—none, F—few, H—half, M—most, A—all)
_____ Chooses reading during free time
_____ Listens attentively to stories
_____ Uses pictures to predict print
_____ Retells stories in own words, including characters, settings, and main events

_____ Connects story events to life experience
_____ Tells personal stories in detail

Print Behaviors (Y—yes, M—most times, S—sometimes, N—no)
_____ Shows interest in writing
_____ Selects own topic for dictation
_____ Communicates more than one thought
_____ Draws a picture
_____ Matches text with picture
_____ Mimics writing (scribbles)
_____ Uses mature pencil grip
_____ Letters float around the page
_____ Uses directionality (left to right, top to bottom)
_____ Writes capital letters (N—none, F—few, H—half, M—most, A—all)
_____ Writes lower-case letters (N—none, F—few, H—half, M—most, A—all)
_____ Letters are legible
_____ Writes numbers 0 through 10 (N—none, F—few, H—half, M—most, A—all)
_____ Numbers are legible
_____ Copies numbers/letters/words randomly
_____ Writes own name
_____ Writes/copies print
_____ Uses space between letters correctly
_____ Uses space between words
_____ Writes phrases/sentences
_____ Begins using punctuation

Math Behaviors (Y—yes, M—most times, S—sometimes, N—no)
_____ Rote counts 1 through 10
_____ Counts objects 1 through 10 using 1-to-1 correspondence
_____ Identifies numerals 1 through 10 (N—none, F—few, H—half, M—most, A—all)
Draws basic shapes
_____ triangle
_____ square
_____ circle
_____ Creates sets of more, less, equal
Knows vocabulary:
_____ same
_____ different
_____ before

_____ after
_____ first
_____ last
_____ Matches equivalent sets of objects
_____ Identifies and names shapes
_____ Sorts and resorts objects using more than one attribute
_____ Orders objects by size
Compares objects by
_____ size
_____ length
_____ width
_____ height
_____ Identifies, extends, and creates patterns
_____ Ability to order pictures according to logical sequence
_____ Estimates
_____ Demonstrates understanding of addition and subtraction
_____ Distinguishes weight

In the next chapter, we'll talk about what to do if your child has delays or learning disabilities, and how to benefit from government-funded services including doctors, teachers, therapists, and even private special-needs schools.

23. Testing for Support Services for Children with Delays

EARLY INTERVENTION AND SPECIAL EDUCATION

Once I adjusted to the fact that my daughter was not a certified genius (at least, according to Stanford-Binet), I became fine with the idea that she was a bright child who would do well in school by working hard like I had. Sam, on the other hand, was bound for glory, at least judging by his Apgar score, which was 9.8, the highest of any newborn at Mount Sinai Hospital nursery during his stay. Not only that, he mastered every activity on his Elmo's Musical Peek-a-Boo Gym before he turned 10 months, a record I'm told. Imagine my shock when Sam was diagnosed with developmental delays and Schuyler was found to have a nonverbal learning disability. I was devastated. Yes, I knew things could be worse, but these were my babies and their struggles were my struggles.

I was lucky. As I began working with Sam to help him catch up, a chance conversation with a mother in my building revealed that I could get additional support from the city and later my school district, and it would be free! These services are offered under the federal Individuals with Disabilities Education Act (IDEA).

Under IDEA, children with physical, learning, or emotional disabilities are entitled to a "free appropriate public education." In most cases, children get support services such as speech or occupational therapy, tutoring, extra time with a special ed teacher in the resource room, that sort of thing. In some cases, if the district can't provide a free appropriate education, you can place your child in a private special education school and the government will pay for it. Of the 6 million children in special education today, almost 90,000 are in private schools with their public school's financial support. These services are available everywhere in the country. Not everyone knows about this, and I want to be sure that you do. Under IDEA, there are two levels of services provided: services for children from birth to age 3 and services for children from 3 to 21 years old.

Early Intervention: Services for Children from Birth to Age 3

Let's say that your 18-month-old daughter can't seem to stay focused on activities the way other children her age can. Or your 14-month-old son has difficulty picking up small objects. After reviewing the milestones children should reach from birth to age 3 at Babycenter.com/milestone-charts-birth-to-age-3, you're worried but not sure what to do. Run (don't walk!) to your pediatrician. She may give your child a screening test that will identify delays in children from birth to 6 years. In many cases the doctor will be able to relieve your anxiety, but you should continue to monitor your child's progress. If, even after seeing the doctor, your instinct tells you that something is wrong, go to nichcy.org/babies/states/ and get the number for your community's early intervention program.

SIGNS THAT YOUR BABY OR TODDLER'S DEVELOPMENT MAY NOT BE ON TRACK

- absence or minimal eye contact or smiling
- does not bring hands together by 4 months
- does not roll over by 6 months
- by end of 7 months, seems stiff, tight-muscled
- by end of 7 months, shows no affection
- head lags when child is pulled into a sitting position at 6 months
- does not sit without support by 8 months
- does not crawl by 12 months
- does not point to objects or pictures by 12 months
- does not walk by 15 months
- lack of interest in surroundings and caregivers
- stops babbling by end of first year
- doesn't respond to sound or loud noises
- seems frightened by new surroundings
- does not use hands to manipulate and explore objects
- other expected milestones are not being met

When children are born prematurely, with cerebral palsy, a chromosome disorder, infections, or other diseases, they are likely have what is called a *global delay*, which affects all areas of development. Hospitals jump on this and make appropriate referrals, so parents in that situation are quickly introduced to early intervention. When children's delays present later, parents often don't know that help is available.

Early intervention is designed to address the developmental needs of very young children with delays. Give them a call and tell them about your concern. Let them know that you want your child evaluated under IDEA. They will refer you to Child Find (Childfindidea.org/) or another agency in your state whose job it is to identify children in need of services. The evaluation is free.

Although the process varies from community to community, here is how it is supposed to work. The early intervention system will assign a coordinator to your case. A team of professionals (i.e., a psychologist, social worker, occupational therapist, speech pathologist, special educator) will observe and evaluate your child, read each other's reports, and decide if her delays meet the criteria necessary for eligibility. She qualifies for services if she is found to have developmental delays in one or more of the following areas: cognitive, physical (including vision and hearing), communication, social or emotional, mastering basic functions (i.e., walking, talking), or if she has a diagnosed physical or mental condition that has a high probability of resulting in developmental delays.

If your child is found to be eligible for early intervention, she will then go through an even more in-depth assessment, which may include doctor's exams, developmental tests, performance assessments, a detailed history, direct observation, feedback from parents and caretakers, and review of any other relevant records about your child.

INFANT AND TODDLER DEVELOPMENTAL TESTS

The Battelle Development Inventory, the Bayley Scales of Infant and Toddler Development, the Denver II Developmental Screening, and the Childhood Autism Rating Scale are tests commonly used to measure physical, motor, sensory, and cognitive development in very young children. They involve an examiner interacting with the child using toys, games and simple tasks. The tester might introduce an object to the child to track with his eyes. Parents are interviewed for information that can't be observed during the test.

After the assessment, you'll meet with your coordinator to develop an Individualized Family Service Plan (IFSP) for providing early intervention services to your child. This is a detailed document that reviews her developmental issues, states the services she should receive, the outcomes expected after services are given, where they will be delivered, who will pay for them, and more. The services your child receives may include speech, occupational, or physical therapy, hearing impairment services, psychological services, special education, applied behavior analysis therapy for autism, or whatever is needed.

Your state's policy will determine whether you or the state will pay for the actual services. In some states, you may be charged a fee based on what you earn. In other states, everything will be free no matter what your financial status. No child is denied services because her family cannot pay. She will continue to receive services until either she meets the IFSP goals and it is determined that services are no longer needed or she transitions out of early intervention, either at age 3 or at age 2 if she will turn 3 during the school year.

If your child has been in early intervention and will continue to need services, you will want to begin planning her transition to special education services about 9 to 12 months before her third birthday. In early intervention, the focus of services is on developmental needs. In special education, the focus is on educational needs. The service coordinator assigned to your case can guide you with this transition.

The "downside" of going through early intervention is that the evaluator or coordinator may "drop a bomb" in terms of a diagnosis. Hearing "autism" or any other scary-sounding condition being used in the same sentence as your child's name can feel like a knife to the heart. The best evaluators are sensitive in the way they break hard news to families. Most parents rise to the occasion, tackling the situation with love and determination. The important thing is to find out if there is a problem as soon as possible so your child can receive early and intensive treatment, giving him the best chance to lead a fulfilling and productive life.

Special Education: Services for Children Age 3 to Age 22

When Schuyler took the WPPSI at age 4, she did poorly on the subtests that measured spatial abilities. Several years later, she was found to have a nonverbal (spatial) learning disability. At the time Schuyler was tested, I didn't appreciate what it meant when she didn't perform well on those particular subtests, and as a result, she wasn't diagnosed until fifth grade. By then, her problems in school had compounded, making it difficult to catch up.

When I was first told Schuyler had a nonverbal (spatial) learning disability, I didn't have a clue what that meant. In fact, labeling someone with a "nonverbal learning disability" is as revealing as calling someone a doctor. Is she a medical doctor or a PhD? Is she a general practitioner, a dermatologist, an oncologist, a pediatrician, a dentist, a podiatrist—what is she? *The Essentials of WPPSI-III Assessment* lists 68 discrete mental ingredients or abilities that are considered nonverbal. Was Schuyler deficient in all of them? Some of them? Who knew? It was only through exhaustive psychological testing that we were able to uncover the specific components of nonverbal intelligence that weren't in place for my daughter.

This is true for any learning issue a child may have, whether it is a language, memory, attention, cognitive, or fine-motor disability. I emphasize this because if a teacher or school counselor ever tells you, "Your daughter has a graphomotor disability," you must get that confirmed by an educational psychologist, and even then, don't stop digging until you understand the specific weaknesses that are impeding her ability to write. The obvious solution to a graphomotor disability would be occupational therapy. However, thorough testing might reveal that there is no fine-motor problem at all. Instead, maybe she has a visual-spatial issue (she can't form symbols known as letters) or a memory problem (she can't remember what the letters look like). Only by diagnosing the exact compromised ability underlying the presenting problem can you determine the support she needs. Where do you get this support? A good place to start is special education services.

Let's say your little one hasn't been in early intervention, but after age 3, you realize that something may be wrong. This was what happened with Sam. We did not recognize his delays until after his third birthday. With Schuyler, it wasn't discovered until fifth grade. Unfortunately, kids don't hold up a sign saying "I have a delay." Often, the signals are subtle. You may have a nagging feeling that something is wrong. Fortunately, at any point during your child's schooling that breakdowns in learning take place, special ed services can be sought.

If your child is older than 3 and isn't hitting the developmental milestones discussed in chapter 6, or is exhibiting worrisome emotional or behavioral symptoms, contact Child Find (Childfindidea.org) and ask that your child be evaluated. Or, go to nichcy.org/Pages/StatesSpecificInfo.aspx where there are local resources you can tap into. Put your request in writing and include consent for the evaluation. In most cases, you'll submit this to your school district, but confirm this. The state will have a specific number of days for you to complete the evaluation from the time your consent is given (it varies by state).

The next step is the evaluation by your school district. There a team will be assembled that may include a psychologist, special education teacher, speech therapist, reading teacher, and/or educational therapist. The evaluation is extensive and will include examinations of your child's health, vision, hearing, social and emotional development, general intelligence, academic performance (for children in school), communications, and motor abilities. She will also be observed in her classroom if she is already in school.

We went through the evaluation process many times with Schuyler. Where we lived, the IQ testing provided by the school district was done in a shoddy manner and came to inaccurate conclusions. This is not always the case. Some districts provide excellent evaluations. Still, watch out for quality of testing issues.

Why is the testing so important? First, only thorough testing by an experienced educational psychologist will uncover the specific weaknesses that underlie your child's learning delays, and you must understand what these are in order to get an appropriate learning plan in place. Second, since so many recommendations for services will depend on how your child performs when tested, you want to know that the testing was reliable.

Although the testing by the school psychologist was free, we eventually came to realize the importance of having own psychologist evaluate her. This second opinion is important because if you don't agree with the conclusions the school district comes to or with the services they recommend, you can appeal. Your own psychological reports may be critical in proving that your child needs different support than what the school district is offering. No matter what, your child will have to undergo a district evaluation since services cannot be provided solely on the basis of an "outside" expert report. If you disagree with your school district's evaluation and can't afford to hire your own psychologist, ask the district to pay for a private evaluation. Sometimes they will. Alternatively, call the psychology department at your local college. Often, there are programs where students test children under their professor's supervision. They may test your child at a reduced rate or for free. All of Sam's hearing and speech evaluations were done this way.

After the assessments are complete, the committee on preschool special education will meet and determine if your child is eligible for services. If they conclude she is, they will schedule an IEP (individual education plan) meeting, which you will attend. Here, they will decide if your child should be placed in a special classroom, which special services she should receive either inside or outside of school, what her educational goals should be, how they will be measured, and more. You can either accept the IEP the school offers or reject it and appeal their decision.

A preschooler might be offered a special education teacher to shadow her at nursery school. She might be given speech and occupational therapy. This is what Sam was given, and the professionals the district provided were outstanding. In my personal experience and having watched friends and clients go through this process, the government is more generous in providing services for children from ages 3 to 5. During preschool, there is federal and state money to cover the cost. Once they enter kindergarten, districts rely on state funding alone, so they offer less support. This is why it is important to apply for special education services as soon as you suspect a problem.

- Ninety percent of children with reading delays will achieve grade level if they receive help by first grade.
- If a child still has reading delays in fourth grade, he will most likely struggle throughout his entire school career.
- If help is given in fourth grade, rather than late kindergarten, it takes four times as long to improve the same skills to the same degree.

If your child is entering kindergarten or beyond, IDEA requires that she be placed where she will have the maximum opportunity appropriate to learn with children who don't have disabilities in academic, nonacademic, and extracurricular activities. You'll hear this referred to as the *Least Restrictive Environment*. This means they will attempt to put your child in a mainstream classroom. Depending on her issues, she may be placed in a regular class and pulled out for individual or small-group time with a speech therapist or reading specialist. Another typical model is called an *inclusion classroom*. Here, there is a regular and a special education teacher who co-teach. Sometimes they break into ability groups for differentiated instruction. Students don't know which children have an IEP so there are fewer stigmas attached. If you do accept the IEP your district offers, you must diligently monitor what is going on in classroom to make sure they are following it. Sometimes they don't.

The first two times we went through this process with Schuyler, she was attending a magnet school. In both instances, the committee on special education gave her only two hours a week in the resource room with the special ed teacher. Big whoopee, right? When it became apparent that this was not enough, we hired our own psychologist and a lawyer to get her moved to a school with teachers trained to deal with her type of learning issues, which were not run of the mill.

Instead of giving us what we asked for, the school district's special ed committee offered Schuyler a place in a particular special education classroom in a nearby school that they felt would be an acceptable "free appropriate public education." We were invited to observe in the classroom and decide if we agreed with their placement. It was a class of twenty kids, half with a wide variety of learning disabilities different from Schuyler's and half with behavioral issues. We were told that if we didn't agree with what they offered (and we didn't), we had the right to appeal the decision (which we did). Under the law, if your school district fails to provide an "appropriate" program to meet your child's needs, they must pay for a private special education school that can. Note that they have to provide only a "suitable" or "adequate" program, not the "best" program for the child.

As a practical matter, if you decide to challenge your school district's recommendation for placement, you'll have to enroll your child in a private special education school, pay the tuition yourself, and then challenge their recommendation. If you win, they reimburse you for the tuition. With our lawyer's help, we won our case two years in a row and placed Schuyler in the school with expertise in nonverbal learning disabilities that met her needs. Although they took forever to pay, the school district covered the entire tuition.

HIRING A LAWYER.

When my friends are seeking significant special education services for their children, I urge them to hire a lawyer. It is extremely difficult to advocate for your own child when you are emotionally involved. Also, the laws in special education are complicated and constantly changing. The school district must follow IDEA procedures to the letter. If they don't, they can be forced to settle and give you what you want for your child. Only a lawyer will know if they have missed a step. Hiring a lawyer can be expensive, but it is less costly than paying for certain therapies or private special education school. If you feel your child isn't getting the services to which he is entitled, ask a special education attorney to assess your case. You can find a list of special lawyers at rsaffran.tripod.com/legal.html.

If you can't afford a lawyer, there are less expensive advocates who may be able to help you. Visit the Council of Parent Attorneys and Advocates (copaa.org) or google "the learning disabilities association of (your state)" for information on local resources. Alternatively, you may qualify for free legal services. Google "free legal advice for children seeking services under IDEA in (your state)." For those of you that want to handle your own case, attorney Pete Wright's Wrightslaw.com is a great website that covers many legal issues in getting special services through IDEA. He has written a book called *From Emotions to Advocacy* that can guide you in managing your child's case.

Can my child get special education services if he is attending private nursery school, private school, or a TAG program?

Yes, Children in private school may receive speech therapy, occupational therapy, tutoring, and other after-school support through their local school districts. Even gifted kids have learning issues, and it is not unusual for their parents to seek support services under IDEA.

Our daughter seems to have language delays. We are trying to get her into the competitive private school that her sister goes to. If she gets special education services, our nursery school director will tell the private school and she'll never get in. Shouldn't we wait until she's accepted to apply for services?

If you think your child might have a developmental delay, do not wait to seek help under IDEA. The earlier you identify these issues, the quicker you can fix them. If you wait, your daughter may fall further behind. If your child does have speech delays, your nursery school director has surely noticed and so will the private school you want. By getting help now, she may be fine by the time you apply her to kindergarten.

My son was diagnosed with a written expression disorder. He gets good marks for participating in class but cannot communicate ideas on paper. I don't understand why he has this or how I can best help him. Any ideas?

If your child has been diagnosed with a learning disability, there is a book I recommend you read. Once you do, I promise you will have a clearer understanding of his disability and you'll know how to go about getting the best help for him. The book is *A Mind at a Time*, by Dr. Mel Levine. Here, Dr. Levine examines each ability, how it works, and how parents can help children who are struggling. Honestly, it wasn't until I read that book that I truly understood my daughter's spatial learning disability.

To any parent who is contending with a learning-disabled child, my hat goes off to you. It takes strength and perseverance. When Schuyler was first diagnosed, she was attending a private school that was absolutely wonderful . . . for any child who learns the "normal" way. They made it clear that this was our problem. Either we hired tutors who could get her to learn what her teachers couldn't, or she should go somewhere else. Unlike public schools, private schools have no obligation to serve learning-disabled children. Many private schools have set up special programs to help children who process information differently. Ours hadn't and didn't feel it could meet her needs.

At that point, I moved Schuyler to a magnet school where they promised to give her extra attention. The board of ed gave her two hours a week with a learning specialist, but that wasn't enough. Though she excelled in English and history, math was torture. Ironically, we call her "the human calculator" because you can ask her, "What's 2,345 divided by 25?" and she can immediately tell you the answer. Still, Schuyler regularly failed tests on long division because she didn't have the spatial perception to line up the numbers and show her work. And don't get me started on geometry. Making a child with her spatial deficits take geometry was like asking a blind person to drive. Every other day we got notices in the mail that she was failing. One day, her principal (who knew about her disability) wandered into her geometry class and inspected the children's notebooks. She picked up one of Schuyler's tests and held it up for everyone to see. "An F," she said. "Are you stupid?" I was relieved to learn that this soul-crushing principal lost her job a few years later. Still, this incident is typical of the kind of indignities suffered daily by children who learn differently.

IF YOUR CHILD HAS A LEARNING DISABILITY

- Tell her what it is so she can understand she has a language-processing problem or a working-memory problem. Otherwise, she might just think she's "dumb." It helps kids to know exactly what they need to work on.
- When you talk to her about her weakness, point out her many strengths.
- Remind her that school is the only place in life where she'll have to be good at everything. When she grows up, she'll be able to specialize and pick a career that capitalizes on her strengths.

Schuyler attended three more schools after that magnet program. Getting her through homework every night was a monumental project. Luckily, she discovered a love for acting and singing and went on to perform in plays and attend drama camp. Besides acting, she has amazing people skills. All the school changes she endured made her fearless when it comes to taking on new situations. She has a natural stubborn streak and refuses to give up when she wants something (just remember "the grape soda" incident). Schuyler may not have the spatial intelligence she needed for school, but her acting, interpersonal skills, openness to change, and persistence will serve her in life.

I always talked to Schuyler about people with learning disabilities who have gone on to achieve great things. Barbara Corcoran, who owned one of the top real estate agencies in NYC, was dyslexic. "I hated school. It was like a jail sentence," she is quoted as saying in *WWD*. "Still, being dyslexic forced me to use my imagination, to be charming and fill in the blanks, which is what good salesmanship is all about." Super chef Jamie Oliver grew up hyperactive and dyslexic, failing all his subjects except art and geology. He says, "The key to life is to know what you're good at and stay away from what you're bad at." Still, he believes it is his disability that allows him to jump from project to project and juggle thirty things at once. Charles Darwin, Walt Disney, Richard Branson, Winston Churchill, John F. Kennedy, and Henry Winkler all had learning disabilities. Dr. Carol Greider, who won a science Nobel Prize in 2009, was dyslexic, forced to take remedial classes, and always believed she was stupid. Sadly, this is a common belief among learning-disabled children.

Charles Schwab, who is dyslexic, once said, "Nobody's good in everything. Advantages and disadvantages come in many forms." He was right. For every parent with a child like this, it is our job to help her discover those advantages. I urge you to do everything you can to help your child identify and develop an interest or activity where she can experience daily success.

Meanwhile, if your child has a learning disability, take heart. There is help available. Alexandra Hindes, a Manhattan attorney who specializes in special education law, put it this way: "Very often when parents start the special education process they believe that their school district will provide all of the services their child needs. They are surprised and do not know where to turn when their child's needs are not being met. Parents of special-needs children should realize that there is an abundance of resources and services available to their children. However, it often takes time and dedication to seek out these services. Parents need to play a proactive role in the special education process and make sure they understand their child's right to a free, appropriate public education."

A Few Parting Words

As I write this, Schuyler has been out of high school for six months, moved to New York City, and gotten a tiny apartment and her very first job. She is studying at one of the finest acting conservatories in the country. With her learning challenges, there were times that I wondered if she would ever graduate. I am so proud of what she has become and how hard she fought to distinguish herself in school, where she never fit the mold. Recently she said to me, "Mom, the best decision I ever made was to skip college and go right to acting school. I've never been happier. It's so hard but I'm doing well." She went on to tell me that she's learned more in the last three months than she did in four years of high school. I ran a victory lap around my apartment when I heard those words. Finally, she's getting an education that matches her passion and type of intelligence. Sam will take a different road. He is an excellent student and is already starting to look at colleges. Your child will chart his own path, being true to his nature, interests, and talents.

In the course of letting my children go, I realize that they were only mine for a brief chapter. Soon, it will be up to them. Regrets, I have a few (hundred). What parent doesn't? In hindsight, I can think of so many things I might have done differently had I known then what I know now. But I didn't. Oh well, next time. Wait: There is no next time when it comes to raising kids. You get it as right as you can the first and only time and then you hope for the best.

If you are reading this, you have a very young child and years to go before you're walking in my footsteps. I know it feels like it will be forever before your little one will be donning her cap and gown and moving out, but the years fly by. Soon you'll be thinking about Botox instead of babysitters. Like me, you will have made plenty of missteps, but you also will have gotten it right plenty of times. By sharing what I've learned about preparing children for testing, school, and life success, I hope this book helps you get it right a few more times than you might otherwise have. One thing I've come to realize is that our children will survive and thrive in spite of everything. As a parent, the more you know, the better you can do, and all you can do is the best you can. So relax, give it your best shot, and enjoy this remarkable time in your child's life. Believe me, it's over all too quickly.

Acknowledgments

They say that necessity is the mother of invention and in this case, I never would have been drawn to testing and early childhood education if not for the special needs of my son, Sam Quinn, and my daughter, Schuyler Quinn. Your struggles led me to a subject about which I am passionate, inspired a business, two books, and an informational website (Karenquinn.net/category/blog/). Your struggles made you the strong, resilient young adults you are today, so perhaps it was all worth it. Thank you to Dr. Shari Nedler, who demystified intelligence tests and showed me how to use them as blueprints to turn Sam's delays around and get him ready for kindergarten. I am so grateful to have been given the perfect mother (and not just because you know so much about teaching children).

As always, thank you to Robin Straus, my agent; Michelle Howry, editor extraordinaire; and all the folks at Simon and Schuster, including Trish Todd, Stacey Creamer, Emily Remes, Josh Karpf, and Patricia Romanowski Bashe. I appreciate your support, enthusiasm, and wise editorial notes.

I am grateful to my early readers, Bonnie Edelman, Judy Mumma, and Wendy Quinn, kindergarten teachers who gave me so many wonderful ideas for activities that young children love. Thank you to Dr. Marion Blank, who taught me what kids need for reading success. The information you provided was invaluable. I also want to acknowledge Kerry Canella, Jan Potter, Amy Sampson, Tatiana Boncompagni, and Kim Chopoorian, who gave me insight into how to make this book even more helpful to busy mothers.

Alex Hindes, I am grateful that you read my chapter on special education and assured me I had gotten it right. Thank you for guiding our family through the special education legal system for all those years. Vicki Goldman,

I appreciate that you took the time to read this when you had your own private school guide to complete. Your feedback was refreshing and straightforward, as always. I must also thank Dr. Suellen Carney. Through the years, I gained so much from you as you tested Schuyler and helped us understand what made her tick (learning-wise, that is). You never failed to recognize and celebrate her unique strengths, which meant the world to us. Meghan O'Leary, thank you for your illustrations that bring the test examples to life.

To Roxana Reid, my partner in founding Smart City Kids, you have done a remarkable job helping NYC families make the best education choices for their children through the years. To the families I was fortunate enough to work with during my time there: It was a privilege to have helped you and your children, and I am confident they are doing brilliantly today wherever they are going to school.

Appendix I

BREAKING DOWN THREE MORE TESTS, SECTION BY SECTION

The Woodcock-Johnson Tests of Cognitive Abilities

The Woodcock-Johnson has two major sections: verbal and performance.

Verbal

Comprehension and General Information. These questions are similar to the knowledge, comprehension, and information sections in the prior tests starting on page 42. *Assesses knowledge/comprehension.*

INFORMATION RETRIEVAL

Your child is asked to name as many items in a category as he can say within a minute. For example, fruit, what you wear, animals. This is a like the old *$20,000 Pyramid* game show, only your child is told the category up front. *Assesses language, knowledge/comprehension, memory, mathematics, cognitive thinking.*

INCOMPLETE WORDS

Your child is orally presented with a word that is incomplete. He must say what the word is supposed to be. For example, *el-phant* is "elephant" and *hol-day* is "holiday." *Assesses language, memory.*

AUDITORY ATTENTION

Your child listens to a tape of someone saying a word against a noisy backdrop. After hearing the word, the child has to point to a picture that represents the word. The pictures shown are of similar-sounding words so he really has to listen. For example, *tree, knee, ski.* *Assesses language, memory, fine-motor skills (pointing).*

MEMORY FOR WORDS.

This is the same as Memory for Words and Numbers on the Stanford-Binet, page 48. *Assesses memory.*

PICTURE NAMING

Your child is shown a row of pictures and asked to name each picture as quickly as possible. *Assesses language, knowledge/comprehension, visual-spatial reasoning, memory.*

Hat, fish, ring, hand, flower, eye, carrot.

WORKING MEMORY

Your child is presented with a series of two to seven spoken numbers and asked to repeat them in reverse order. Item: 2–5–4 Correct: 4–5–2

Your child is presented with spoken words and numbers in mixed order and is asked to reorder the information with numbers first and then words. Item: clock, 3, 2, fish. Correct: 3, 2, clock, fish. *Assesses memory.*

VISUAL-AUDITORY LEARNING

Your child is taught pictographic representations of words. Symbols are first taught orally and then they are combined to make a sentence. The child is shown a line of these symbols and asked to interpret what it says. This test assesses decoding skills as well as *language, memory, visual-spatial reasoning, cognitive skills.*

Here are some symbols
and what each means:

ate   the   dinner   girl

Can you read this sentence?
The girl ate dinner.

CONCEPT FORMATION

Your child is shown drawings inside a box that are different from drawings outside of the box. They are asked to identify how they are different. *Assesses visual-spatial reasoning.*

How is the clover outside the box different from the clover inside the box? *It is a three-leaf clover and the one in the box is four-leaf.*

Performance/Nonverbal

SPATIAL RELATIONS

Your child is shown a drawing of a whole shape along with several other partial shapes that, when combined as though they were puzzle pieces, would make the complete shape. He is asked to point to the partial shapes needed to form the whole shape. *Assesses visual-spatial reasoning.*

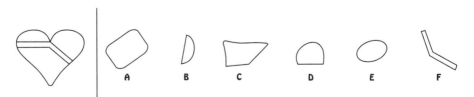

A   B   C   D   E   F

Look at the shape above. Can you point to all the puzzle pieces that, when put together, would make the shape in the box? *B, C, D, F.*

VISUAL MATCHING

Your child is asked to circle two identical numbers in a row of numbers. *Assesses visual-spatial reasoning, fine-motor skills.*

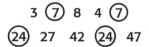

PICTURE RECOGNITION

Your child is shown pictures of two items that are then removed. Then, the child is shown the same two items within an array of other items. He is asked to point to what he saw before. *Assesses memory, visual-spatial reasoning, fine-motor skills.*

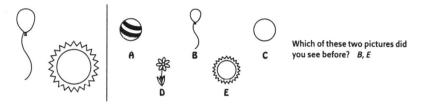

Which of these two pictures did you see before? *B, E*

PLANNING

Your child is asked to trace over a pattern without retracing or lifting his pencil. *Assesses visual-spatial reasoning, cognitive skills, fine-motor skills.*

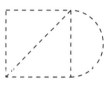

Can you trace this design without lifting up your pencil or retracing?

PAIR RECOGNITION

Your child is shown an example pair of pictures (for example, an apple and a pencil). These two pictures are randomly repeated among rows of three pictures (an apple, a pencil, a flower). The child is asked to scan the rows and circle the example pair of pictures every time it shows up as quickly as possible. *Assesses memory, visual-spatial reasoning, fine-motor skills.*

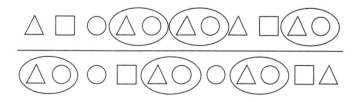

Scan the rows of shapes and each time you see a △ ○ in that order, circle it.

The Bracken Basic Concept Scale (BBCS)

This test is also used by many public schools to screen for giftedness. It assesses children's knowledge of the concepts and information that parents and preschool teachers traditionally teach children in preparation for school. It takes about thirty minutes. The questions are presented orally, so a child can complete a sentence and visually point to one of four colorful pictures that fits the description read by the examiner or just answer the question. The test covers:

Colors. Identify colors pointing to the correct color on a chart.

Letters. Identify upper-case and lower-case letters by pointing to the correct answer on a chart.

Numbers/counting. Identify single- and double-digit numbers, and count sets of objects.

Size. Show an understanding of words that describe size (e.g., *tall, small, wide, narrow*).

Comparisons. Match or differentiate objects based on a specific characteristic (e.g., "Point to the animals that can climb a tree," "Choose between a horse, a monkey, a cat, an elephant").

Shapes. Identify circle, square, and triangle by name.

Direction/Position. Show understanding of words that describe direction (e.g., *above, center, right*).

Self and Social Awareness. Demonstrate familiarity with social concepts and relationship terms (e.g., *happy, hungry, tired, old, mother, son*).

Texture/Materials. Show an understanding of words that describe texture or materials (e.g., *soft, rough, solid, metal, wood*).

Quantity. Show an understanding of words used to depict quantity (e.g., *full, empty, a lot, double*).

Time/Sequence. Demonstrate an understanding of time or sequence (e.g., *after, before, last, first, spring, winter*).

The Kaufman Assessment Battery for Children—Second Edition (KABC)

The KABC measures verbal and nonverbal abilities in children. It is often used to screen for kids who might benefit from a gifted program.

Verbal

WORD ORDER

Your child touches a series of silhouettes of common objects in the same order that the examiner names the objects. ***Assesses language, memory, visual-spatial reasoning.***

I'm going to name some pictures that you see here and I want you to point to them in the same order in which I say them. *Butterfly, ant, balloons.*

NUMBER RECALL

Similar to the memory for words and numbers subtest on the Stanford-Binet, page 48.

LEARNING

The examiner teaches the child nonsense names for fanciful pictures of fish, plants, and shells. The child shows learning by pointing to each picture (out of an array of pictures) when it is named. Or the child demonstrates delayed recall of paired associations learned about fifteen minutes earlier by pointing to the picture when the examiner reads the nonsense name. *Assesses language, memory, visual-spatial reasoning, cognitive skills.*

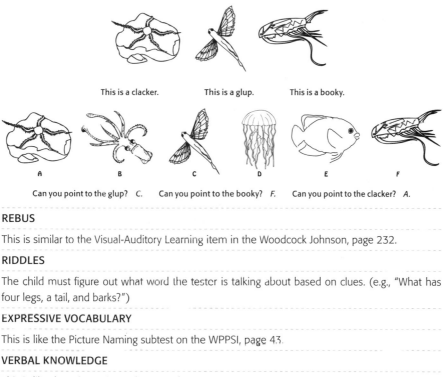

This is a clacker.   This is a glup.   This is a booky.

A   B   C   D   E   F

Can you point to the glup? C.   Can you point to the booky? F.   Can you point to the clacker? A.

REBUS

This is similar to the Visual-Auditory Learning item in the Woodcock Johnson, page 232.

RIDDLES

The child must figure out what word the tester is talking about based on clues. (e.g., "What has four legs, a tail, and barks?")

EXPRESSIVE VOCABULARY

This is like the Picture Naming subtest on the WPPSI, page 43.

VERBAL KNOWLEDGE

This is like the Information Subtest on the WPPSI, page 42.

HAND MOVEMENTS

Your child copies the tester's sequence of taps on the table using his fist, palm, and the side of his hand (e.g., fist—fist—palm—side of hand). *Assesses memory, visual-spatial reasoning, fine-motor skills.*

TRIANGLES

Your child assembles several three-dimensional triangles to match a model constructed by the examiner or a picture of an abstract design. *Assesses visual-spatial reasoning, cognitive skills, fine-motor skills.*

Can you copy this design using these triangles?

FACE RECOGNITION

The child briefly examines photos of one or two faces. Then he identifies the same face or faces in a different pose in a group photo. *Assesses memory, visual-spatial reasoning.*

CONCEPTUAL (ABSTRACT) THINKING

This is just like the Pictorial Classification subtest on the OLSAT ("Which picture doesn't belong?"), page 53.

GESTALT CLOSURE

The child mentally fills in the gaps in a partially completed drawing and names or describes the object or action depicted in the drawing. *Assesses knowledge/comprehension, visual-spatial reasoning, memory, cognitive skills.*

Can you tell me what this is?
An elephant.

BLOCK COUNTING

The child counts the number of blocks in various pictures of stacks of blocks. The stacks are configured in ways that one or more blocks is hidden or partially hidden from view. *Assesses mathematics.*

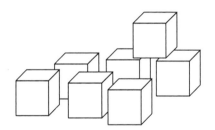

Can you tell me how many blocks are in this picture? *7.*

PATTERN REASONING

This is similar to the Matrix questions on the WPPSI, page 44.

Appendix II

GAMES AND ACTIVITIES: CRIB NOTES

Here are the games and activities mentioned in the book. There are many other things you can choose to do besides these. For more activities to build each ability, go to Testingforkindergarten.com.

Chapter 8. Reading to Build All 7 Abilities

Chapter 9. Instruments to Strengthen All 7 Abilities

Chapter 10. Conversing to Support 6 Abilities

Chapter 11. Language and More

Chapter 12. Knowledge/Comprehension

Chapter 13. Memory

Chapter 14. Mathematics

Chapter 18. Beyond Testing Success Page

If you have ability-building games and activities that your child loves, let me know about it so I can share it with other parents on my blog (giving you credit, of course). You can reach me directly at karenquinn1@aol.com.

Appendix III

THE 25 MOST IMPORTANT LIFE LESSONS: POST THIS ON YOUR REFRIGERATOR

1. Allow lots of time for play.
2. Encourage your child to devote himself to mastering something he enjoys. Support him in practicing what he isn't good at.
3. Praise your child for trying, not for being smart.
4. Teach patience.
5. Foster curiosity.
6. Respond to your child's babbling, pointing, or gazing.
7. Talk to your child about everything and anything and always say why.
8. Practice Ping-Pong conversation.
9. Insist that your child listen and respond at home.
10. Follow through on promised consequences.
11. Use dialogic reading.
12. Fill your home with music and get your child moving to the beat.
13. Don't solve problems for your child. Help him do it himself.
14. Show that it's okay to make mistakes.
15. Encourage experimentation.
16. Give your child a voice in simple decisions.
17. Encourage your child to be independent, dressing herself, brushing her teeth, tying her shoes, get her own snacks, pour her own cereal, etc.
18. Read concept books, but also go to zoos, the beach, museums, and plays.
19. When talking about everything and anything, include all the information children are supposed to be exposed to before kindergarten.
20. Build math questions into your dialogic reading.
21. Children need repetition and variety to learn.
22. Help your child make connections.
23. Children learn best when they're involved and having fun.
24. No TV for children under 2; no more than two hours per day of high-quality media for children 3 and older.
25. Set the bar high for your child to keep her motivated, but not so high that she can never meet your expectations.

Appendix IV

Here are some books that I particularly recommend and believe you might enjoy. I included my own novel about school admissions in New York City because I think every parent needs a good laugh.

Bronson, Po, and Ashley Merryman. *NurtureShock: New Thinking About Children* (Hachette Book Group, 2009).

Colvin, Geoff. *Talent Is Overrated* (Portfolio Hardcover, 2008).

Gardner, Howard. *Frames of Mind: The Theory of Multiple Intelligence* (Basic Books, 1993).

Gladwell, Malcolm. *Outliers: The Story of Success* (Little, Brown & Co., 2008).

Goleman, Daniel. *Emotional Intelligence: Why It Can Matter More Than IQ.* 10th anniversary edition (Bantam, 2006).

Guernsey, Lisa. *Into the Minds of Babes: How Screen Time Affects Children from Birth to Age Five* (Basic Books, 2007).

Hirsh-Pasek, Kathy, Roberta Michnick Golinkoff, and Diane Eyer. *Einstein Never Used Flash Cards* (Rodale, 2004).

Levine, Mel. *A Mind at a Time* (Simon & Schuster, 2003).

Nisbett, Richard E. *Intelligence and How to Get It* (W. W. Norton & Co., 2009).

Pohlman, Craig. *Revealing Minds: Assessing to Understand and Support Struggling Learners* (Jossey-Bass, 2007).

Quinn, Karen. *The Ivy Chronicles* (Plume, 2006).

Schulman, Nancy, and Ellen Birnbaum. *Practical Wisdom for Parents* (Alfred A. Knopf, 2007).

Sternberg, Robert. *Successful Intelligence: How Practical and Creative Intelligence Determine Success in Life* (Plume, 1997).

For more information on the sources and research used to create this book, a direct link to every website mentioned, and a list of all the toys, games, and materials I recommend, you can visit Testingforkindergarten.com to find my detailed notes section.

Index

About the Author

Karen Quinn cofounded Smart City Kids, a New York City-based company dedicated to helping families survive the application process to Manhattan's most competitive public and private schools. Her first novel, *The Ivy Chronicles,* was based on that experience. Now a full-time writer, she recently moved from New York City to Miami. Karen has written four novels including *Wife in the Fast Lane, Holly Would Dream,* and *The Sister Diaries. Testing for Kindergarten* is her fifth book.

Karen loves to hear from readers. She invites you to write to her at karen quinn1@aol.com and to visit her website at Testingforkindergarten.com. There you'll find links to all the games, toys, and materials she recommends; references to all the studies and sources she relied on when writing this book; a place to sign up for daily one-minute practice test questions you can do with your kids (that's all the time it should take); along with her blog, which covers valuable bonus material that didn't fit inside these chapters.

In addition, this book recommends many websites. For direct links to these sites, go Testingforkindergarten.com/wp/book/links-to-websites-by-chapter, where the sites will be updated in the event that they change (as websites so often do). You can also find Karen on Facebook at Karenquinn.net/facebook and on Twitter at Karenquinnnyc.